The
Best
Strangers
in the
World

Stories from a Life Spent Listening

ARI SHAPIRO

HARPERONE

An Imprint of HarperCollinsPublishers

HarperCollins books may be purchased for educational, business,
or sales promotional use. For information, please email the Special
Markets Department at SPsales@harpercollins.com.

FIRST HARPERCOLLINS PAPERBACK PUBLISHED IN 2024

Designed by Bonni Leon-Berman

Library of Congress Cataloging-in-Publication Data is available
upon request.

ISBN 978-0-06-322135-2

24 25 26 27 28 LBC 6 5 4 3 2

For Mike, who doesn't read books but promises
he'll listen to the audiobook of this one

CONTENTS

INTRODUCTION:
THANK YOU
FOR LISTENING

I became a public speaker in the first grade. In Fargo, North Dakota, my older brother and I were the only Jewish kids at our elementary school, and so, every year at Christmastime, he and I would go from classroom to classroom with a menorah and a dreidel, explaining to children descended from Scandinavian immigrants what Hanukkah was. It was my first experience presenting to an audience, and also my first experience as a sort of ambassador—a storyteller, making the foreign seem a bit less strange.

Somehow, Fargo had not one but two synagogues in those days. My parents, who never wanted to be exclusionary, took us to the Reform temple on Friday nights and the Orthodox shul on Saturday mornings. My most vivid memories, naturally, are of the food. Dum Dum lollipops from old Joe Paper and pickled herring from a jar in the shul basement after services. My family kept kosher, so our meat was delivered once a month on a truck from Chicago that pulled into the synagogue parking lot, where we would pick it up and load it into a deep freezer in the garage. For Shabbat dinner every Friday night, my mom made matzoh ball soup and challah from scratch.

My parents both taught at North Dakota State University, my mother in communications and my father in computer science. Visiting their offices meant walking past pastures and waving at the grazing cows. My dad would take me to his computer lab, which in the 1980s was a room filled to the edges with one enormous machine. I'd walk the perimeter of the hulking device and look at the blinking lights, wondering about the mysterious workings going on inside.

When I was eight years old, in 1987, we left Fargo for Portland, Oregon, as the city was drenched in the unselfconscious pre-*Portlandia* weirdness of the late twentieth century. If you've seen early Gus Van Sant films like *My Own Private Idaho* and *Drugstore Cowboy*, that was the vibe. Five years after we arrived, there was a ballot measure that would have allowed the state to, among other things, fire teachers for being gay. The language of Measure 9 lumped in homosexuality with pedophilia, sadism, and masochism. Most of us teenagers didn't know what those words meant; these were still pre-internet days. But thanks to the debate over Measure 9, everybody figured them out.

All the kids at my big, mostly white, suburban high school had an opinion about Measure 9, even though most of them had never knowingly met a gay person. They wore pins that read "Nein on Nine" or "Straight but Not Narrow." (Congrats on your heterosexuality, bro!) That was the world into which I came out of the closet at the end of my junior year.

My decision to come out at sixteen wasn't spurred by a secret boyfriend or even a specific crush. I wasn't living a double life. I just decided that I didn't ever *want* to live a double life. Once I realized that I would have to come out to my parents and friends someday, I concluded that I would gain nothing by postponing the inevitable. "The sooner I do this, the sooner it will be over with," I told myself. And so I ripped off the Band-Aid and asked my parents if I could talk to them about something. Their reaction was more open-minded than many coming-out stories I've heard from the 1990s.

"Are you sure?"

"Yes, I'm sure."

"Well, we still love you."

They asked if I wanted to see a therapist, I declined, and they decided that they would go see one themselves.

I don't know whether I was actually the first openly gay student at Beaverton High School, but nobody could remember a teenager admitting it before. There had been rumors about me, of course. Nothing specific—I hadn't even kissed a boy before I came out. But I decided that the best approach was to drown out the whisper campaign with a bullhorn. When I showed up for the first day of school senior year, I plastered my locker with postcards of hunky men—Tom of Finland drawings and photographs by Herb Ritts and Tom Bianchi. On Halloween, I came to school in drag. After that, my calculus teacher stopped calling on me when I raised my hand in class. I also carried Mace, since not everybody was excited about having a gay classmate. Thankfully, I never had to use it.

On the weekends, I would go to an all-ages gay nightclub in downtown Portland called the City, where remixes of Whitney Houston and Madonna blasted through a haze of CK One and cigarette smoke. Afterward, my friends and I walked a couple of blocks through the inevitable Portland drizzle to a twenty-four-hour diner called the Roxy, for coffee and cheese fries.

My club look was harvested from "the bins," the Goodwill surplus store in an industrial part of town. All the clothes that didn't sell at the regular Goodwill stores got piled into endless heaps and sold for ninety-nine cents a pound. My friends and I would spend hours rifling through blouses and blazers, kimonos and fake leather jackets, playing mix-and-match with no rules about what went together.

I paired polyester shirts with corduroy knickers or flowy culottes in paisley patterns. Add a ceramic pendant charm or a homemade hemp necklace woven with wooden beads, and I had something you could call an outfit. A strange outfit. But we were strange teenagers. To complete the look, I wore an ear cuff shaped like a small human, a mountain climber clinging to the side of my head. My hair, parted in the center, fell to my chin in a sort of Nirvana-meets-Prince-Valiant bob.

I guess today my fashion choices would be labeled "gender non-conforming," but that wasn't a term we knew. Nobody around me identified as queer; calling yourself gay seemed radical enough. People routinely shouted *faggot!* from car windows as they drove past us on the street, and we reflexively replied with *breeder!* and a middle finger in the air. After weekends at the City and the Roxy, I would show up at Beaverton High Monday morning (strutting the halls in a *Phantom of the Opera* T-shirt over a red turtleneck and acid-washed jeans) for my packed schedule of honors classes and extracurricular activities.

It felt like a superpower, this ability to move between worlds. And by the time I graduated from Yale and became a journalist, I realized that these boundary-crossing skills I had picked up as the Jewish kid in Fargo and as the gay teen in Portland could serve me as a reporter. I found a career where I could perform those acts of translation, and be a liaison, for groups to which I had no personal connection beyond my journalistic interest. My microphone and headset served as a snorkel and mask. When I strapped them on, I could enter colorful hidden worlds that were invisible to people on the surface. And then came the important part: sharing those worlds with others.

..

MY FIRST JOURNALISM GIG, IN 2001, was as an intern to NPR's legendary legal affairs correspondent Nina Totenberg, who is still a friend and mentor. She's the dean of the Supreme Court press corps and a force to be reckoned with. One of the most valuable lessons she taught me during my internship: "Grow a pair!"

Years after that internship, I became NPR's Justice correspondent, working alongside Nina to cover major investigations and federal trials. People would often ask, "Do you want to be the next Nina Totenberg?" I always gave the tongue-in-cheek reply, "No, I want to be the first Ari Shapiro." I said it with a laugh, aware of how presumptuous it sounded. And I never would have admitted this at the time, but . . . I wasn't really joking. I didn't know what it might mean to be "the first Ari Shapiro." But I knew that I wanted to do something that felt new.

Since 2015 I've been one of the hosts of *All Things Considered*, a role in which I've interviewed world leaders and narrowly avoided fatal explosions. And for more than a decade, I've also toured the globe with the band Pink Martini, performing in venues from Carnegie Hall to the Hollywood Bowl. At first I didn't see a common thread. In fact, the band felt a bit like an affair I was having on the side. (Though really, how secret can the affair be when it literally plays out onstage in front of thousands of people?) My different projects felt meaningful, but I couldn't put my finger on what they shared. There was always an audience. There was always a story, whether it was told through journalism or music. And in the best moments, there was also connection.

I can see now that, as the self-reinforcing bubbles we live in become more impenetrable, I keep seeking out ways to help people listen to one another. As algorithms pull us into feedback loops and congratulate us for dunking on perceived opponents, Pink Martini goes to Texas and performs songs in Farsi and Arabic to an audience that might see Persians or Arabs as suspect. Crowds in Istanbul clap along with us to songs in Greek, and in Seoul they dance to our rendition of a Japanese tune.

In my work at NPR, I have traveled to rural Louisiana, where guards at a federal prison were struggling during a government shutdown—working without pay, sleeping on cots at the prison because they didn't have gas money to commute to and from home. And when one of those men told me through tears that he couldn't afford to buy a gift for his son's birthday, people from around the country who heard his story emailed and tweeted at us, asking how they could send toys. They didn't ask whom he supported for president or how he felt about immigration or guns. They saw him as a father who cared about his son.

Later that same year, I went to rural Mississippi to tell a different story of struggle, about undocumented chicken plant workers who had been caught up in the biggest work-site immigration raid in US history. And listeners responded the same way. They asked what they could do to help.

Of course, my mission isn't entirely selfless. When my grandma Sylvia turned ninety, the whole family flew to Chicago to celebrate. She presided over the party in her blond wig and false eyelashes, staples of her look since her days as a carnival fortune-teller. Each of her children described their own nuclear families for the assembled relatives. When it was my mother's turn, she got up to talk about her three sons. There was Dan, the oldest, an inventor and start-up tech CEO. She introduced my younger brother, Joseph, a university professor studying environmental economics. "And then there's Ari," she said, "who was so ignored as a middle child that he had to go find a job where millions of people would pay attention to him every day."

My mom got a big laugh. I was dumbfounded. Was that why I had made a career as a journalist? Is that why I host a nightly news program? Is the totality of my professional life just one long bid for attention?

"Really, I was neglected?" I asked her later. "I don't think you and Dad ignored me."

"You don't remember that rash on your face?"

I flashed to my third-grade school portrait in Fargo. A child with a bowl haircut, in an Ernie-style striped shirt, grinning wildly through an eczema-induced facial disfigurement.

"We ignored it for weeks," my mom said, "and by the time we finally took you to the pediatrician, it was infected." Maybe she was onto something.

Years later, the Spanish author Javier Cercas told me, "Probably you are on the radio because you want to be loved." We were in the middle of an interview, and I had never met the man before.

So, yeah, I liked being the kid in front of the classroom with the menorah and the dreidel. I liked being the only teenager at school with a gay pride symbol on his backpack. I get a rush from hearing the roar of thousands as I walk on the stage at a music festival in Casablanca, and I feel a thrill when someone in a restaurant leans over to my table and says they recognize my voice from the radio.

But more than that—I like handing the microphone to someone else, whose voice wouldn't otherwise be heard. To a survivor of political violence in Zimbabwe, or a Venezuelan migrant walking hundreds of miles through the mountains of Colombia. I like introducing you to them, and bringing their experiences into your life.

I'm Ari Shapiro, and I like that people listen to me. I like having a megaphone, and sharing it, and holding you rapt when I do it. Particularly in our distraction-filled lives, the fact that millions of people have given me their attention over the years—that you are giving me your attention now, in these pages—is not something I take for granted. I mean it when I say, *Thank you for listening.*

That phrase, *Thank you for listening*, can serve many purposes. I think of it as the "shalom" of journalism. It can mean hello, goodbye, peace, and it is also my go-to response to listener hate mail. In that respect it's a bit like *Bless your heart.* Let me explain:

I've always considered hate mail to be a badge of honor. My first paid job at NPR, after that internship for Nina, was as a temporary editorial assistant on *Morning Edition.* One of my duties was to go through the show's email inbox and forward listener messages to the correspondents. I became intimately familiar with the taxonomy of hate mail. There were partisan messages, nitpicky ones, misogynistic ones. (NPR was one of the first news organizations to put women on the front lines covering wars, and the first to hire a woman to anchor a nationally broadcast nightly news program, Susan Stamberg on *All Things Considered.*)

I dutifully forwarded all those messages. And if a listener wasn't writing in about a particular correspondent but, rather, ranting about our programming in general, I would anonymously respond on behalf of the show, ending my generic reply with "Thank you for listening."

When I started reporting my own stories for NPR and getting my own hate mail, it felt like a sign that I had finally arrived. I savored it. I started to keep a file folder of the ones that came on actual paper. And after the arrival of Twitter, I created a photo album on my phone for screen grabs of hate tweets. (I have another photo album for genuinely kind fan mail, for days when I need a pick-me-up.)

By the time I became a host of *All Things Considered* and graduated from a cubicle to an office, I decided that it was time for the world to see the best of these messages. The side of my office bookshelf faces an interior window at NPR headquarters. So I taped some of my favorite letters to the window-facing side of the bookshelf. This was inspired by something Susan Stamberg used to do. Her office door was plastered with letters from people who misspelled her name. Susan Strombag, Stormbridge, Stembage . . .

People waiting to meet with me in my office could kill time reading these messages. There's one from a man (they're usually men) who called me a "faggy, pushy, annoying smart-ass." Another comes from a listener who told me I made his "hair hurt" by referring to "the Queen of England." ("The person of interest is, officially, 'Elizabeth the Second, by the Grace of God, of Great Britain, Ireland and the British Dominions beyond the Seas Queen, Defender of the Faith,'" this listener explained.) One letter writer wanted to inform me that a man may be "hanged," and he may be "hung," but the two words have very different meanings. And there is one letter from a person who objected so strongly to the way I pronounced *data* that they felt compelled to write in and let me know that "each time you say DATTA (which was MANY times) it is as if you want to slap your listeners."

My all-time favorite listener letter isn't on that wall, though. It is a postcard that arrived the first time I guest-hosted *Morning Edition*, more than a decade ago. The one that really made me feel like I was on the path to figuring out what it meant to be the first Ari Shapiro, and not just the next Nina Totenberg. The postcard has a picture of tulips, and the stamps are doves of peace. It reads (punctuation and capitalization as written):

> Dear Ari, Please Butch up.
> I find a daily dose of your personality, annoying.
> I'm a person too.
> *D. Emerson, Miami, Fl*

I framed it when it arrived, and it has sat in a place of pride on my desk ever since, as I have steadfastly refused to butch up year after year. I don't know who D. Emerson is. I don't know their gender, though one can assume. I'm sure he had no idea that his postcard would have such staying power. He included no return address, so I've never been able to contact him. If I could, I would simply tell Mr. Emerson, "Thank you for listening."

1

NATURE BOY

My first hike in Oregon was memorable for reasons that I would prefer to forget. I was eight years old, and my family had just moved to Portland from Fargo. Not five minutes down the trail, a banana slug the size of a Twinkie sat in the middle of the path. I had never seen anything like it. I screamed and started to cry, refusing to advance another inch. My parents offered to hold my hand while I stepped over the slug. Nope. They tried to pick me up and lift me over it. No ma'am. They showed me a detour, to go around it and continue the hike. Nuh-uh. I turned around and went back to the car.

But kids are adaptable. A few hikes later, I saw a pair of banana slugs curled around each other to form a perfect circle. I admired the way each thick slimy body tapered toward the other, making a perfect yin-yang. (I didn't know that they were also making baby slugs.) By the time I was in sixth grade, I was daring friends to lick one—because it makes your tongue go numb. What started as disgust had become curiosity and had led to something like affection.

My parents raised me to believe that the more you learn about the world, the more interesting life becomes. They encouraged their three boys to apply this philosophy broadly to life, most especially to nature. For instance, I didn't realize until I went to college that waterfalls are a vacation destination for most people. I took it for granted that trails through old-growth forests and sweeping mountain vistas were just a short drive from our modest one-story house in Portland.

My parents' own upbringing didn't provide any obvious clues for where they learned to value lifelong curiosity or the natural world. My mom, Elayne, grew up with her sister and brother in Chicago. Her father was a strict disciplinarian who served in World War II, and her mother was a flamboyant fortune-teller who worked at carnivals wearing the blond wig and false eyelashes that would become her signature look. Not exactly an outdoorsy family.

My dad, Leonard, grew up in the San Francisco area, raised by a working mother who was widowed when my dad was twelve. Teenage Len and his younger brother would come home from school each day to an empty house and heat up a can of beans while their mother was at work. One night, Len got an idea to avoid dirtying a pot that he'd have to wash. He put an unopened can of beans directly on the stove and turned on the burner. He went off to play and forgot about the can until he heard a thunderclap from the kitchen. The kid who'd grow up to be my father spent weeks cleaning a film of beans off the ceiling and walls. Hiking and camping weren't ingrained in his family's DNA either.

Nevertheless, my two brothers and I spent most of our weekends outdoors. Our parents would take us to the Columbia River Gorge, or we'd drive west to the fog of the coast. (In Oregon nobody calls it the beach, maybe to discourage false hopes of warmth and sun.) Late in the summer, we would drive east to Mount Hood, where hiking trails wound through alpine meadows in kaleidoscopic blooms under the cables of ski lifts.

My mom kept a diary of the wildflowers we saw during our hikes. Week after week, she would fastidiously log the date, trail, and species we found along the path. In those years of the late twentieth century, before smartphones and plant ID apps, she would pore through field guides and consult strangers on the trail to figure out what each flower was. (Picking a blossom was absolutely forbidden in my family. "Let it live!") Over the years, that hiking journal became her personal almanac and guidebook.

Each bloom got equal billing. It wasn't just the phallic bear grass, popping its fluffy white stalks out of mountain hillsides like towering cartoons from a Dr. Seuss book. She got equally excited to peel back the ground-hugging leaves of a wild ginger plant and discover its three-pronged purplish brown flower like an ancient rune bearing a secret message.

My dad pursued his own seasonal hobby in the woods: wild mushroom hunting. While wildflower hikes required us to stay on the path, foraging for mushrooms gave my brothers and me the illicit thrill of leaving the trail behind and bushwhacking through the forest in pursuit of our quarry. One autumn day I stumbled onto a fawn as I plunged through the underbrush. It was so camouflaged that I nearly stepped on it. The fawn let out a feeble cry and teetered off on its wobbly legs.

We searched for morels in the spring, boletus (also known as porcini) in the summer, and chanterelles in the fall. On a good day, we would emerge into the sunlight with overflowing bags of loot. On our way home we'd stop at a ranger station, spread out our haul on the counter, and let a professional sort through our harvest to make sure we weren't bringing home anything that could kill us. On a bad day, we'd be rain-drenched, empty-handed, and itching with poison oak. But even the bad days were pretty good.

My dad's rule was to harvest only mushrooms that looked nothing like toxic varieties, which narrowed our options to a small fraction of all the edible mushrooms in Oregon. But we tried to identify as many other types of fungus as we could, just for the fun of it. There were puffballs that released a cloud of spores into the air when you squeezed them, witch's butter that oozed like Cheez Whiz out of fallen logs, and warty crimson deadly amanitas that we were never allowed to touch. We came to understand which ones grew under leaf litter or on decaying stumps, which species were more likely to appear just after a rain or in an area that had recently been logged.

The first time I saw chanterelles for twenty-five dollars a pound at a grocery store as an adult, I called my dad in shock. I had no idea we'd been eating delicacies all those years. It made me think of how different my upbringing was from his daily childhood ritual of heating up a can of beans on the stove.

Our curiosity wasn't limited to wildflowers and mushrooms. My older brother introduced us to tidepools, thanks to an engaging ocean-ography teacher who showed him the wonders of liminal spaces. We scanned the charts looking for the most extreme tides of the year, then we'd tromp out to see what we could find when the waves were at their lowest ebb. Darting fish like sculpins, always. Anemones waving their green and purple tentacles, same. Orange starfish, check. My favorites were the nudibranchs. They were difficult to find and spectacular once you clocked them. These sea slugs were smaller than my thumbnail, hiding their psychedelic neon colors under waving kelp leaves. Occasionally they would crawl on the underside of the water, spinning a path of slime to stay suspended just below the surface. Actual punk rock didn't appeal to me, but the nudibranchs were the tiny punk rebels of the tidepools, and in them I saw fellow renegades.

Tidepools taught me patience. I would squat over a puddle of sea-water and see only a rock garden at first. Then, slowly, my eyes would discern movement. After a few minutes, camouflaged creatures might reveal their outlines. Details that I had overlooked would eventually emerge. These little ecosystems showed me that nothing entirely reveals itself to the casual observer and that to fully see something requires more than a perfunctory glance.

When we went tide-pooling at the base of Haystack Rock, I would bring binoculars and aim them up at the towering stone monolith to spot puffins preening and wheeling. If each of us had a niche—flowers, mushrooms, tidepools—then birds were my thing. I kept a life list, checking off species as I spotted them. (My younger brother, always game to join us on these outings, was a bit of a black sheep, more enthusiastic about sports than anyone else in the family.)

I came to understand the difference between the gray wings of an urban scrub jay and the black mohawk of a woodland Steller's jay. And when kids at school would point out the window at a "blue jay," I would inform them that blue jays were not a West Coast species. This did not make me especially popular with my classmates.

Our summer vacations were always domestic. We would caravan across the US with uncles, aunts, and cousins, talking over CB radios as we visited national parks or far-flung relatives. We all had broadcast handles—code names. Mine was Waiter, the joke being that if I followed through on my threat to pursue an acting career, I'd wind up as one. Visits to my card-reading grandmother in Chicago meant we got to see the scarlet flash of a cardinal and actual blue jays. On a summer trip to the Grand Canyon, I finally checked a roadrunner off my list.

Great blue herons were so common around our house, we would point out the window at one flapping overhead and say, "GBH." Over time I figured out how to distinguish the silhouettes of soaring turkey vultures from red-tailed hawks from golden eagles. And as we drove through Oregon farm country, I would scan the power lines for kestrels perched on the wires in their hunt for sparrows.

On the drive to a hiking trailhead, we would slide an Audubon Society cassette into the minivan's tape deck and listen to the warbles of birdsongs in hopes of identifying the ones we couldn't capture with our eyes. We'd rewind the tape and tune our ears to the *fee-bee* of the black-capped chickadee, the *weet* of the western meadowlark, and the *bzeet* of a cedar waxwing. They were like audio flashcards. Before I ever conducted an interview for the radio, I had gained close listening skills from birds.

Sometimes my parents hiked on a trail while my brothers and I hopped from rock to rock in a streambed along the route below. This slowed down our progress significantly, but completing the hike was never the mission. The goal was to find interesting things along the way. We turned over rocks to spot insect larvae and crayfish, scanning deeper pools for the shadows of trout.

At school, I was taught to acquire knowledge as a means to an end. I studied history to write a paper; I practiced math problems to pass an exam. My experiences in nature were different. Curiosity didn't lead to knowledge in pursuit of some kind of end point. There was no destination to be reached. Curiosity just led to more questions, which led to more curiosity. The more I learned, the more complicated, nuanced, and interconnected the world seemed to become—like exploring a house with endless rooms. Even without the satisfaction of a letter grade, I found that infinite trail of curiosity to be a more rewarding path than studying to pass a test.

Peering up at the underside of bridges in search of swallows' nests, we would also spot bats roosting. Then I wanted to know what species of bats they were and what kinds of insects they preferred. When the bats emerged at dusk, I would lob pebbles into the air to make them swoop down toward me. I told my classmates that I had trained bats, which didn't win me any more friends than the line about the blue jays. So I sought out my fellow nerds and signed up to compete in

Science Olympiad, where I chose insect identification as one of my events.

I made flash cards and drilled myself on the Latin names of the orders of insects, reciting them like an incantation: Coleoptera, Lepidoptera, Hymenoptera, Ephemeroptera. That gave us something else to look for during our hikes, and even at home. Housefly: Dipteral Stink bug: Hemipteral The world seemed to deepen as my perception expanded. Things that had been invisible to me materialized as I became aware of them.

In college I pivoted from hard sciences to liberal arts, but my reputation as a nature boy followed me. My friends at Yale would impersonate me with a mocking "Did you know . . . ?" followed by some obscure unverifiable fact. "Did you know that tarsiers have the largest eyes, relative to their body size, of any mammal?" (True, but unverifiable at the time for my friends, because we weren't all carrying supercomputers in our pockets.) I was probably insufferable, but so were a lot of kids at Yale. At least my tree-hugging made me insufferable in a way that was different from most of my classmates.

In my a cappella group, everyone was given a nickname at the end of freshman year. I was dubbed Forsythia because, according to my fellow singers, when we went on tour I couldn't stop saying things like, "Look, the forsythia are in bloom!" I know that this was not literally true, because I was not familiar with forsythia when I was given my nickname. But by the end of freshman year, that yellow flowering shrub had become a part of my personal taxonomy. I now grow it in my backyard.

I never thought of my curiosity as a skill. Hiking and tide-pooling weren't covered in any classes I took, and they've never appeared on my résumé. But today, when journalism students or interns ask me the most important trait for a reporter, I always give them the same answer: curiosity. It doesn't matter whether you're curious about nature, or people, or finance, or politics. The best journalists are people who always want to learn more, who enjoy the feeling of moving from ignorance or confusion to understanding.

And somehow I have found my way to a job where every day I get to scratch my childhood itch to understand the world more deeply. My favorite part of hosting *All Things Considered* isn't the interviews with celebrities or the world travel or the front-row seat to history. It isn't any single topic at all. It's the totality, the range of what I get to do. I conclude each day knowing about something I hadn't understood when I woke up in the morning. I still find it surreal that I basically just get paid to ask questions, and experts in almost any walk of life will answer them. It reminds me of standing at the park ranger's counter in front of a pile of mushrooms, asking, "How do I tell which ones could kill me?"

2

IMPACT

I was hoping to find a job during a dinner party.

My NPR internship was wrapping up in the spring of 2001, and I had no real prospects for what came next. I had already applied for a few positions in public relations and at nonprofit organizations—a process that had gone nowhere. I'd had a dismal interview for an entry-level job in a senator's office, where my ambivalence about Congress might have torpedoed my chances. I was thinking about looking into graduate school (in something-or-other . . . I hadn't quite nailed down what exactly). Then my boss, NPR matriarch Nina Totenberg, had an idea.

She knew that I loved to cook, and that my living situation as her unpaid intern hadn't exactly allowed me to spread my culinary wings. I went home every evening to a one-room apartment that I was sharing with a lesbian I had found on Craigslist. I slept on her pullout sofa bed, and we shared a half-size refrigerator. So, no, I wasn't having many adventures in the kitchen.

"Why don't I hire you to cook for a dinner party that I'll throw at my house?" Nina said. "You'll also join us for dinner, and I'll invite a bunch of guests who might be able to offer you jobs." She had never actually tasted my cooking, so this was a true leap of faith on her part.

In my parents' household, Nina Totenberg was a celebrity on par with Meryl Streep. So she was more than just my first boss; she was a larger-than-life trailblazer who'd shown an interest in me and my career at a moment when I was hitting walls everywhere else. And now, beyond merely offering me advice on next steps, she was creating a scenario that could, perhaps, give me a legitimate career.

Nina's guest list included former deputy attorney general Jamie Gorelick and Congressman John Dingell. The powerful Michigander Dingell attended with his wife, Debbie, who would go on to win John's House seat after his death in 2019. I spent days weighing possible menus and landed on salmon Wellington—a riff on the retro classic beef Wellington. It was a complicated recipe involving salmon fillets individually wrapped in puff pastry. It would be a stretch for me, but I wanted to impress these people.

Cooking for any dinner party makes me a bit nervous. Part of the magic of playing in the kitchen is casting culinary spells, and sometimes they fail no matter how many times you've practiced the incantations. Add a guest list of powerful Washington VIPs you've never met, and it becomes more nerve-wracking. Layer on top of that the fact that this particular dinner was hosted by my boss, and that my future job prospects hinged on its success, and—well, if I hadn't been concerned about keeping my wits sharp, I would have downed a glass or two of wine over the sink.

As the guests arrived, I said a prayer to the kitchen gods, removed my apron, and joined the fray. I had set out a cheese and charcuterie plate;

Congressman Dingell was bringing a cracker to his mouth when an oily black glob of olive tapenade oozed off the crisp and plopped onto Nina's expensive rug. He scolded himself, apologizing as he dabbed at the smudge with soda water. Nina's husband, David Reines, leaned over and whispered in my ear, "You've just witnessed the humanization of an icon." I breathed more easily.

The biggest hitch of dinner was one that Nina had predicted early in the day: the salmon Wellingtons were enormous. I'd been cooking for my own appetite—that of a six-foot-three twenty-two-year-old—and most of the guests didn't come close to finishing. Not the worst kitchen offense I had ever committed, and at least it tasted good.

I went big on dessert, too, making cherry shortcakes on homemade biscuits threaded with dark chocolate and kirsch whipped cream. As the guests fought drowsiness and stared down the final bites, Nina announced, "As you all know, the food you've eaten tonight was prepared by Ari here. He's one of the best interns I've ever had. He needs a job. And not as a chef." I wanted to kiss her hand.

It was a noble effort, and I was grateful to Nina, but it didn't work. The salmon hooked zero job offers. Part of me wished that I had put as much effort into my professional pitch as I had into the meal. But another part wasn't entirely sure I wanted what Nina was trying to serve up for me. I cared about people, how they lived, and what motivated them. I wanted work that would allow me to keep caring about the world in that way. And I wasn't sure I would find that as a low-level aide on Capitol Hill.

··

THE FACT THAT I HAD landed in the world of DC journalism at all surprised the people who knew me best. I had spent my free time at Yale performing in plays and musicals. In the spring of my senior year, I had actually completed an application for the acting program at Juilliard and was about to mail it in when my friend Rachel Levy suggested a thought exercise. "Let's imagine the best-case scenario," she said. "You're fifty years old and still going to auditions. You have no job security. You spend long stretches performing in other cities, living in hotels. Are you sure you want that life? And if so, are you sure you want to go deeper into student debt applying for a school that will train you for that life?"

She made a good point. So Rachel and I each started to brainstorm lists of things we might conceivably do with our lives instead. My list included working at Club Med, joining the Peace Corps, and doing LGBT advocacy. Her list included getting a job at NPR. That sounded intriguing, even if I had never dipped a toe into journalism. I added NPR to my list and applied for an internship. I was rejected. Six months later, while working at a summer camp in Southern California, I learned that Nina Totenberg hired her own interns, separate from the broader NPR internship program. I applied to her, and she said yes.

The following year, as my internship end date grew closer, I sent out more résumés and job applications. But I didn't seek out openings in other newsrooms. I wasn't confident that the journalism business was for me. It felt too hard-boiled. I found the obsession with what was happening in Congress and on Wall Street puzzling at best. Plus, I suspected that maybe I would struggle to set aside my emotions and biases for a "just the facts" outlook on the world.

NPR has always stood half a step apart from other news organizations. But even public radio, with its flair for the quirky and personal, often seemed to get sucked in by the gravitational pull of CNN chyrons and *New York Times* headlines. A senior NPR executive once walked by my desk and paused. He took in the potted peace lily blooming on a shelf, the flamboyantly colored betta fish swimming in a vase, and my hair coiffed into a faux-hawk. "What are you doing here?" he quipped. "You look like you should be working for the CW or the WB," the

TV networks famous for cheesy teen soaps. I don't know whether he thought he was making a lighthearted joke or just toying with some mild sexual harassment. Whatever his intention, it landed as a strong hint that even my Ivy League degree and the support of Nina herself wouldn't be enough to make me feel at home in journalism, at NPR or anywhere else.

With a week to go before my internship ran out, a two-month temporary position as an editorial assistant on *Morning Edition* opened up. It was my best (read: only) option, and Nina put in a good word for me with the person doing the hiring. I went for it despite my doubts. I'd be doing research, finding guests for the show, and lining up interviews.

This was my first paid full-time job out of college. I had worked side gigs for years as a waiter, a barista, a Hebrew school teacher, and more. But this contract—even without any job security—was something new for me. I told myself that despite the lack of tenure, it was an opportunity to further my education without adding to my debt. Plus, I could finally leave the pullout sofa bed behind. I rented a one-bedroom apartment in the same building, and my boyfriend, Mike Gottlieb, who had been on a Fulbright fellowship in London for the previous year, moved to Washington to join me.

Morning Edition went on the air at 5 a.m., so the staff worked in a twenty-four-hour rotation. As my temp contract got extended month by month, I spent stretches working the night shift from 1 to 9 a.m. Rationalizing that caffeine before noon was okay, I would drink coffee for eight hours straight. This schedule wasn't great for my quality of life or my stomach lining, but the upside-down hours paid more than the day shift. I would stumble home in the morning sun and pass out by ten. On the weekends I'd try to realign my schedule with Mike's for forty-eight hours. All I ever thought about was sleep.

On one clear blue September morning near the end of my workday,

I went up to NPR's roof deck to get some fresh air as the sun rose over the Capitol. Before I left for the day, I scribbled a note to Nina saying hi and dropped it off at her third-floor desk. When I came back to my second-floor cubicle to grab my backpack, the TVs were showing smoke coming out of the World Trade Center.

NPR was embarrassingly slow to report the breaking news that morning. We still thought of ourselves as more of a scrappy alternative news outlet than a primary news source. Public radio was a place where listeners found context to help them make sense of the noise and chaos around them. Reporting on chaos in real time wasn't our strong suit. Self-deprecating NPR staffers sometimes summed up this approach to journalism as, "Report it a day late and call it analysis."

As we all tried to understand what was happening, I was assigned to call people who worked at the businesses on the upper floors of the World Trade Center. I reached a secretary at one of the financial firms. She apologized and told me she couldn't talk; everybody was being evacuated.

I kept dialing any numbers I could find, searching for businesses in the buildings and calling them as we threw out our planned broadcast and went into live special coverage. Every time I reached someone, I would patch them through to the studio to describe what was happening. A plane hit the second tower, and I started calling businesses in the streets around the World Trade Center. Bodegas, diners, drugstores, anywhere with a view of the towers.

When we learned that a plane had hit the Pentagon, Mike called my desk and asked if I was okay. "I'm busy!" I shouted. We didn't have a TV in our apartment, so he had gone across the street to a hotel to watch the news in their lobby.

Everyone around me was so immersed in their own specific tasks, I don't know if anyone was looking at the TVs as the first tower fell. I don't remember a shout in the newsroom. I just glanced up at the TV screen and saw that the tower wasn't there anymore. "It can't be gone," I thought. "Did the camera angle change? Is one tower blocking the other from view?" The idea that it had crumbled wasn't conceivable to me. I kept calling strangers, putting guests through to the studio to tell the story of what was happening.

Streets around DC were shut down, and a voice over the NPR intercom informed us that a suspicious vehicle had been identified on our side of the building. We were advised to move away from the windows. But I couldn't. I was in my cubicle, glued to the phone. I wondered if the suspicious vehicle was a car bomb and started to weigh what this temp job was really worth to me. What would people think of me if I just stood up and left? *I could walk out of the building right now.* I kept dialing.

Our team went off the air at noon that day and passed the baton to a call-in show called *Talk of the Nation*. I watched the *Morning Edition* host, Bob Edwards, fly out of the studio to the men's room faster than I had ever seen him move. He, too, had been drinking coffee all morning, and he hadn't left the microphone for hours. When he returned, the staff huddled to talk about our plan for the next day.

Bob never spoke more than he had to, which is unusual for broadcast journalists. He certainly wasn't the type to give an inspirational speech. But on that day, he did. He told us, "People all over the country right now are wondering what they can do. And we're lucky that as journalists, we know what we're supposed to do. We tell the story. We document what's happening. We give people information. We make them feel less alone, less in the dark. That's our role."

Decades later, when the world nearly shut down in the coronavirus pandemic, I was one of the hosts of *All Things Considered*. I shared that story with the staff, telling them what Bob said to us on 9/11 when I was the most junior person on the team. Even decades later, I still feel that sense of relief and purpose in a crisis; the knowledge that when the world comes to a stop and nobody knows what they are supposed to do, we have a role to play.

I left the newsroom at noon on the day of the attacks, returned at 9 p.m., and worked again until noon. In those days after 9/11, people all over the country lined up to donate blood. As a gay man, I was prohibited. But I could show up to work every night and help tell the story of what was happening.

One of my tasks that first week was to write brief remembrances of people who had died. We slotted them into the show for the host to read whenever there was a bit of extra time in a segment. Researching those obituaries in the middle of the night, I found the names of Ronald Gamboa and Dan Bradhorst. They were passengers on Flight 175 with their three-year-old son, David. Theirs was the plane that crashed into the second tower. Gamboa and Bradhorst were founding members of a group called the Pop Luck Club, an organization in Los Angeles for gay men interested in adoption. They were on their way home from a vacation on Cape Cod, and their son, David, was one of the youngest people to die on 9/11.

As I wrote a paragraph about them, I thought about the importance of using the word *family* to describe a gay couple and their adopted son. In 2001, we didn't have many public examples of gay families. I knew that someone else in my job might have written the story differently or chosen other victims to highlight in an obituary. Even though it was less than a minute long, when I heard the segment on the air, I felt like I had left a small fingerprint on the record of the day.

Maybe my logic in not applying for jobs in newsrooms was backward, I thought. Maybe I didn't care too much about the world to be a reporter. Maybe caring about the world was instead a reason to pursue journalism. That moment was part of an awakening for me—a realization that whether or not journalism already had space for people like me, I could make space. And then, maybe I could carve out space for others. I didn't have to accept the hard-boiled world of news for what it was with all its flaws; I could be part of a new generation of journalists, with the power to nudge our industry and shape it from the inside.

··

AFTER I HAD WORKED AS a temp for more than a year, NPR gave me some job security and hired me as a full-time employee. I resolved to treat the newsroom as a free journalism school. I borrowed a microphone and minidisc recorder and asked an engineer to teach me how to use them. Then, after leaving the office at nine each morning, I'd go out and report stories during the day. I wasn't precious about it. I knew from studying the piano that if you do something a little bit every day, you'll get better at it. So I told myself that I didn't need to create the perfect radio story. I just needed to start practicing.

On a piece of paper, I scratched out a pitching hierarchy for where I would try to place my stories: first NPR, then Marketplace, then my local station, WAMU. If they all declined, then I would pitch it to a website for radio freelancers. And if they weren't interested, then I'd add it to my clip file and go out to report the next story.

My first outing with a microphone was a feature about an event called the "Peace Cafe," where an Iraqi American restaurateur in DC named Andy Shallal brought Jews and Arabs together for falafel and conversation. WAMU agreed to air the piece on its local weekend show. And just like that, I was an on-air reporter.

Even in that first story, I see themes that thread through my career. I didn't confront a news event head-on; I came at it from a human perspective. I used people's personal experiences to explore intractable struggles. I focused on individuals who were trying to change the world for the better. And another signature, as producers who've worked with me over the years will attest, is that I ate well while I was doing it.

I decided to stick with food and did another story for WAMU, about fancy restaurants in town discovering Greek wine. After that piece aired, the tourism arm of the Greek embassy invited me on an all-expenses-paid trip to visit wineries in Greece with other food journalists. It would have been a hell of a junket for a beginning reporter. I called Nina to get her advice, and she suggested that I politely decline. As she explained, news organizations generally frown upon journalists accepting expensive freebies from the industries they've reported on. (When I finally did make it to Greece for the first time years later, it was to perform with Pink Martini in Athens.)

I reached out to editors at NPR whose work I respected, even if I didn't know them well, and asked for feedback on my stories. Their notes were helpful, but I was also being strategic. Beyond just trying to learn from my elders, this was a way of saying to people in powerful positions, "Look, I am a reporter now! I am on the air! I am using my free time to practice journalism!" And the tactic worked. Some of the NPR editors I'd been sending my stories to eventually suggested that I try reporting freelance pieces for the network. My inroad would be the obituary.

Every news organization keeps a long list of people who could die at any moment. Movie stars, politicians, musicians, athletes, and other towering figures from earlier generations are all on the list. Often, obituaries are written long before the celebrity takes that last breath. But beat reporters covering arts or politics generally don't want to spend their time reporting stories that could sit on a shelf gathering dust for years.

So for someone like me, obituaries were a perfect stepping-stone from the local station to the network. I could learn from an NPR editor and report a radio piece that would air all over the country, eventually. But I had no deadline, and the correspondents on staff didn't feel like I was encroaching on their turf.

I scanned the list of names and chose the actor Hume Cronyn, who had won a lifetime achievement Tony with his late wife, Jessica Tandy, in

1994. I decided to call the legendary actress Marian Seldes for a quote. I had seen and admired Seldes in a Neil Simon play called *45 Seconds from Broadway*, and Mike and I still quoted her most famous line from the show to each other—a long, drawn-out "*Las Pallllllmas*," ideally delivered in a caftan with a swoon. I wasn't used to interviewing famous people, so once I got Seldes on the phone I stammered my way through some kind of introduction, explaining that I was hoping to speak with her for a story that would be a tribute to the great (at that point still very much alive) Hume Cronyn.

She began to describe her dear friend's approach to acting and his relationship with Tandy, speaking in that precise, patrician diction found only in performers of a certain generation. The only problem was, she was describing him in the present tense.

"I'm so sorry to interrupt you, Ms. Seldes. Um, this tribute for Mr. Cronyn, it's—ahh—a tribute that will be broadcast after he is no longer with us."

Her silence could have had so many motivations. Shock, confusion, fury, disdain . . .

"It's, mm, an obituary." I figured I should make sure there was no further ambiguity. Probably should have led with that.

"Oh."

More silence. I imagined this woman with her flagpole posture, growing taller as her inner monologue unfurled.

I plowed ahead. "So, you're making some wonderful points, but could I ask you to speak about Mr. Cronyn in . . . the past tense?"

Another pause. A sigh. Finally, "Couldn't you just explain that you spoke to me before he, ah, passed?" I now think she was right. Why not be transparent about it and let someone talk about their living friend in the present tense, even if that interview will air after the person has died? But at the time, I believed this act of artifice to be crucial. I somehow persuaded her to briefly play the role of a person remembering her dear departed friend and colleague, and I got the quote.

Cronyn died in 2003 at the age of ninety-one, and that afternoon NPR listeners heard Seldes say of his relationship with Tandy, "They were absolutely straightforward. They were so—funny to say this about actors—but they were so real in their real life, and they made so many people happy to be in their presence."

I ended the piece with the voice of Cronyn himself, quoting a poem by Christopher Logue that he called his credo.

> Come to the edge.
> We might fall.
> Come to the edge.
> It's too high!
> COME TO THE EDGE!
> And they came.
> And he pushed,
> And they flew.

I listen to that story now and hear the effort I was making to sound like someone who belonged on NPR. I was an intensely earnest, overarticulate, tightly wound spring. But I also appreciate that when that piece aired in 2003, the final moment of poetry gave listeners an opportunity to pause—a breath of relief from the chronicle of wars and politics that filled *All Things Considered* that day.

I wish I could say that my exchange with Marian Seldes was the only time I embarrassed myself before a legend. In my day job as an editorial assistant, one of my responsibilities was to coach commentators on their delivery. I would ask the naturalist to convey the sound of the oriole with a bit more verve in his voice. I'd tell the essayist to look up from the page and pretend she was talking to a friend. But one day the commentator Marvin Kalb popped up on my schedule, and I didn't know who he was.

I should have looked him up. Today, I'm fully aware that he was the last correspondent personally hired at CBS News by Edward R. Murrow. After a career spanning decades, Kalb founded the Joan Shorenstein Center at Harvard's Kennedy School. I could go on. The point is, on the day I was asked to bring in his commentary for *Morning Edition*, I thought he was just one more person with an opinion.

I took my coaching responsibilities seriously. "Excellent delivery, Mr. Kalb." (I'd been taught to always begin a coaching session by offering praise.) "Now, could you do me a favor? Read it again. But this time, maybe go a bit more slowly. And I'm going to ask you to *lean* into certain words. You might try to pretend you're talking to an old buddy. If it helps you to underline these phrases on the page, feel free! Would you like a pen? I have one here."

This was a man who had covered the Cuban Missile Crisis and Martin Luther King Jr.'s "I Have a Dream" speech. And I was attempting to tell him how to do broadcast journalism.

To his credit, Kalb nodded and said, "Thank you." Then he delivered his commentary again, beginning to end, with exactly the same delivery. "*Much* better!" I beamed.

By the time I realized what I had done, he had long since left the building. He was gracious enough to say nothing about it.

The benefit of these mortifying experiences was that, when I was given my first assignment to report a news story on deadline for NPR, I had some practice barreling through rough patches. The piece would be a two-day project, about grandparents who raised their grandchildren when the mother and father were incarcerated, addicted, or otherwise absent. The grandparents were gathering in Washington, DC, lobbying for the kinds of federal benefits they'd get if they were raising their own children.

Day one was a peaceful, festive rally at the Capitol building. White-haired men and women milled around with the little kids they were helping to raise. I proudly wore my NPR badge around my neck and held out my microphone to capture the speeches, the music, the sounds of chants and cheers. At home that night, I spent hours transcribing the interviews and then agonized over my script long past bedtime. I left one hole in the piece for a quote that I planned to get the next morning at a press conference.

I woke up giddy to Nina Simone singing "Here Comes the Sun." It was the first track on the CD that I had put in my alarm clock, the same song I started my day with nearly every morning. This was the day I would be on *All Things Considered*, with a proper hard news story, for the first time ever! I took the DC Metro to a hotel in the Virginia suburbs for the press conference, humming to myself.

I plugged my equipment into the box that would provide an audio feed from the microphones on the dais and inserted a minidisc into my recorder. The disc was full of . . . something. "Hmm, that's odd," I thought. "I could have sworn this was blank." I formatted the card to erase whatever junk was on it. *DELETE.*

The moment the formatting was complete, I knew what I had done. It hit me like a January cold plunge. All the audio from the previous day was gone. I felt nauseated and dizzy. That's when the press conference started. I was sweating through my blazer. I hit record and walked out into the hallway to think.

My first plan was—I'll leave my things behind, get on a train, and go as far as it will take me. I'll never return, riding the rails as an anonymous hobo for the rest of my life. That way, I won't have to face what just happened.

That was plan A.

I decided to go with plan B. Call my editor, hyperventilating, and explain what I'd done. "Well, what do you want to do now?" she asked me.

I hadn't actually thought about an answer to that question. I had expected her to tell me what to do. Likely pull the plug on the story. I knew the day's news agenda wasn't riding on my piece. I was the only person at NPR who would mourn if the story vanished.

Then I heard the words coming out of my mouth, "I think I can do this story anyway. I'll use more tape from the press conference than I had planned, and I'll call back some of the people I interviewed yesterday. And maybe we can find footage of the rally online, or get sound of the event from the organizers.

"And you'll make your deadline?"

"I'll make my deadline."

The day was a mess, a blur, a panic. But by the time *All Things Considered* aired that night, my story was ready to join the lineup. It wasn't great. It might not have even been good. But it checked the box.

And then I moved on to the next story. And the one after that. One of the things I love about making radio is that it's a volume business. You do a piece, and it's great or fine or boring or moving or forgettable. And the next day, the slate is blank again. You've written the first draft of history. The second draft is someone else's job. I find it reassuring to start from zero each day. I like showing up each morning with the possibility of success or failure, regardless of what happened the day before.

I've always been attracted to forms of expression that are short-lived. I like to cook, and to sing with a band. If the meal is terrible, you can throw it out and scramble some eggs. If you forget your song lyrics, you'll do another show the next night. (I have forgotten song lyrics in the middle of a concert more than once. I quote the performer Taylor Mac to myself: "Perfection is for assholes." If audiences wanted something flawless, they'd listen to the album.)

I can't imagine making an oil painting. The canvases just pile up and stare at you from the corner of the room. This might also be why I've never wanted children. You don't get to wipe the slate clean and start again if they turn out a mess. But radio? It can be wallpaper. Go in one ear and out the other. It can move you, then move on. And so, after my story about grandparents, I got back to work.

I did a short piece for *Morning Edition* about the first sandwich in recorded history. (Food again.) The feature, tied to the Jewish holiday of Passover, turned into a jaunty history of the sandwich, from biblical times to the military's efforts to formulate a shelf-stable PB&J that could survive in a war zone. When I showed up at my desk the day after the story aired, there was a note scrawled on a napkin.

Best in show!—Mrs. Stamberg.

As one of NPR's founding mothers and the first woman to host a nationally broadcast nightly news program, Susan Stamberg is the heart and soul of NPR. When the Newseum opened on Pennsylvania Avenue in Washington, DC, her tape recorder was on display in one of the exhibitions. Her favorite cousin was also married to my distant cousin, so when we saw each other around the building, we affectionately called each other "Cuz."

The very same Susan Stamberg, that legend of broadcast journalism, had stopped by to congratulate me on my story about sandwiches. When she didn't find me at my cubicle, she had scribbled that note.

I held the napkin and recognized that I had guardian angels in the building. Just as I aspired to shift the culture of journalism in a direction that would be more welcoming to people following in my footsteps, I saw that I'd been benefiting all along from the work of a generation that came before me, promising to do the same. Nina, Susan, and others whom I may never know spent their careers chipping away at a solid rock face so that, years later, I could get a toehold and start to climb. I treasured the napkin, vowing to keep it forever.

After more than a year of doing freelance stories alongside my day job, I landed an NPR reporting fellowship at the local station in Boston. I'd be given a three-month leave of absence from *Morning Edition* to work as a reporter at WBUR. At least for a few months, I would no longer have to squeeze my own reporting projects into off-hours. Mike and I sublet our apartment in DC and crammed everything we owned into a rental van, planning to leave before dawn for the drive north.

We went to sleep in our empty DC apartment and woke up to a 3 a.m. phone call from the police. Someone had smashed the window of the van and stolen everything inside it. My passport and laptop were gone, along with other valuables. But the thing I was most distressed about losing was the napkin from Susan. I'd been planning to frame it and hadn't yet gotten around to doing so.

A few months later, Mike gave me a birthday present. I unwrapped a silver frame, with a napkin under glass. Scrawled on the napkin, in ballpoint pen:

Best in show!—Mrs. Stamberg.

"How the hell did you find it?" I asked him.

He laughed. Of course he hadn't found it. He'd asked her to write me another one. It has sat on my desk in that silver frame ever since. It reminds me that the torch I carry today was lit by others before me, and that it is one I will someday pass to those coming up behind.

3

HAPPY ENDINGS

For most of my adult life, I've started every day the same way. I turn to Mike and say, "Good morning. How are you? It's a beautiful day." Then he repeats the same words back to me, verbatim. Sometimes he goes first and I reply. If we're in different cities, the exchange happens by text.

Our ritual started the first time we stayed together at his parents' house in San Francisco. We were still in college, and so, like most college students, we slept in. When I looked at the clock and saw how late it was, I bolted up in a frenzy, panicked that his parents' first impression of me would be that I was lazy.

While I hopped crazily around the bedroom trying to pull on my pants and rouse Mike, he said, still shaking off sleep, "No, no no. That's not how we start our day. We start our day by saying, *Good morning. How are you? It's a beautiful day.*" He recited it in a sweet, musical way, almost like a kids' song. I repeated those words back to him in just the same way, and it stuck. By now it has become one of our many shared marital passwords, the key we turn to unlock whatever lies ahead for the day: *goodmorninghowareyouitsabeautifulday.*

Five years later, when Mike and I decided to get married, I felt like I had to ask permission to do so. Not from my parents or future in-laws, who were all thrilled. In fact, by that point, our mothers talked to each other on the phone more than either of us talked to them. I think their shared view was, "If we'd known you were each going to settle down with a nice Jewish Yalie from the West Coast, we wouldn't have freaked out when you told us you were gay." They were ecstatic that we wanted to make it official.

No, I thought I should ask permission from my employer, NPR. I was about to step into the middle of the culture wars at a time when the country was undecided on whether gay couples should be allowed to legally commit to a life together. As a journalist, I would be publicly placing myself at the center of a national controversy, becoming a participant in a major news story. I didn't feel especially good about that. If I could have kept my head down and gotten married without making a political statement, I would have. I didn't want to be a standard-bearer or a flag-waver; I just wanted to do what all my straight friends were doing, tie the knot, and get on with my life. But the low-key option wasn't available to me.

After years of "goodmorninghowareyouitsabeautifuldays," Mike and I took it as a given that we would spend our lives together. Early on we said to each other, "If you meet someone who's a better fit for you than I am, then Godspeed. But I don't think that's gonna happen." And that's proved true. We always figured we'd get married whenever it was eventually legal. *If* it ever became legal. But in those early years of our relationship I wasn't holding my breath for the country to grant us permission.

I had heard of same-sex couples where one partner adopted the other, since it was the only way for two men or women to legally become a family. Having come of age during the AIDS crisis, I was familiar with the horror stories of men who were barred from a dying partner's hospital room after a parent decided he wasn't *actually* family. So getting a piece of paper seemed important to me, whether it was an adoption certificate or something else. For Mike, it was about claiming a right to which he felt entitled. (For the same reason, he later joined the military as an air force reservist. He couldn't tolerate the idea that gays weren't permitted to serve. That, more than anything, drove him to become one of the first openly gay officers commissioned in the US military immediately after the repeal of "Don't Ask, Don't Tell.")

When marriage rights slowly began to take hold in the early 2000s, for the first time I saw happy same-sex couples publicly declaring their love and commitment to each other in large numbers. Sometimes they had kids; other times they were my grandparents' age and had been living together for decades. Maybe there were people on the sidelines marching with signs reading "GOD HATES FAGS," but that was nothing new. Queer people getting married? That was new. For a man to even use the word *husband* felt foreign. More than one person asked me, "Does that make the other one the wife?" Friends of mine opted for the word *spouse*, just because it seemed less like a full frontal assault against the status quo.

There was this strange trend where people would get married a bunch of times to the same person. First they would have a commitment ceremony, which was like the alcohol-free beer of weddings. Then, once civil unions were a thing, they'd go someplace like Vermont to get one of those. (Civil unions were considered radical when Vermont governor Howard Dean supported them, before social conservatives decided that they could stomach civil unions as a last-ditch bulwark against same-sex marriage.) The couple who got a civil union might then cross the border into Canada when actual marriage became legal up there. And when their home state finally let gay people marry, they'd go to city hall and add that piece of paper to the pile.

These couples weren't addicted to bouquets and toasts. Okay, maybe some of them were. But many of them just felt an urgency to make sure the systems that had been weaponized against LGBTQ people for centuries wouldn't be used against us again.

When Massachusetts first legalized same-sex marriage in 2003, Mike and I considered going, then decided against it. Neither of us had a connection to the state, and it was clear that the movement was spreading. We assumed we'd soon have other options. Sure enough, San Francisco mayor Gavin Newsom suddenly decided to start allowing same-sex marriages in early 2004—without any legislation or court ruling—and as a San Francisco native, Mike wanted to be a part of history in his hometown. Of course, I was game.

Mike and I were in a long-distance relationship at the time. I was living in Atlanta, on a temp assignment for a few months, filling in for an NPR reporter who was on maternity leave. Mike was in his second year at Yale Law School in New Haven. Neither of us got down on one knee. We made the decision over the phone. The conversation was along the lines of, "We're doing this, right?" "Of course we are."

Political commentators declared that by sticking his neck out for LGBT people, Newsom was throwing away his political future, his chance to be "the next Bill Clinton." Fourteen years later, he would be elected governor of California. Whatever the political risks might have been in 2004, Newsom was legally way out on a limb. And eventually the branch snapped. California's Supreme Court would rule that a mayor didn't have the authority to legalize same-sex unions on his own. All the weddings performed under his declaration would be annulled in August 2004, including ours.

But in February of that year, when the window cracked open in San Francisco for the first time, couples lined up outside City Hall for hours. Families, including ours, flew in to celebrate weddings that had been thrown together in less than a day. The mayor deputized volunteers to perform weddings. People from all over the world phoned up San

Francisco florists asking to have bouquets delivered to anyone waiting in line at City Hall, all of the bouquets addressed "To the happy couple."

By the Monday after San Francisco's gay wedding mania started, the city was taking appointments instead of the chaotic first come, first served scenario of the initial few days. Mike spent hours trying to get through the jammed city hall phone lines and finally booked us for that Friday at noon. We had four days to put together a wedding and get across the country for it.

Mike popped into the jewelry store across the street from his dorm. "I need to buy four men's wedding rings," he told the baffled man behind the counter. Mike told me that the reason he got two extras was in case either of us lost our first one. I knew that he believed he needed to buy an extra only for me: I'm the type to lose my wedding ring; he's not. I appreciated the gesture of buying a backup for us both, and Mike appreciated that I knew what the gesture meant without his having to explain it. The guy at the jewelry store had never made a sale of four men's wedding rings, but he didn't ask questions. (The money we saved by skipping the caterer, the florist, and all the other typical wedding accoutrements meant we could splurge on backup rings.)

Jewish tradition states that no matter how rich or poor you are, there are two things that everyone gets exactly the same, with no signifiers of class or wealth: everyone gets buried in a simple wooden casket, and everyone gets married with a plain gold wedding band. I told Mike to make mine white gold. One does want a bit of flair.

I didn't have time or the budget for a new suit, so I went to a mall in Atlanta and picked out a pale blue Ralph Lauren tie with tiny white dots. It cost more than one hundred dollars, an exorbitant amount for a young public radio reporter working on a temp contract. I told myself that the splurge was appropriate for a once-in-a-lifetime occasion.

My last-minute plane ticket had me landing in San Francisco on Thursday night, and Mike's flight was scheduled to get in on Friday morning, a few hours before our noon appointment at city hall. It would be a true "running from the airport to the wedding" scenario, straight out of a rom-com. He flew in his wedding suit.

The marriage extravaganza was dominating national headlines. The religious right predicted the downfall of civilization. Of course it was happening in San Francisco, they said, "the land of fruits and nuts." It all gave me a strange sense of déjà vu. When I was in high school, some of those same protesters had told us that gays shouldn't be protected from discrimination because we were too promiscuous and couldn't settle down. Now they were trying to block us from doing exactly what they had insisted we would never commit to doing.

..

WHEN I WAS GROWING UP in Portland in the nineties, my classmates would toss around the word *faggot* as casually as *idiot* or *loser*. The epithet wasn't particularly directed at feminine boys; it was a generic put-down, used against all, since being gay was generally the last thing anyone at my school would have wanted to be. As a kid, I tried saying it once or twice, but the word always thudded out of my mouth with the limp flop of a baseball falling short of home plate.

There was obviously a gap between the abstract way my classmates deployed the word and the lived reality of gay people. My classmates, for the most part, didn't even recognize that gay people lived in reality. They couldn't name one, apart from maybe a swishy pop star. And then in 1992, when I was fourteen, everything changed. A group called the Oregon Citizens Alliance put a measure on the statewide ballot that would have added this text to the state constitution:

> All governments in Oregon may not use their monies or
> properties to promote, encourage or facilitate homosexuality,
> pedophilia, sadism or masochism. All levels of government,
> including public education systems, must assist in setting

a standard for Oregon's youth which recognizes that these behaviors are abnormal, wrong, unnatural and perverse and they are to be discouraged and avoided.

Measure 9 would have required sex education classes to teach that gay people were "perverse." Gay teachers could be fired. And of course, you couldn't overlook that familiar pairing of homosexuality and pedophilia, as classic as wine and cheese.

Oregonians voted no on 9. A similar proposal a few years later, called Measure 13, went the same way. But the debate mobilized everyone. Suddenly students at my school were choosing sides, which meant that by the time I came out to my parents the summer after my junior year in high school, I was a vessel into which my classmates could pour all their feelings about gay people. They no longer had to shout their political opinions into the void—they could shout them at me! Or about me. Or near me. Or all three.

As I've already established, I've never shied away from attention. And I soon realized that in this case, I didn't have a choice. People at school were going to gossip about me no matter how I felt about it. Before my senior year began, I went to talk to my younger brother, Joseph, in his bedroom. He was about to start his freshman year at the same school where I, as a senior, would be the only out gay student.

"I hadn't really planned to be out to everybody at school this year, but I think at this point it's out of my hands," I told him. "You may get bullied for having a gay brother, which isn't fair. So, I'm sorry for making your freshman year more difficult. I know you didn't ask for this."

I will never forget his reply. "You don't deserve it either," he said. "You didn't ask to be gay. And you shouldn't be bullied for it any more than I should for being your brother." He was thirteen years old.

So I showed up at the first day of school senior year with a pink triangle button pinned to my backpack. (The pink triangle originated in Nazi

Germany as a symbol to identify gay men and lesbians, before LGBT activists reclaimed it decades later as an expression of pride.) I strutted through the halls like it was my own personal catwalk. The French teacher and the drama teacher gave me knowing nods, which have long been the language of queer people, but they couldn't exactly come out to me. After all, powerful institutions were telling us that homosexuality was adjacent to pedophilia. And those teachers still lived in fear that they might someday lose their jobs if they confirmed what everyone already assumed.

When closeted people ask me whether they should come out, I sometimes tell them that it can give others an opportunity to surprise us by being their best selves. I saw that in many of my classmates at Beaverton High, as people stood up for me in ways that I hadn't expected. A football player offered to defend me from bullies. (Hindsight: Was he hitting on me? Probably.) The star of the women's basketball team, who came out herself a few years later, was the student council member in charge of morning announcements each day. On my seventeenth birthday, less than a month into the school year, she opened the announcements with ABBA's "Dancing Queen." It felt like a serenade and a celebration as the whole school started their day bopping to *Young and sweet, only seventeen* . . .

I tried to start my school district's first gay-straight alliance, but the principal was afraid of a backlash from parents. He suggested that I start a "diversity club" instead. I saw it as a cowardly dodge . . . a convenient way for him to gloss over the specific discrimination against me (and presumably other students whose identities fell under that squishy "diversity" label). As a teenager, I couldn't understand where the principal was coming from. His job was to protect students, to make the school a safe place for us to learn. Why would he allow his fears of conservative parents to stop him from doing his job? I wish I had asked him those questions and held his feet to the fire. Instead, I swallowed my resentment and started the diversity club.

Imagine my shock, years later, when I came back to Portland to sing in a Pink Martini concert and the GSA at my old high school invited me to drop in. The openly gay Japanese teacher, who was also the wrestling coach, was the staff coordinator for the club. People introduced themselves with their pronouns. I felt like Rip Van Winkle waking up in a different world.

As lucky as I was to have a supportive family and friends, I got the message growing up that gay stories don't have happy endings. Maybe you would die young—of AIDS, a gay bashing, a drug overdose, or suicide. You might get fired from your job, or marry a woman to get by, potentially ruining someone else's life while trying to salvage yours. Those were the only stories I saw on TV and in movies, and I didn't personally know any queer people with happier stories to prove them wrong. I stewed when *Philadelphia* won big at the 1993 Oscars. I got it—gay people's stories ended in tragedy. I didn't need a straight actor weeping along to a Maria Callas aria to drive the point home.

In that context, I guess I shouldn't have been surprised that when I came out at sixteen, many people confessed that they expected the next words out of my mouth after "I'm gay" to be "and I have AIDS." Even before I had had any sexual contact with anyone, I had absorbed the message that gay sex equaled sickness and death. So, it seemed, had everyone around me.

In the best-case scenario, you would wind up sad and alone, self-medicating like the guys in *The Boys in the Band*. Soon after I came out, I decided to watch that film from 1970—one of the few movies at the time to revolve around openly gay characters. The only line I remember is "Show me a happy homosexual, and I'll show you a gay corpse." It left me feeling grim and defeated. Even *Will and Grace*, which was groundbreaking when it debuted in 1998, made gay men seem as sexually potent as Ken dolls.

As a teen, I assumed that I'd have to wait at least until I was an old man (which I defined as "in my twenties") to meet anybody my age who was openly gay. So I was surprised to discover a thriving queer teenage scene in downtown Portland. An organization called Lambda Rising hosted a weekly drop-in youth group called Windfire. (That's the name you end up with when you let queer Portland kids in the nineties choose the name for their group. *Windfire*.) I would take a city bus downtown every Thursday after school to attend. It was sort of like group therapy, where the other teens shared stories about getting kicked out of the house, doing sex work, or fighting addiction. I became friends with them and started to learn what life was like for people way outside my suburban bubble of privilege.

The tight network of queer kids in Portland looked out for one another. I'd drop by Pioneer Courthouse Square in the center of town, and someone I knew was always there. Maybe I'd run into a few of the gutter punks, or members of the baby bull dyke gang that protected my little posse of femmy teenage boys. A girl everybody called Julie the Junkie gave me a studded leather wrist cuff and dog collar as a gift. It didn't matter that I was a middle-class honors student who came from a supportive family; we were all on the same team.

I was surrounded by teenage peers, but I still didn't really have any queer role models. When I got to college, I read books by and about gay men who'd gone to Yale before me. There was the aching loneliness of the poet and essayist Paul Monette, who died of AIDS in 1995. Calvin Trillin (not gay) wrote a book called *Remembering Denny*, about the golden boy and Rhodes scholar who was in Yale's secret society Scroll & Key with Trillin in the 1950s. Denny killed himself, because—let's not forget—stories of gay people always end in tragedy.

I watched people take one of two paths after they came out. The first group of us tried to compensate for letting everybody down. We insisted that we would excel in every other facet of life, conform in every respect, prove our worthiness. It's what the author Andy Tobias (a Harvard grad, but close enough) called the "best little boy in the world" syndrome. As you can imagine, Yale had a lot of those folks.

The other group of us recognized that we had been lied to. That we weren't "abnormal, wrong, unnatural and perverse." And so we wondered what other lies we'd been told. The sky didn't fall when we broke the cardinal rule of sexual partnership. So what other rules were ready to be broken? What fictions had we swallowed about the way society should function—about immigrants, or people of color, or other marginalized groups?

I can see now that I contain both of these archetypes, wrestling like fraternal twins in utero. Sometimes I'm a secret agent faggot behind enemy lines; other times I just want to impress your parents. I itch to torch oppressive and exclusionary institutions, even as I long to prove myself worthy of membership in them. To rewrite a slogan from a T-shirt that I've spotted at countless pride parades over the years, I am both "gay as in happy" and "queer as in fuck you."

So at Yale, I dug into queer theory. It was a way for me to understand the hidden architecture of society that may have been invisible to those who had always been able to take their membership in the Club of Acceptable Humans for granted. I wrote about how monsters in gothic literature reflected society's evolving attitudes toward social deviance. (Dracula: combining archetypes of the homosexual, the foreigner, and the Jew. Discuss.) I worked for an AIDS organization in New Haven. And at the end of my freshman year, I met Mike.

He was, and still is, the most charismatic person in any room. Charming and witty, but reserved enough to leave everyone wanting more. He was the one everybody yearned to be friends with (or more), who kept most of his admirers at arm's length. He wore a personal uniform—white button-down shirt, khaki pants. He was not "queer as in fuck you." In fact, my friends weren't sure whether he was gay or straight. He was drawn to my radicalism; I was drawn to his conformity. He saw someone who might pull him out of his comfort zone; I saw someone who might temper my extremes.

A group of Yale undergrads always puts on a commencement musical, thrown together in twelve-hour rehearsal days for a week between final exams and graduation, culminating in an intense weekend of performances for graduating seniors and their families. Somehow, even though Mike and I ran in similar circles at Yale (a cappella, improv comedy, plays and musicals), we had never crossed paths until the first day of rehearsals.

That year's commencement musical was *Little Shop of Horrors*. Both of us had small roles, just a step up from the chorus. I couldn't tell if he was interested in me romantically. But I could tell we were hitting it off. I sat next to him at that first rehearsal. Like everyone else, I wanted to be close to him. To my shock, he wanted to be close to me too. For the week that we spent putting the show together, we were inseparable—and platonic. We shared a dressing room at the theater, where he lay down a red carpet on the ugly tile, hung up a clock in the shape of Elvis swinging his hips, and played the overture to *Candide* on his portable stereo. And after the opening night party, we slept together.

Two days later, we went our separate ways for the summer. He flew to Japan on an a cappella tour; I went to New Hampshire and worked at a summer stock theater. We wrote actual letters to each other, on paper. But when we got back to campus for our sophomore year, it became clear that we were in different places. After a quasi-coming out in high school that didn't quite achieve lift-off, he wasn't yet ready to make another attempt at going public; I wasn't ready to go back in the closet. He had another complicated romantic entanglement going on at the same time; I didn't. Our relationship imploded, and we spent the year keeping each other at arm's length.

Midway through our junior year, we started to piece together a friendship again. The weekend before Thanksgiving break, we decided to take the train from New Haven down to New York to see a show. After the theater, we wound up at a gay bar in Chelsea. Making out on the dance floor, he said, "I'm not ready for a relationship." I snorted, "The last thing I'd want is a relationship with you." And then we saw that we had missed the last train back to New Haven. Mike offered to pay for a hotel room. I said, "Only if we get two separate beds." The guy at the hotel's front desk said the only room they had left was a king bed. I vehemently insisted on sleeping on the floor. I did not sleep on the floor, and we have been together ever since. (His second coming out was therefore less of the "I have an announcement" variety and more of the "Well, I guess Mike and Ari are together" variety.)

When we finished college and I arrived at NPR as an intern in 2001, it never crossed my mind to try to conceal who I was. I'd been out to everyone I knew for years. The effort it would have required to undo that seemed absurd. Besides, I wasn't even very good at passing as straight *before* I came out. The idea of trying to do it at that point was laughable.

There weren't many out public figures in journalism when I started working in news. This was the age of the "glass closet," when lots of people, from Anderson Cooper to Rosie O'Donnell, were *obviously* gay but not *publicly* gay. If I had had a career plan, I might have thought more about whether being out would get in the way of that plan. But I wasn't that strategic, and I definitely wasn't going to pretend that Mike didn't exist.

When San Francisco started performing same-sex marriages in 2004, older gay reporters from other news organizations told me they planned not to tie the knot, at least until there was a national consensus on the issue. As journalists, they didn't want to wade into the controversy.

I recognized their impulse, but I wasn't going to let my fear of becoming a combatant in the culture wars override my excitement to marry Mike. I called my boss and explained the situation to her. "Of course you should go get married," she told me. I assured her that I would keep a low profile and leave my NPR tote bag at home. After all, I wasn't flying to San Francisco because I wanted to take a stand or jump on a political bandwagon. I just wanted to wed my college boyfriend.

..

MY PARENTS FLEW DOWN FROM Portland, and my soon-to-be in-laws drove downtown from the house where Mike was born. His flight landed on time, and we all converged on city hall just over an hour before our appointment. A jubilant sort of order had replaced the frenzy of the first few days. We waited in line for our wedding license, and the clerk handed us a pamphlet about avoiding unwanted pregnancies. She shrugged and told us it was required under California law.

The central vestibule had a long staircase, with joyous same-sex couples exchanging rings and vows every few steps. Bouquets were laid out on a long table—gifts from strangers who wanted to support the celebration. We were encouraged to choose our own. I picked up a bunch of flowers and read the card, which offered best wishes from a straight couple in upstate New York.

The man who performed our wedding had white hair and a close-cropped beard. He told us he'd been with his partner since before the Stonewall riots. They had gotten married on Valentine's Day, and then Mayor Newsom had deputized him to perform weddings himself. I didn't expect to be as emotional as I was. Looking into that older man's eyes, I thought of the history that he had lived through, from antigay employment laws to the AIDS crisis. In that moment, I felt a small part of something enormous. I realized that we were helping rewrite the narrative, one in which gay stories could actually have happy endings. I was so caught up in the moment that I didn't notice the TV camera over our shoulders.

Mike and I were at least twenty years younger than most of the other couples at city hall, and it seemed unusual to have all four of our parents there, snapping photos and wiping away tears. Maybe that was why the crew for the local NBC affiliate decided to film us exchanging rings and saying our vows. They didn't interview us, just recorded our wedding as part of the public event causing so much celebration and controversy. After the ceremony we went back to Mike's parents' house for lunch, where his mother had ordered an elaborate chocolate wedding cake.

That night, our wedding was in the B-roll footage for the local news story about the San Francisco gay marriage boom. A few days later, the footage of our wedding was part of a national package. We were no longer just background for the San Francisco affiliate—our exchange of vows showed up in a story on the *NBC Nightly News*. Then the video made its way to MSNBC, CNBC, and a few documentaries.

The reports never identified us. I don't think anybody had asked for our names. But there we were, me in my brand-new blue necktie and Mike just off the plane from New Haven. I cringed, even as I also felt proud and defiant. I aspired to moderate national debates, not to embody them. It was one of the happiest days of my life, and also a day that I had promised my boss I would keep out of the spotlight. She wasn't bothered by it. (I realize how much luckier that makes me than many other queer people.) I think I was more conflicted than she was. It was the first time my identity as a reporter felt at odds with my identity as a queer person. I had no models for the two labels coexisting.

And since the same-sex marriage debate remained a huge issue for years, our faces kept showing up—day after day, year after year. I didn't want to ask to have the footage removed from the NBC archive. That felt like giving in to shame and public pressure. At the same time, I felt a bit queasy every time someone reported seeing me in the B-roll. I kept waiting for the other shoe to drop. I expected a tap on the shoulder and an Edward R. Murrow–esque voice to say, "You got gay married? On TV? Your journalism career path ends here."

Of course that never happened. About five years after our wedding, I was a full-time correspondent for NPR, covering the Justice Department and legal affairs. I generally recused myself from reporting stories about same-sex marriage litigation, which came up a lot. On a day that the issue was in the news yet again, my office phone rang. It was Pete Williams, the veteran Justice correspondent for NBC News, who is also gay. Pete is a consummate gentleman, always friendly and polite.

"Ari, I think you're in the background of my same-sex marriage story tonight," he said.

I explained the situation and told Pete that I was ready to pass the tiara and let someone else take the throne as the face of same-sex marriage on NBC. He was gracious as ever, and assured me he would have us removed from the files.

..

A FEW MONTHS AFTER OUR 2004 shotgun wedding, we got a check in the mail from the city of San Francisco. It was a refund of our marriage license fee, along with a letter explaining that our legal union had been annulled by the California Supreme Court. We had seen this coming, so it wasn't a shock. In fact, we'd already started planning to have a religious ceremony the following summer, jointly officiated by Mike's family rabbi and mine. It would be an opportunity to invite all our extended relatives and friends whom we hadn't been able to include in the San Francisco whirlwind, a more traditional wedding than the one we had pulled off on four days' notice with only our immediate family. We would buy entirely new outfits this time.

We were married for the second time in Napa Valley in 2005, overlooking vineyards, surrounded by loved ones. We exchanged the same rings we'd been wearing for a year. At that point, same-sex marriage was still not allowed in California. So it was a religious ceremony, but not a legally binding one.

Which means that today Mike and I are, technically, not legally married. We've had two weddings now. And someday we'll probably have a third, just like those pioneers in the earliest days of same-sex marriage. But we're not in a hurry. The world has changed so much since I came out; I no longer fear that we'll be barred from seeing each other in a hospital room or that one of us will have to adopt the other in order to prove that we're a family.

I'm not naive. I see governors all over the country enthusiastically signing anti-LGBTQ policies into law. Those bills remind me of the anti-gay ballot measures Oregon defeated in the nineties. I hear members of Congress accuse queer people of "grooming" children, reviving pernicious conspiracy theories that I hoped had been debunked long ago. I know that the Supreme Court could take away our marriage rights as easily as five justices granted them in 2015.

I've reported on gay people being killed in Chechnya and Uganda. I covered the Pulse nightclub shooting in Orlando. And I serve on the board of an LGBTQ youth organization in Washington, DC, called SMYAL (Supporting and Mentoring Youth Advocates and Leaders). It reminds me a lot of Lambda Rising, where I attended Windfire in the nineties. At SMYAL, I hear queer teens share stories of discrimination and violence, addiction and homelessness. But those aren't the only stories I hear. The youth also talk about romance and role models, ambitions and aspirations.

Today, I no longer believe that every queer story has to end in tragedy. But just for the record, Mike and I are both still wearing wedding ring number one. I have the backup in a drawer, somewhere.

4

MUSICAL INTERLUDE 1:

JE NE VEUX PAS TRAVAILLER

I think the waiter was doing me a favor by continuing to hang out with me. We weren't exactly dating. We weren't even sleeping together. We definitely weren't in a relationship. I was a teenager; he wasn't. I was newly out of the closet and had no idea what I wanted. Actually, I did know one thing: I wanted to go to the Ron Paul Bakery staff holiday party. Because I knew that my favorite local band, Pink Martini, would be playing. The waiter benevolently kept me around long enough to be his plus-one.

This was in 1995, when I was at Beaverton High, and Pink Martini had yet to release its first album. They were a local band of close to a dozen people, Portland's own "little orchestra." Their music felt worldly, glamorous, and bubbly. Just campy enough without being silly. The members of the band wore dapper suits, beads, and feathers. (Sometimes the bandleader and pianist, Thomas Lauderdale, wore the feathers.) In those days, they would play shows anywhere that would have them. That worked for me, since I'd go see them anywhere they played.

The band's first album, *Sympathique*, came out while I was at Yale. To this day, the title song remains Pink Martini's most well-known tune, with its chorus of "Je ne veux pas travailler," "I don't want to work." The melody feels so classic and timeless; I once heard a misguided man in the audience of a Pink Martini show loudly insist to his date that the track was first recorded by "Edith Pilaf." (He was wrong, on multiple counts.) The release of the album meant I could finally share this music that I'd been telling my college friends about. The record had songs in Greek, Japanese, Spanish, and French. I learned how to host dinner parties, stirring risotto to the rhythms of "Amado Mio."

In the early 2000s, I was temping at the bottom rung of the ladder in NPR's newsroom and just beginning to make my way on the air as a reporter, when I pitched a profile of the band to an arts editor. "The story will be about the sophomore curse," I explained. "These relatively unknown artists released *Sympathique* with no pressure and no expectations, to massive global acclaim. The title track was nominated for song of the year in France. Years later, why is it taking so long for them to release their second album?

The editor gave me the green light. I called Pink Martini's manager, who immediately shot down the idea. "Why would we want NPR to do a story about the band's creative paralysis?" My heart sank.

I'm very good at holding two contradictory ideas in my head at once. After all, I'm a Libra. And I don't believe in astrology. And so, I do not believe people come into our lives for a specific reason. Also, I believe that Ryan Offutt entered my life for this specific moment.

Ryan was an impossibly cute blond rugby player who was drinking a beer at the DC outpost of a gay bar chain called Hamburger Mary's when a friend of mine started chatting him up. My friend learned that

Ryan had gone to Reed College in Portland and called me over, thinking maybe we'd know some of the same people. My first serious boyfriend was a Reedie named Michael Kelley. I asked whether Ryan knew Michael. "Yes, I know Michael." He winked.

Ryan and I started to assemble the puzzle pieces over pints of lager. Just as I was breaking up with Michael to start my freshman year at Yale, Ryan was moving to Portland to start his freshman year at Reed . . . where he soon met my ex. And slept with him. Ryan told me he was also a Pink Martini fan, and friendly with Thomas Lauderdale. Then our conversation got weirder.

"Where did you grow up?" I asked.

"Fargo, North Dakota."

"Wait a minute. Did you go to Washington Elementary School?"

"Were you . . . in Mrs. Swenson's first-grade class?"

"And Mr. Stigman's third-grade class!"

He squinted at me. "You were a bit chubby."

"You brought Burger King for lunch," I squinted back. "And wore the paper crown the rest of the day."

This was the first time we'd seen each other since we were both eight years old. And now we lived a few blocks from each other in DC, having slept with the same guy in Portland. I left the bar that night knowing that this had to be more than just a coincidence.

So a few months later, when Pink Martini's manager shot down my dreams of doing a story, I remembered what Ryan had told me about his friendship with Thomas. Certain that our reentry into each other's lives had been a preamble to this very moment, I asked Ryan if he might call Thomas and lobby on my behalf.

Ryan said yes. Thomas said yes. Suddenly I was cleared to do the story. I flew to Portland on my own dime and stayed with my parents.

Microphone in hand, I arrived to meet Thomas for the first time at the studios of Kung Fu Bakery (formerly a kung fu school, formerly a bakery). He's hard to lose in a crowd, a self-described "mystery Asian gay guy" with platinum blond hair who wears vintage suits and bow ties even in casual settings. (He was adopted into a Josephine Baker–esque rainbow tribe and never had any interest in learning about his biological origins. "I was quite content being from nowhere and everywhere," he once told me.)

Thomas pulled up to the studio in his 1959 Nash Metropolitan, a car that looks more likely to hold clowns than be a viable mode of transportation. Indeed, it wasn't all that viable; I would come to learn that the Nash spent more time getting repaired than it did getting Thomas where he needed to go. After an enthusiastic greeting, Thomas offered me Pocky—the Japanese chocolate-dipped cookie snack. It was Passover, so I wasn't eating bread products. As I demurred, I experienced a wave of despair—certain that with this one snack rejection, I had alienated Thomas forever. I reminded myself, "You're here as a journalist. It's not your job to make him like you."

I needn't have worried. After a long day in the studio followed by hours of interviews, Thomas suggested we go out on the town. At dinner, a very excited young woman came up to tell him how much she loved Pink Martini's music. He didn't brush her off. He made eye contact, asked her name, and introduced her to the rest of us at the table. She seemed shocked that he related to her as a person, and not just as a fan. In that moment, I didn't dream that I would one day experience something similar. But when people approach me these days to say how much they enjoy my work on *All Things Considered*, I try to channel the spirit of Thomas. This is true even when people gush, "I wake up to you every morning!" I smile, nod, thank them, and don't mention that my program is on in the evenings.

..

IN THE YEARS THAT FOLLOWED, I kept in touch with Thomas. His personality charmed me as much as his music, and he embodied everything I loved about my hometown. When Pink Martini passed through Washington, DC, on tour, I'd invite a few of the band members to my house for brunch, drinks, or dinner.

One such night, in 2008, Pink Martini and another Portland band called Blind Pilot both had the same Monday off in DC. I decided to go all out, inviting both bands over along with a bunch of my DC friends. I spent all weekend cooking. Then on Monday morning before work, I panicked that there still wasn't enough food and decided to crack a few dozen eggs for a precautionary frittata. I raced home that evening and set out platters of salads and dips with cases of cheap vinho verde and lager, manning the grill as people arrived.

The cliché of Washington is that the city is an industry town. "Hollywood for ugly people" is the overused phrase—a place where the only thing anyone cares about is what your boss can do for their boss. But that night the crowd included chefs, choreographers, and photographers. On my kitchen's chalkboard wall, Blind Pilot's drummer drew a mouse-size ladder leaning against the electrical outlet near the floor. On top of the outlet, he chalked out a small Icarus-like figure, wings strapped to his arms, taking a leap. Looking around the sea of faces that night, I felt a sense of pride that I had managed to defy the Washington stereotype.

A few people from my parkour gym showed up. Yes, at that point in my life, I was living out my Spider-Man fantasies at a converted firehouse called Primal Fitness, where we learned to vault over boxes and run up walls. At my cookout, one of the parkour trainers scaled the gap between our row house and the neighbors'. He slipped into our second-floor bathroom window from the exterior brick wall, then popped his head out and grinned at everybody gaping below. Mike, observing my utter indifference to the safety of our lemur party guest—let alone our potential liability if he were to fall—murmured, "This is why we will never have children."

As the night wore on, the cookout morphed into a sing-along in our piano room at the top of the stairs. Thomas sat at the keys, taking requests. I have wine-blurred memories of "Home on the Range," "Lilac Wine," and "9 to 5." Blind Pilot's lead singer, Israel Nebeker, harmonized with me on "Hallelujah."

When Thomas called me at work the next morning, my head was pounding. "You're a really good singer!" he said. "We're writing a song for the next album that needs a male singer. Can you come to Portland and record it with us?" My headache disappeared. "Come early to tonight's concert at Wolf Trap so we can talk about it!"

I had sung in choirs and a cappella groups before. I'd been in musicals. But I'd never sung with a live band, let alone on an album. I wondered if this would be a violation of journalistic ethics, since I'd reported on them. I decided that since I'd done the story more than five years earlier, the statute of limitations had expired.

Backstage at Wolf Trap's outdoor amphitheater, Thomas sat at an old, out-of-tune upright piano. He was playing an original song, based on a Schubert melody, with an Afro-Cuban rhythm. The lyrics told the story of a woman who'd had enough of her faithless man. *My dear Lorenzo / you come and go / and never know / the tears that I have cried . . .* The title? "And Then You're Gone." This was not the song he wanted me to record. That tune would be sung by the band's lead singer, China Forbes.

It would be followed by a yet-to-be-written song based on the same Schubert theme, this time with a big band rhythm, sung from the perspective of Lorenzo—the man standing outside, hoping to be let back in. *My dear Maria / I'm here to see ya / won't you please, please open the door . . .* This one would be called "But Now I'm Back." That was the song they wanted me to sing. I was certain this would never actually happen. I couldn't say yes fast enough.

..

BACK BEFORE EVERY TV SHOW was available on demand, I used to watch *The Dog Whisperer* when nothing else was on. One of the Dog Whisperer's techniques for handling a crazy dog was to bring in Calm Dog. Crazy Dog would yap his head off, and Calm Dog would stand unfazed. Crazy Dog would twirl and snarl. Calm Dog would yawn. Crazy Dog would whine and bark. Calm Dog would sit down. Eventually, Crazy Dog turned into a calm dog too.

We've all had Crazy Dog moments in our lives. And we've all been Calm Dog to others. My default place on the spectrum tends to be more Calm Dog. But when I arrived in Portland to record with Pink Martini for the first time, I was full-fledged Crazy Dog, spun up into an anxious frenzy. This Crazy Dog needed a Calm Dog.

I found him in Martin Zarzar, a bushy-eyebrowed Peruvian percussionist with a wild mane of black curls, who exuded an air of chill. His steady drumbeat reassured me that everything would be fine.

I don't know how many takes of a song is typical. But after about a thousand takes of "But Now I'm Back," we ended our recording session and Thomas turned to me with an impish smile. "Now, let's pick a show where you can perform the song live with us."

That was how I wound up making my debut at the Hollywood Bowl in September 2009. The audience size? 17,500 people.

··

BACKSTAGE AT THE BOWL, huge framed black-and-white photos spanning decades gazed out from the walls of dressing rooms and dimly lit hallways leading to the wings: Judy Garland, Jimi Hendrix, the Beatles, Aretha Franklin. These weren't close-up portraits; they were wide-shot panoramic images of those artists incinerating audiences from the exact spot where I was about to stand.

I stepped out from the darkness and walked in their footsteps. The spotlight tracked my path. And the roar came rushing in, like an ocean swell lifting my feet off the sand. Thousands of strangers in the darkness were cheering me on. From the lip of the stage, I could make out the first few rows of people. After that, it was just camera flashes and applause, scored by a thrumming undercurrent of crickets and cicadas in the surrounding Hollywood hills on a late summer night. I opened my mouth, and sang.

When I finished the last note, my scalp was tingling and I was sure that I would deliver an electric shock to anyone I touched. I suspected that the audience was applauding me more as a novelty than as an artist, but I was okay with that. I was the journalist who sang with a band one night, and I hadn't embarrassed myself. That was enough for me.

The last song of the set, as usual, was "Brasil." The band's three percussionists weave a tight samba rhythm, and other members of the band join in with shakers. Rather than a shaker, I picked up a tambourine. Now, there are a lot of instruments in Pink Martini. And they're loud. But a poorly played tambourine can drown out even a trumpet, a trombone, a violin, a cello, a piano, a guitar, a bass, and three percussionists who know what they're doing. I let out all of my nerves and excitement shaking that thing during "Brasil," and it sounded like a hailstorm on a tin roof. After the concert, Thomas congratulated me and kindly told me that I was banned from ever playing the tambourine in concert again. "Now if you're going to keep performing with us, we're going to need to find some more songs for you," he smiled. That was my first clue that this wasn't going to be a one-off.

I hadn't mentioned this side gig to most of my colleagues. I was a little afraid to jinx it, a little afraid that people in the newsroom would think that singing with a band would undermine my credibility. The Edward R. Murrow–esque voice in my head piped up again, asking, "Would Walter Cronkite have sung at the Hollywood Bowl?" It's not that I aspired to be Walter Cronkite, but a nagging judgmental part of me wondered whether I was being a little too campy, a little too frivolous, and whether it would come back to bite me the next time I tried to interview the attorney general of the United States. (This is probably the same internal voice that wondered if I sounded too gay on the air. In any case, I muzzled Murrow as best I could and forged ahead.)

As it happened, someone in the audience filmed that first performance at the Hollywood Bowl and posted a grainy video on YouTube. The recording immediately made the rounds at work. I couldn't tell if people were applauding, snickering, or both. My colleague and friend Linda Holmes, who covers pop culture for NPR, wrote a blog post about it. The headline: "Step Aside, Cat Videos: NPR's Own Ari Shapiro Sings (Beautifully) with Pink Martini." As she put it, "not to be all root-for-the-home-team, [but] it is delightful and grand." I felt grateful for the reminder and reassurance that despite my insecurities, my home team was rooting for me.

..

SINCE THAT 2009 DEBUT, I've spent much of my vacation time on tour with Pink Martini. I've recorded one or two songs on each of the subsequent albums, in half a dozen languages that I don't speak. Going on tour feels like a reality TV show where nobody gets kicked off. We might wake up in London, take the train to Paris, do a show at L'Olympia, sleep a few hours, then go to the airport and fly to Rome to do it all again. (There are also less glamorous tours, with long overnight bus rides over winding, bumpy roads.)

One way Thomas has kept the band fresh over more than twenty years is pulling other interesting people into his menagerie, like a bird weaving shiny ribbons into his nest. His collaborators have run the gamut from civil rights icon Myrlie Evers-Williams to Emilio Delgado of Sesame Street to the great-grandchildren of the Captain and Maria von Trapp. Phyllis Diller's swan song was a Pink Martini collaboration—a recording of the song "Smile," written by her old friend Charlie Chaplin.

I didn't really believe that I had earned my place in this dazzling parade of talent. I thought of myself as a sort of party trick—the guy people recognized from NPR, surprising the audience as a fish out of water. During tours through American cities, I always got a reaction when I stood onstage and said, "From the Hollywood Bowl (or wherever we were), this is Pink Martini. I'm Ari Shapiro." It was the juxtaposition of the familiar voice and phrasing in an unexpected setting. I could almost hear the audience say "It really is him" as they laughed in recognition. Those laughs made me suspect that it didn't actually matter whether I was a good singer or not.

And then our lead singer, China Forbes, suddenly needed emergency vocal surgery. The band had a full schedule of upcoming concerts, and Thomas decided to go forward with them, without China. He asked his friend Storm Large to fill in.

Three sold-out shows at the Kennedy Center with the National Symphony were coming up in just a couple of weeks. This was going to be the first time since I had started singing with the band that we'd be playing DC. My friends had all bought tickets, and some of my colleagues from NPR were planning to come. I felt a sinking sense of dread, like I was in the backseat of a car speeding toward a cliff with no one at the wheel.

If I'd been asked, I would have suggested canceling the shows. All I knew about Storm was that she'd been runner-up on a reality TV competition called *Rock Star: Supernova*. And that her most well-known song had the chorus *My vagina is eight miles wide / Absolutely everyone can come inside*. It actually is very catchy.

Storm had a few weeks to learn a dozen songs in almost as many languages. The morning of the first show, everyone arrived at the Kennedy Center to rehearse. I sat in the audience with my head in my hands, waiting to hear what would come out of her mouth. She stepped up to the microphone, and an arpeggio on the harp announced the opening of "Amado Mio." On the first word, Storm's voice soared through the room like a blazing phoenix, and I knew that we would be okay.

Storm and the band ran through most of the set list . . . no problem. Then came Pink Martini's most famous number, the French tune, "Sympathique." On this one, her mouth just would not cooperate. Thomas didn't want to cut the number. I don't think they've done a set without that tune in decades. So I offered an idea.

That night, it felt like we were including the audience in a thrilling adventure. *Watch Storm launch herself into Turkish! Spanish! Croatian! Will she fall? She triumphs again!* When it came time for "Sympathique," I took the mic. I explained that Storm had exceeded all expectations, clearing every hurdle, with one tragic exception. So, I said, it was time for a French lesson.

I began very slowly, overenunciating: "Ma chambre a la forme d'une cage."

Storm furrowed her brow and gave me an exaggerated "kah-ZHUH."

"Le soleil passe son bras par la fenêtre."

Storm spit out a "TRUH."

We turned the song into a Henry Higgins / Eliza Doolittle routine. By the time we got to the chorus, the two of us were dancing and singing in harmony. Storm, who's almost as tall as I am, said we probably looked like wedding cake toppers standing side by side. The audience that night loved it, and I felt like I had broken through a barrier. Even though I know it sounds backward, our gimmicky novelty act helped me see my role in the band as more than just a gimmicky novelty act.

··

NPR DEMANDS VETO POWER OVER any outside activities that could be considered political. Everybody has to follow the ethics code, which evolves over time. We're not allowed to donate to political candidates, obviously. At various points we've also been told we can't march for Black lives, or women's reproductive rights, more controversially. Gay pride parades have been a gray area. ("Which float are you hoping to be on?") I'm not allowed to attend most gala fundraiser dinners (a blessing, really). And any time I pass someone on the street seeking signatures, I have an easy out. "Sorry, I'm a journalist. Not allowed to sign petitions."

As the years went on and my involvement with the band deepened, nobody at NPR raised a flag about Pink Martini's politics. And understandably so. On the surface, the band falls far outside the danger zone. I mean, the chorus of our most popular song translates from French as *I don't want to work; I don't want to lunch; I want only to forget. And then, I smoke.* We're not exactly Pussy Riot.

But there's also a not-so-subtle undertone to the band's mission. Pink Martini was founded in the culture wars of the 1990s. Thomas was working as an organizer on the fight against Measure 13, the anti-gay rights proposal that made it onto the Oregon ballot in 1994. The band's first performance was a fundraiser for the "No on 13" campaign.

And although the band doesn't play at overtly political events today, there's a clear element of musical diplomacy to what we do. Pink Martini goes to the reddest parts of Texas and sings songs in Arabic. In Greece, the band performs Turkish songs. We're not opining on the Iran nuclear deal or NATO from the stage. But as the singer Andra Day once told me, music is the only thing that can enter your psyche without permission. It's hard to view someone as an enemy when you're dancing and clapping along to their songs.

Even the finale feels like a subtle way of breaking down barriers. When the band plays "Brasil," everyone is encouraged to do a conga line around the room. Thomas calls it being neighborly, putting your hands on someone's waist and dancing around, even in an august temple of music like Carnegie Hall.

Very rarely, the politics of the place we're in collide with the band's ideals. We were invited to play a music festival in one of the Middle East's less autocratic countries—a relatively liberal place, as long as you don't stir up trouble. We would be the guests of Her Excellency, performing especially for her. The thousand or so other people in the audience would be there through her magnanimity. (I'm leaving the details vague, because the band would probably like to play there again someday.)

Just before the show began, Her Excellency's aides informed us of one crucial rule. There was a wide-open area between her front row seat and the lip of the stage. No one was to cross it, period. Her view of the band was to remain completely unobstructed at all times.

Thomas explained that an exception would have to be made for the conga line at the end of the show. With the crisp clarity of those accustomed to representing the views of an autocrat, Her Excellency's aides explained that this would not be possible. The audience was seated. The show was about to begin. Her Excellency's assistants informed us that if we did not wish to perform under these terms, we were free to leave the country. Presumably immediately, presumably forever.

At last, someone suggested that just before "Brasil" began, perhaps guards could be stationed at the appropriate spots to direct foot traffic around Her Excellency's line of sight. The conga line would double back in a U, rather than circling the auditorium. Eureka! Problem solved, we took the stage, and the show began.

Midway through the set, Thomas was introducing a Turkish tune called "Aşkım bahardı" when he decided to ask if any Turks in the audience would like to come onstage and dance. A handful of people jumped to their feet and flew down the aisle like contestants on *The Price Is Right*. We watched with horror as they rushed to the front of the house. I wanted to dive off the stage and physically stop them. It was too late. They passed in front of Her Excellency. There was an audible gasp.

Thomas cued the band. We started to play, and our patroness stood up, clapping and dancing while her aides scowled. At the end of the show, the conga line dodged her as planned, while she twirled and grinned. At the VIP reception with Her Excellency and the US ambassador after the concert, no mention of the infraction was made.

..

THE MOST MEANINGFUL SONG I'VE recorded with Pink Martini was actually a rewrite of a tune from *Sympathique*. For years, I'd been singing "La Soledad" in concert. It was an original song in Spanish that the band wrote in the 1990s. In 2016, Thomas asked our friend Iyad Qasem to write new lyrics, in the Egyptian dialect of Arabic.

Thomas and Iyad met on a flight from Paris to New York. He was a handsome Jordanian Palestinian TV producer and documentary filmmaker with a close-cropped silvery beard and a soft British accent. The two of them became close friends and collaborators, dreaming up new projects until Iyad's untimely death of pancreatic cancer at the age of fifty-two.

When Thomas asked Iyad to rewrite "La Soledad" in Arabic, Iyad took the new title from something his mother, a Palestinian refugee, used to say: "There is no breeze as sweet as the breeze of home." He retitled the song "Finnissma Di," which means "In this summer breeze." Although the new lyrics sound like they are about pining for a lost love, Iyad told us that he imagined these words being sung by a refugee, longing for the homeland he may never see again.

When I recorded that song, the Syrian refugee crisis was at its peak. It was a story that I had covered during reporting trips to Turkey, northern Iraq, and refugee camps across Europe. As I sang "Finnissma Di," I thought of the people I'd met on those assignments—doctors, teachers, students, parents who'd left everything familiar behind, piling onto overcrowded rafts and hoping to find a better life across the water.

In New York, I sang "Finnissma Di" at Pier 17's rooftop concert venue, where I could see the Statue of Liberty from the stage. Iyad drew on his years working in the entertainment industry in the Arab world to produce shows for the band in Casablanca, Tunis, and Abu Dhabi. At each of these concerts, before I began to sing, I would introduce Iyad to talk about the song's meaning. He would always end by saying, "And it is an honor to have this piece performed by my Jewish friend, Ari Shapiro." We would hug, Arab and Jew. Despite the cliché, or maybe because of it, the audience would stand and cheer. There were often tears. I would take a deep breath, and sing the song.

It felt especially significant to perform the song in Lebanon, a place that had taken in more Syrian refugees per capita than any other country. Iyad booked us at the Beiteddine Festival in the mountains outside Beirut, where the air smelled like roses and night-blooming jasmine. The backdrop to the stage was an ancient palace, dramatically uplit against the darkening sky.

When Iyad introduced "Finnissma Di," the applause felt more tepid than usual. After the concert ended, the festival organizer crisply informed Iyad that while the music was excellent, it was "unnecessary" of him to mention that I was Jewish. Iyad bristled as he recounted the conversation to me backstage. We resigned ourselves to the reality that musical diplomacy can only do so much and decided not to let our hosts' bigotry spoil our night. We walked into the after-party arm in arm and stuffed ourselves with baklava and knafeh under a starry Lebanese sky.

··

I KNOW THAT MOST BANDS never reach Pink Martini's level of success. Those that do often implode or run out of steam before they've lasted a decade. The fact that Pink Martini has continued touring for nearly thirty years makes the band something of a unicorn.

When I've asked Thomas what he thinks the secret is, he gives an answer that's both self-deprecating and unusually pragmatic for him. He says the band's success comes from having built relationships with orchestras across the US, which program Pink Martini shows into their pops repertoire. And, sure, I guess the Harvard Business School paper about Pink Martini that has yet to be written would cite relationships with symphony orchestras as one factor. Thomas also points to the band's early decision to record in other languages as key to building an international fan base. It's a bizarrely boring nuts-and-bolts explanation coming from him. Of course what he says is true, but there's obviously more to it than that.

If you ask me, part of Pink Martini's secret is that they've fully embraced what makes them different from everyone else. And in so doing, they've nestled into a spot that is authentically and singularly theirs, without ever chasing a trend or a fad. That is to say, even if you're the most talented singer-songwriter with a guitar in the world, hundreds of other talented guitar-playing singer-songwriters are coming up right behind you, breathing down your neck. There's not really anybody else competing to be "The UN's house band from 1962," as Thomas describes Pink Martini's style. They are enthusiastically, unapologetically themselves.

And I think another secret is that Thomas has never stopped evolving. At most concerts you'll still hear songs that I was dancing to back when I was in high school. But any time things began to feel stale, Thomas pivoted and branched out in new directions, whether the rest of the band liked it or not. He pulled in collaborators across generations and continents. People like the von Trapps, Phyllis Diller, and . . . even after more than a decade of touring the world with them, it still feels surreal to say this . . . people like me.

When I walk onto the grounds of the Hollywood Bowl these days, it no longer feels like an imposing fortress. Performing there still feels like a wildly outrageous gift, but it doesn't turn me into a Crazy Dog. One thing that has not changed is the feeling I get walking to center stage, as the roar of the crowd rushes in. Every time it washes over me, I feel caught up in a powerful ocean swell, lifting me off the sand, in those final seconds before I plant my feet and start to sing.

5

THE BUBBLE

The first day I set foot in the West Wing, in May 2010, I accidentally walked into the Oval Office while President Barack Obama and Vice President Joe Biden were in there. To state the obvious, that's not supposed to happen. They were meeting with congressional leaders to talk about a Supreme Court vacancy. The event was, in the jargon of the White House press corps, "pool only." The press pool is a small rotating group of journalists who represent the entire press corps at events that can't accommodate a crowd. The pool has spots for a print reporter, radio journalist, still photographer, videographer, and so on. On my first day at the White House, I was *not* the radio reporter in the pool.

A few minutes before the event was scheduled to begin, I saw a cluster of journalists gathering at the briefing room's exit door. I assumed that they were headed out to the driveway to watch the congressional leaders arrive. Maybe a lawmaker would toss us a quote on their way in to see the president. That wasn't a totally unreasonable assumption, but you might think that as the new guy I would have asked a more experienced journalist what the huddle was about. I didn't. I was intimidated. It was my first day, and so I clammed up. I would eventually learn that the White House press corps is a very supportive group and that they would have been happy to steer me in the right direction if I'd bothered to ask. But on that day, all I saw was a bunch of more experienced people who knew more than I did and might judge me for admitting my ignorance. So I joined them and stood there, waiting for whatever happened next.

The pool operates on good faith, the assumption being that folks covering the White House know what they're doing and won't try to take advantage of the system. So there was no roll call or head count that day. Our knot of journalists started to move, and as we wound through hallways, heading away from the driveway, I understood that I had made a mistake. The full extent of it hit me only when we walked through the doorway into the room where Obama and Biden were sitting. At that point I couldn't exactly peel off from the crowd and retrace my steps back to the briefing room. Once again I clammed up, hoping Secret Service wouldn't clock me and forcibly remove me from the premises.

I had seen variations of this tableau a million times on TV, but I never imagined that I might accidentally stumble into it. Obama's White House photographer, Pete Souza, took a photo of the meeting. It shows the leaders of the country perched on couches, hands folded in their laps. Flowers and lamps anchor the side tables, and big boom microphones on telescoping poles stretch across the central coffee table toward the president. Behind the elected leaders, a Greek chorus of journalists hunches over notebooks, microphones, and cameras, intently focused on capturing Obama's every word and gesture. In the photo, you can see my face popping out from the back of the cluster, taller than most of my colleagues, like a meerkat who wandered off the savanna into the Oval Office.

In my early teens, I used to have dreams where I showed up to school and discovered I was a few heads shorter than everybody else. I would strain to make out my friends' conversations, desperate to participate but unable to engage. In the dream, it took me mere seconds to sprout up like a cornstalk, growing too fast until I towered above everyone, now struggling to join in the social scrum from the opposite direction. It doesn't take a psychoanalyst to figure out the symbolism here, embodying every teenager's anxieties about fitting in (and even more so the queer ones'). When I look at the photo Pete Souza snapped of my first day on the White House beat, I see the image from my dream transplanted into real life, in a room that represents the global center of political power.

It's not that I had impostor syndrome, exactly. In fact, I was pretty sure I could check the boxes required of a White House correspondent. By the time I joined the beat, I had covered the Department of Justice for five years. I had spent months leading NPR's investigation into US abuse of detainees at Iraq's Abu Ghraib prison and chronicled post-9/11 debates over torture, spying, and indefinite detention at Guantánamo Bay. Reporting on Justice trained me to cover politics and to quickly crank out stories about major news events, from Senate hearings to court cases.

On paper, moving my focus a few blocks up Pennsylvania Avenue to cover the White House was a logical next step. NPR had actually offered me the White House job a year earlier. I declined it that first time. I was afraid that I would wind up a stenographer to power, parroting what the president said and did each day without adding much value. I wanted to report stories that people would remember, and I had a hard time recalling any story about the White House that had moved me. Also, the prospect of pack journalism made me wince. Besides, I reasoned, Nina Totenberg had basically spent her entire career covering the Supreme Court. Why couldn't I do the same with the Justice Department?

I pictured myself playing reporter Mad Libs on the White House beat, writing stories so familiar that you could draft them before a news event even happened and then fill in the blanks with the details. I imagined having copy-paste shortcuts for lines like "The proposed legislation angers Republicans, who argue that it amounts to reckless spending." Or, "Activists say the president is violating his campaign promise to prioritize their agenda." It hardly even mattered what the "proposed legislation" or "campaign promise" might have been. We all know these stories, and I doubted that I could find a more compelling way to tell them.

My concerns weren't totally off-base, but I can also see now that I was being a bit precious about it. A hurdle for anyone covering the White House is figuring out how to find original stories, or how to tell familiar stories in an interesting way. That doesn't have to be a trap; it can be an exciting challenge. And by 2010, with some gentle nudging from my bosses, I decided I was up for it. I figured it would be an education, I'd undoubtedly have some memorable experiences along the way, and having a front-row seat to power would help me understand more deeply how our political system works (or doesn't). If it turned out not to be a perfect fit, it wouldn't be forever.

When I arrived at the White House on my bicycle for work that first morning, Secret Service agents told me there was nowhere within a couple of blocks of the complex that I was allowed to lock it. The benches and lampposts in Lafayette Square were off limits. I rolled away from my new workplace in search of a bike rack with a sinking feeling that maybe I'd made the wrong choice. As the photograph in the Oval Office later that day would capture, I felt a bit like Cinderella's stepsister, trying to force an ill-fitting shoe onto my misshapen foot.

Journalists who cover Washington often treat politics as a sport. Political junkies follow budget debates with the same fervor that others dedicate to their fantasy football leagues. (To be honest, I'm not *totally* sure how fantasy football works, but I think the analogy holds?) This city is full of people who will confess that they were weirdo kids who spent Sunday mornings with Cocoa Puffs watching *This Week* and *Face the Nation* instead of cartoons. Even when I covered the White House, I resisted spending my Sunday mornings that way.

When I pick up (or click on) the newspaper, political stories aren't the first articles I read. I don't yearn to know who's next in line for a powerful committee chairmanship in Congress. Instead I gravitate toward investigative reports, profiles, and articles that illuminate the entire world by zooming in on a tiny sliver of life. In my reporting, and in my news consumption, I'd rather talk *to* people than *about* people—focus on the folks affected by legislation rather than the ones writing it. Entire media empires have been built on the opposite approach—analyzing who's up or down and speculating on how the war in Syria or Yemen will determine which party controls Congress.

I have learned how to speak that language—more fluently than I can speak the language of sports, anyway—but even after years immersed in Washington, it still feels slightly foreign in my mouth. It took me a few weeks on the new beat to learn that I could lean on other members of the White House press corps for help with translation. The lesson really sank in on my first trip with the president outside Washington.

..

OBAMA WAS SET TO MAKE a two-day swing through Illinois and Iowa, and his big plane was too heavy for some of the small-town runways we'd be landing on. So he would take what the press corps and staffers casually called Baby Air Force One. Technically, any plane bearing the president is Air Force One for the duration of the trip. But this wasn't the iconic big bird he usually flies. This one was typically used for cabinet secretaries and looked more like a regional Jet Blue plane than anything from a Harrison Ford action movie.

The size didn't matter to me. I was just excited to be able to sign off my stories "Ari Shapiro, NPR News, Traveling with The President." My editor, Beth Donovan, told me that if you ever walk up to Air Force One without a shiver of awe, it's time to leave the White House beat. I couldn't sleep the night before we left. This time, I *was* a member of the press pool. And as the radio pooler, my responsibility (on top of my regular job) was to record and share audio and observations with the radio correspondents who weren't on the trip. I would send radio pool reports to our email list over the course of the day, perhaps a dozen or more, ranging from the perfunctory "motorcade rolling" to a detailed account of what Obama had for lunch and whom he ate with, including audio when I had access to moments that others did not.

Every drink, every snack, every meal served on Air Force One comes with a napkin that reads "Aboard the Presidential Aircraft" in deep blue ink with the presidential seal. On that first flight and many that followed, I carefully squirreled away each napkin as a gift for nieces, nephews, and NPR interns. As my stash grew over the years, I eventually stopped treating the napkins like precious jewels and started using them as intended.

(My horde of napkins did prove unexpectedly useful once. I was arriving in Israel, via a cruise ship where I had been hired to give some speeches, and confronting immigration at the border. The uniformed agent flipped through my passport and saw Iraq, Afghanistan, and other countries that aren't typical tourist destinations. When he asked why I'd been to those places, I explained that my job covering the White House required me to travel all over the world. The Israeli man looked skeptical. "Do you have any evidence to prove that you actually fly with the president of the United States?" I reached into my backpack and pulled out a crumpled Air Force One napkin. "Aboard the Presidential Aircraft." I handed it to the immigration agent and said, "You can keep that.")

On our 2010 trip to Iowa and Illinois, Obama decided to start his day in Des Moines with a workout at a gym in a strip mall. The pool bided our time at a nearby shop called Coffee + Comics. On a shelf in a back corner of the store, I unearthed a comic book called *Barack the Barbarian*. It was Volume 1, Issue 3: "Quest for the Treasure of Stimuli." As my pool report dutifully informed the rest of the press corps:

> The cover shows a shirtless Barack, abs rippling, ax in his right hand and elephant tusk in his left. Atop the elephant is a laughing "Red Sarah" wearing a gold bikini, gold bicep cuff, and signature Palin glasses.

> Sample dialogue: "Drat! That pesky Barack and his rat pack have got the lead on us . . . but we can still beat them to the top, can't we, Red Sarah?"

> Also: "What part of derivatives do you not understand?"

I patted myself on the back for finding a story that nobody else on the White House beat was covering. Okay, maybe "story" was overselling it. I'd found a goofy satirical comic book. But to me, it counted as a small victory. I could truthfully state that on my first trip with the president, in addition to reporting actual news about biofuels and the White House plan to create renewable energy jobs, I had loosened one little buckle on the straitjacket of pack journalism.

I paid $3.50 to get the store's only copy of the comic book and wrote a blog post about it for NPR's website. (I would later expense that $3.50.

And this is where I thank sustaining members for supporting your local public radio station.) White House spokesman Bill Burton even asked to borrow the comic and obliged me with a quote for my blog post. "I liked it because it had few words and lots of pictures, which made it easy to understand," he said. The comic still sits in a drawer in my office. I only regret that I never asked the president to sign it.

On our flight back to Washington after that swing through the Midwest, I allowed myself to exhale. I had been a fizzing ball of nerves for two days, and I thought I could finally relax. The crew served us a lunch of spaghetti and meatballs swimming in red sauce. I would eventually learn that the food on the plane leaned heavy. The White House press corps came to suspect, only half-joking, that this was a deliberate strategy to keep us sedated by piling on the meatloaf and mashed potatoes. I slid my recorder, microphone, and headset under the seat in front of me to make room for the saucy lunch plate.

Air Force One is split up into sections. You can't just wander around and make small talk with the White House staffers. Even Baby Air Force One had a curtain dividing press from staff. On any flight, the president rarely comes back to see the press, and when he does, a spokesman generally gives everybody a heads-up beforehand. So what happened next on that flight back to Joint Base Andrews was very unusual. I looked up from my marinara-painted plate and saw Barack Obama walking up the aisle to where we sat in the back of the plane, his shirt collar open, sleeves rolled up.

He stopped next to my row. "How's everybody enjoying lunch?" At this point, my only responsibility was to record the president's words, for NPR and every other radio news outlet that covers the White House. My equipment to do that was at my feet. I looked at the plate in my lap and concluded I had three choices. I could dive for the microphone, splattering the leader of the free world in pomodoro. I could hand my dirty dishes to the president of the United States: "Nice to meet you, sir.

Please hold this while I grab my gear." Or I could fail at my new job on my first outing.

I panicked, craning my head around the cabin, looking for some kind of deus ex machina. It came from behind me. The TV sound guy in the press pool stood in the aisle at the back of the plane with a big boom mic stretching down the aisle toward Obama. The engineer saw me flailing and gave me a wink. He understood exactly what was happening and why I was panicking, and his wink was a way of saying, "I got you." He would later give me the audio he had recorded—the first of many times another member of the White House press corps saved me from myself.

Outsiders who hear only about competition among newspapers and TV news outlets might not guess how tightly knit and mutually supportive the press corps can be. Even though we vied to get scoops before anyone else, we also looked out for one another. Piling into the motorcade after a speech, I would often hear reporters from competing news organizations ask each other, "What was that quote?" or "How do you spell the name of the official who introduced him?" Photographers would let print reporters scrutinize an image to accurately describe details of the scene that they might have missed in the scrum.

During the Obama administration, MSNBC journalists fought to keep the Fox News team from getting shut out. And when the Trump White House suspended press credentials for a CNN correspondent, the entire White House press corps came to CNN's defense. (I'm not equating the two. The Trump White House went to extraordinary lengths to punish journalists for exercising their First Amendment rights, to a degree that the Obama White House never did.)

On that flight home, once I saw that the TV audio engineer had me covered and that this midwestern sojourn wasn't going to end in disaster, my pulse started to slow down. I allowed myself to look up at the president standing next to my seat. And I noticed razor bumps on his neck. It was a mundane, inconsequential thing. But the very ordinariness of it struck me. Those razor bumps were the first time I saw Barack Obama as just a guy, with the same annoyances and inconveniences that everyone else experiences. My whole life, the president had been a symbol. He was "Hail to the Chief"; the suit behind a podium with the presidential seal; the portrait that hangs in government buildings and schools all over the country. Looking up at the bumps on his neck, it hit me that he shaves in the mornings like the rest of us.

Just as he was about to wrap up the Q&A, Obama turned to me and said, "I'll give the new guy the last question, since this is his first ride on the plane."

··

TRAVELING WITH THE PRESIDENT IS known as being in the bubble, but playing dominoes seems like a more apt analogy to me. White House staffers and volunteers spend weeks or months meticulously placing each domino in the right spot. Once the first domino falls, the president, his team, the media, and the rest of the entourage zoom from the airplane to the helicopters to the motorcade to the rally to the town hall.

Given how slow and grinding government can be, it is shocking to see the efficiency of the presidential travel machine in action. One evening in 2012, we were sitting in the press van on a street in New York's Greenwich Village. Inside a townhouse belonging to Anna Wintour, people had paid thirty thousand dollars each to hear the president speak at a campaign fundraiser. I looked at the clock, and at the schedule. We were supposed to be landing at Joint Base Andrews in forty minutes. Impossible, I thought.

Then the president climbed into "the Beast," his armored limo, and the motorcade roared into action, sirens blaring. No stoplights, no traffic; every other priority in New York City was shoved aside so that our long line of cars could reach the helipads in Lower Manhattan. We ran from the motorcade to the thumping helicopters and zoomed low over the glittering river to the airport where Air Force One awaited, ready to fly south. Sure enough, forty minutes after our departure from Wintour's place, we touched down at Andrews.

There is a less glamorous side to these events. A White House staffer once told me that presidential travel smells like stale beer and trash. That's because the motorcade rarely arrives at the front of a building. For security reasons, we would more often pull up to the loading dock in the back. Moments before the president entered the event, the commander in chief would be surrounded by dumpsters and recycling bins.

Sometimes the local Democratic Party would let a volunteer drive the press van in the motorcade. They would never entrust a civilian to drive the president or his staff, but I suppose they deemed us more expendable. After an event in Los Angeles, a volunteer who looked like he might not yet have finished college gripped the wheel, giggling as our motorcade zoomed down I-10 in late afternoon. Ours were the only vehicles on the seven lanes of freeway, and I'm sure LA commuters were cursing us. A *New York Times* reporter noticed our driver's phone propped up on the dashboard against the windshield. The young man was filming the drive, glancing at the screen while we hurtled down the interstate. "Would you please put your phone down and concentrate on the road?" the journalist politely requested through gritted teeth. "I can't!" he gasped. "Doing 80 on an empty I-10 at rush hour? I'll never experience this again in my life—this is like seeing God!"

The trips were often as much of a blur as the palm trees whizzing by outside those windows. Sometimes I would make a point to end the night with a local beer from the hotel bar. No matter what city we were in, when every press filing center in every chain hotel looked the same, with endless patterned carpet leading the way to cookie-cutter bedrooms, I could get a literal taste of a place by drinking what they brewed there in the area. It was a way to ground an otherwise surreal experience in reality.

··

I FOUND THAT ONE OF the best ways to set my stories apart was to pop the bubble, or—choose your metaphor—take a step away from the chain of falling dominoes. When a BP offshore rig started spilling oil into the Gulf of Mexico in 2010, I flew with the press corps to the Gulf Coast, where Obama toured cleanup operations. It was a humid early summer day with a heat index near 110. I crouched with my microphone, trying to stay below the TV cameras' shot, my big black headphones sticking to my ears like sloppy wet suction cups. As best I could see, Obama didn't break a sweat walking between the oil-soaked booms. We traveled through three states in as many days—Mississippi, Alabama, and Florida—by car, airplane, helicopter, and boat. That trip was the first time I experienced a "floatercade," a motorcade on the water.

When the president gave his one big speech of the trip in Pensacola, I decided not to listen to it from the filing center with the other reporters. Instead, I went to a local hangout—a waterfront oyster bar called Peg Leg Pete's. The TVs over the bar usually showed sports, but they made an exception for Obama's address about the oil spill. Here, the stakes of reporting felt all the more real. I wasn't talking *about* the impact the oil spill was having on a community. I was talking *to* members of that community.

A restaurant worker named Mark Griffith watched the speech while shucking oysters in back, a chain mail glove on his left hand. He told me even after five years of doing this job, he still ate his share of the harvest raw every day. If the oil came ashore, he told me, "I'm afraid I'm not going to be able to get oysters, period." I asked what that would mean for his livelihood, and he replied, "I could sum it up in one word, but I can't say it on the radio." All these years later, I still wish I'd followed his line about a word he can't say on the radio with "and with a flick of his wrist, another oyster was *shucked*." But I can take solace in the fact that nobody else in the White House press corps had that particular angle on the president's Pensacola speech.

I have a reporting philosophy that applies to covering not just the White House but any assignment on any beat. With every story, there are two bars. First comes the low bar. You clear it when you have something that you can get on the air. It might not be scintillating, but it checks a box and does the job. It's the bare minimum. Once you've crossed that first line in your reporting, you're out of the crisis zone. And then, you're on a mission to inch your way closer to the second bar. The second bar is the platonic ideal of a perfect work of journalism. It is vivid, surprising, transporting, distinctive, and true. Every finished story falls somewhere between those two bars. During my four years on the White House beat, I may have spent more time near the lower bar than the higher bar. But knowing that I constantly had that reach goal, thinking every day about how to get closer to the higher bar, kept me motivated. It also didn't hurt that the job provided some perks in the form of once-in-a-lifetime experiences that you only get when you're inside the presidential bubble.

..

IN DECEMBER 2010, MY BOSS told me that he had been asked to come to Press Secretary Jay Carney's office for a meeting. I'd never heard of this happening before and immediately assumed that I'd committed some sort of grave offense. I mentally scrolled through the last few days of White House briefings. Had I asked a taboo question? Was one of my stories so incendiary that the press secretary felt he had to go over my head to yell about it to the head of NPR's Washington Desk? I was still pretty new to the beat, so I didn't know that this was protocol for a presidential trip to a war zone.

After our bosses were informed of the plan, those of us who would be in the traveling pool were brought into Jay's West Wing office to discuss the trip in person. Security precautions were so tight, we couldn't talk about it over the phone. We were allowed to tell one editor, face-to-face, and a spouse if we had one—no one else. I was heading to Afghanistan with the president.

My only car was a bicycle, and Air Force One always departs from Andrews, far from my home in DC. So in those pre-Uber days, I typically used a car service to get to Andrews for presidential trips. Jay told us that this time, hired drivers would not be allowed. The White House just couldn't afford to take a chance of word leaking out. We'd have to use our own vehicles or carpool, and we would enter the military base through a back gate so base staffers wouldn't see the White House press corps showing up at the front entrance. Another correspondent offered me a ride. The schedule had us taking off in the middle of the night and landing on the other side of the earth in the middle of the night thirteen hours later.

Ordinarily, Air Force One would be parked on the runway when we arrived at Andrews, ready for departure. On this night, the plane was still in the hangar. Two of them, actually: mirror images parked nose to nose at a ninety-degree angle. I didn't know until that moment that the plane had an identical twin.

Typically, after the press corps boards Air Force One, we'd briefly disembark to watch Marine One, the presidential helicopter, land. Obama would salute as he jogged up the stairs, and then we'd follow right behind for takeoff. Not this time. The president silently motorcaded from the White House to Andrews. We were told to keep our window shades drawn, so light from inside the plane wouldn't give us away as we rolled out of the hangar. We knew that Obama was on board only when we felt the rumbling plane start to move for our takeoff.

On the flight around the world, I struggled to sleep. Every time I started to drift off, I would remember what we were doing and a shot of adrenaline would jerk me back to awareness. In my semiconscious nervous haze, I wondered whether I was the first person to bring Kiehl's facial moisturizer into Afghanistan. Perhaps? Avocado under-eye cream, surely.

The plan was to spend six hours on the ground: three at Bagram Air Base, where Obama would thank US troops spending the holidays in Afghanistan, then a quick helicopter flight south to Kabul, where he would meet with Afghan president Hamid Karzai. The staffers who had been to Kabul on previous trips raved about the banquet the Afghans always provided their American visitors. There would be endless platters of food, they promised, the famous Afghan hospitality extending even to the press corps and White House staff in a war zone.

A few hours before landing, the press was brought into a conference room near the front of the plane to talk about the itinerary. I had never been in this section of Air Force One. Sitting around a long wooden conference table, the White House staff told us that the plan had changed. Due to high winds and low clouds, the helicopter trip to Kabul was canceled. Instead, Presidents Obama and Karzai would have a videoconference. Our six hours on the ground were cut to three.

Bad weather may have been the real story. It's also possible that the trip to Kabul was canceled for political reasons. Wikileaks had just dumped a pile of documents that showed the Obama administration griping about Karzai and his government's corruption. It was a particularly delicate time between the two countries. We would also learn later that word of the trip had leaked before our touchdown. So security concerns could have been another reason for scuttling the Kabul leg of the flight. Regardless, we wouldn't experience the famous Afghan hospitality that night.

We closed our window shades again for a darkened descent into Bagram. When we got off the plane, most of the visual cues on the ground could have put us on any military base in the US. Signs were all in English; buildings flew American flags. But there were a few ripples in the facade, subtle clues that we weren't in Ohio or North Carolina. Every surface was coated in a soft, fine sand. The night sky was a wild pointillist tapestry. And at the press catering table, between the deli sandwiches and bags of chips, I picked up a can of Sprite to find that the logo was in English on one side, Pashto on the other. It was no Afghan banquet, but the soda was easier to take home as a souvenir.

As soon as we were on the ground, I sent out a pool report and uploaded a few radio spots that I'd recorded on the plane. I did a live hit on *Morning Edition*, recorded some quick interviews with a few of the troops on base, and plugged in my recorder for Obama's speech, in which he thanked the troops for their service. Our three hours on the ground zipped by.

It was a Friday, and I had worked out a detailed plan with my editor, Beth. After filing a story from Bagram for that night's *All Things Considered*, I would write a piece on the first leg of the flight home for broadcast on Saturday morning's *Weekend Edition*. When Air Force One stopped to refuel at Ramstein Air Base in Germany, I would call Beth to edit the *Weekend Edition* story and file from the plane on the ground before we took off again for the final leg home to Andrews. The story would run while I was in the air.

Timing was key, because we had no Wi-Fi at cruising altitude. The schedule said we'd have thirty minutes on the ground in Germany. That's a narrow window to edit and file, but I work fast. I was confident it would be long enough to put the piece to bed before we took off and lost connectivity.

We touched down at Ramstein, I called Beth, we ran through the story, and she gave me the green light to file. Sitting in my seat aboard the plane, I started recording my tracks. Someone started chatting next to me. I stopped the recording, moved to a different part of the press cabin, and started again. Again, my microphone started to pick up someone talking near me. I decided to relocate to the only private area with a door that was available to the media: I shut myself in the bathroom, lowered the toilet lid, sat down, and locked the door.

A minute or two after I had started recording my piece on the toilet, I felt a rumbling. I thought it couldn't possibly be the plane moving; the schedule said we still had another ten minutes on the ground. I kept reading my script into the microphone as the vibrations got more intense. I tried not to let my voice reflect my growing panic. There was no other possible explanation. We were taking off early, and I hadn't filed yet. Once we were above the clouds, our communications would be totally cut off.

Finally I reached the end of my script. "Ari Shapiro, NPR News, Aboard Air Force One." (I did not say, "in the bathroom.") My laptop was still on my airplane seat, on the other side of the bathroom door. I burst out of the restroom in a mad panic and scrambled to plug my recorder into the computer. Of course my laptop had kicked me off the Wi-Fi while I was sitting on the toilet. I took deep breaths and muttered, "More haste, less speed." I tried to keep my hands from shaking as I typed in my password. Air Force One was speeding down the runway. *Wi-Fi: reconnected.* I clicked "upload" as the plane's nose lifted into the air. We were off the ground over Germany as the progress bar inched along . . . 32 percent . . . 47 percent . . . 76 percent . . . and as we entered the clouds, the screen read, UPLOAD COMPLETE.

In those most intense moments, I try to remind myself of something that an NPR producer once told me when I was an intern. It's only radio. We're not emergency room doctors. Nobody's life is on the line.

The stakes here are actually very low. It's easy to lose that perspective when you're crashing on deadline aboard Air Force Once with seconds to go until you're cut off from the world.

My Afghanistan story filed, I shut my laptop and ordered a gin and tonic. We had a long flight ahead of us, and I had done my job.

··

AFTER I HAD SPENT ABOUT four years covering Obama's presidency, NPR's London correspondent unexpectedly volunteered for an open position in Islamabad. I had never seriously considered taking a posting overseas. But the job in London was suddenly available, and being able to explore the entire world from a home base in a highly developed country where I speak the language was too appealing to resist. I raised my hand for the job, and suddenly my tenure as a White House correspondent had a looming end date.

Obama usually mispronounced my name when he called on me at White House press briefings. I didn't hold it against him. He has a lot on his mind, and people have called me *Airy* my whole life. My last day in the West Wing, he happened to hold a news conference in the briefing room. In a funny echo of that first flight on Air Force One, he said, "Since this is his last White House briefing before he goes to London, lemme give a question to Ari Shapiro." I don't remember what was in the news that day. I don't even remember what I asked him about. But I do remember that in my final White House press conference, the president said my name right.

6

WAR PEOPLE IN WAR PLACES

My daily routine as a correspondent in London included a run along the River Thames, following a path that took me past the Tower of London week after week. It was 2014, and as winter turned to spring, I watched the empty tower moat fill up with hundreds of thousands of red poppies. These blooms weren't sprouting from the soil; they were ceramic works of art mounted on metal stems. Each day as I approached the tower, I'd hear the *tink tink tink* of hammer on metal as volunteers pounded them into the soil one by one. I'd pause my run, lean over the railing, and watch these people who'd donated their time to help commemorate the centennial of the First World War.

The poppies were an art installation by the ceramicist Paul Cummins. He had taken the name of the piece from a poem written by an anonymous British soldier during the war. It was called "Blood Swept Lands and Seas of Red." Over the year, the volunteers planted 888,246 ceramic poppies in the Tower of London's moat—one flower for each soldier from Britain or the British colonies who had died. Each was unique, handmade, planted by the living to commemorate the dead. "I'm almost in tears just talking to you now," a volunteer named Lynne England told me. "Just look at it. Every single poppy, every poppy you hold, is somebody's life."

The flowers weren't lined up in orderly rows. From where I stood at the railing, they swelled in an undulating crimson sea, crashed like a wave of blood against the walls of the tower, and cascaded from one of the windows to the earth below in a frozen waterfall, while a thirty-foot curl of red poppies crested over the tower's main entrance.

One of the Yeomen Warders, wearing his iconic beefeater hat, escorted me through the growing field of blooms. "Every morning when you walk through the site just to make sure everything's ready, you get your own moment of inner peace," Jim Duncan told me. "You get the goose pimples, you get the lump in the throat, and then you get a great bunch of people that come in, work hard, work together as a team. It was raining this afternoon, and nobody left." A staffer overseeing the art project reminded me that more than one hundred thousand Americans died in the war. She handed me a ceramic red poppy on a metal stem, and I hammered it into the dirt myself.

I had always had a hard time wrapping my head around World War I. Other conflicts had a clear narrative, a more obvious reason for occurring. But "the Great War" felt so needless, the trigger so amorphous. Twenty million people were killed, and I was never quite sure why, or who they were. I knew the story of Gavrilo Princip assassinating Archduke Franz Ferdinand. In fact, I spent a week in Sarajevo reporting on the one hundredth anniversary of that assassination. So I understood the facts. But it still never made intuitive sense to me. How could so many millions of people kill one another, and for what? The poppies didn't answer those questions, but the artwork at least helped me picture the scale of the loss.

Years later, my *All Things Considered* cohost Robert Siegel said something to me in the NPR studio that gave me a bit of perspective. We were listening to a reporter's story about growing waves of nationalism and anti-EU sentiment when Robert turned to me and observed, "Not that long ago, if you tried to tell someone that Europe was somehow more peaceful than the Middle East, Africa, or other parts of the world, they would have laughed at you. Until the end of World War II," he said, "the story of Europe was basically centuries of uninterrupted bloodshed." Viewed through that lens, World War I seemed less like an aberration and more like a resting state, albeit one amped up by new technologies.

To better understand whom the poppies represented, I went underground, literally. I boarded the tube to the outskirts of London and emerged at the British National Archives. In the basement, I read diaries from some of the men who had fought in that war a century before.

> All the hedges are torn and trampled. All the grass trodden in
> the mud. Holes where shells have struck. Branches torn off trees
> by explosions. Everywhere the same hard, grim, pitiless sight of
> battle and war. I've had a belly full of it.

That entry, from Captain James Patterson, was written on September 16, 1914. It ends, *I must try and write to my mother now.* He died six weeks later.

On the day of my visit, British archivists were in the process of digitizing 1.5 million pages of diaries describing life in the trenches. They hoped that people around the world would read the pages, as I was doing, and gain some insight into the daily reality of the people who fought the war. The diaries were a chronicle of explosions, death, frigid marches, and rare moments of joy, like pickup soccer games. A historian named William Spencer told me those were the diary entries that helped him understand what these young men were thinking a century ago. "If you want to get your people pointing in the right direction, you kick a football over the top, and they followed it," he said.

I emerged from the basement into wan sunshine, and in the archives' cafeteria I met an eighty-four-year-old sipping coffee. Michael Brookbank told me he was the son of a World War I veteran. "My father very rarely talked about the war," he told me, "and I think that is common with most of the veterans of the war. The experiences that they went through, and the conditions that they lived in were just something that, unless you were actually there, nobody could really comprehend."

As the centenary commemorations continued across Europe over the year, I, too, felt distant from the narratives of wars, bombs, explosions, and death. I didn't have my war correspondent colleagues' experiences of covering conflict firsthand, but at least I could read fiction. I bought the novel *Birdsong*, by Sebastian Faulks, and Ernest Hemingway's *Farewell to Arms*.

Back at my flat in East London some months later, the second World War roared into my life. The neighborhood adjacent to mine, Bethnal Green, was evacuated. Workers at a construction site had stumbled on an unexploded German bomb in a basement, one of about thirty thousand that were dropped on London in just three months during the Blitz. That bombardment virtually flattened Bethnal Green, but not all of those bombs exploded. The one that contractors unearthed in the basement was a yard long and about five hundred pounds.

These kinds of discoveries are common enough in London that in certain neighborhoods, Realtors point out damage from the Blitz when they're selling a house. But it felt utterly foreign to me. I tried to imagine how I would react if a yard-long World War II bomb turned up in the Portland neighborhood where I spent my childhood. It would be like aliens landing at my neighbors' house. A seventy-five-year-old lifelong Bethnal Green resident named Bernie Lewis told me it brought back some of his earliest memories. "Aw, it was terrifying," he said. "I was three years old. You know, like, you could hear the bomb, the V-2 bombers, *bum-bum-bum*. They whistle, *wheeeeeeeeee*. And once the whistle stops, they drop."

It hit me how much I had taken certain aspects of my comfortable American life for granted. The distance from San Francisco to New York is three thousand miles. Travel the same distance from London, and you're in Moscow or Damascus, having crossed up to a dozen countries on the way. I could take a train two hours from London and emerge in Paris. If I took a train two hours from Orlando, I would be . . . well, nowhere, because Florida killed the high-speed train proposal. But if I got in my car and drove two hours from Orlando, I'd still be in Florida.

From my perch in London, I could see that my cozy American bubble had distorted the way I viewed the rest of the world. When I heard stories about wars and revolutions on other continents, as empathetic and well informed as I might have imagined myself to be, some part of my brain filed those away as unfortunate events happening to "war people in war places." In my mind, the humans who lived through those experiences never took shape as more than two-dimensional characters in a distant drama.

These are not ideas that I expressed aloud. Instead, they stayed on a low simmer in the back of my mind during the year London commemorated the centenary of the start of the Great War. I occasionally turned them over in my head, but didn't engage them too deeply. And then, I volunteered to go cover some wars.

By 2015, ISIS had taken over massive parts of Iraq and Syria. The black flag flew over Mosul, the largest city in Iraqi Kurdistan. I booked a ticket to Erbil, the Iraqi city just an hour's drive east of Mosul.

Before I took off for the assignment, I called my friend Alice Ford-ham to ask for her advice. She was a Middle East correspondent, so reporting trips to dangerous war zones like Syria, Yemen, and Iraq were a regular part of her routine. I asked her how to keep everybody safe, how to navigate cultural differences, how to lead a group that might include an interpreter, a fixer, a driver, and a security adviser.

"The best advice I can give you," Alice said with utter seriousness, "is don't skip lunch. People get cranky if they don't eat." The more she talked, the more sense her advice made. Carving out time for lunch is a way of showing that you care about the people on your team, she explained. It demonstrates that you see them as real people with needs, not just hired labor or worker bees. I still follow that advice diligently, no matter how wild or urgent a day of reporting in the field might get.

..

IMMIGRATION OFFICERS IN ERBIL WELCOMED me warmly, eager for another American to tell stories of Kurdish forces fighting to reclaim their land. Erbil had dreams of becoming the next Dubai, a hub for Western oil investment and international business, but the rise of ISIS put those aspirations on hold. Half-built towers dotted the skyline as a private car took me to my hotel. NPR's security team deemed taxis a safety risk, even though Erbil itself was largely peaceful.

The city felt bizarrely normal, with few signs that everyone was living adjacent to a war zone. At an American-themed pub called T-Bar that offered the best buffalo wings and cheesesteaks in Kurdistan, I met a US expat who had come to Erbil to teach English. "It's life in a border town," Ryan McCarthy told me as he drank Budweiser and played trivia. The biggest difference from an American bar was that everybody was smoking cigarettes indoors. Ryan found it easy to forget about the atrocities happening just an hour to the west. "I suppose you can ask people in South Korea who live right next to North Korea if they feel the same way," he said.

Instead I asked the bar manager, a Yazidi man named Ayas Murath-adji. He told me that if the American expats heard the same things he did about what ISIS was doing to his countrymen, they might not be so relaxed. The Yazidis are an ancient religious minority in northern Iraq, and they've been singled out for persecution over many generations. ISIS massacred Yazidi men and kept women as sex slaves. Ayas told me that even on the days when he heard horrific stories about Yazidis slaughtered by ISIS, or trapped and starving on a mountaintop, he came to work at the bar, serving beers and burgers like any other shift. It seemed that even in a city on the border of a conflict, Americans were able to dismiss the people in the crossfire as "war people in war places."

A map of Erbil looks like a dartboard, with a series of concentric rings narrowing in on an ancient citadel at the bull's-eye. After six thousand years, that walled city on a hill may be the oldest continuously inhabited site on earth. Even as American bombs fell on Mosul, archaeologists at the Erbil citadel continued their research, and UNESCO continued its restoration project of the ancient city. It was a strange juxtaposition, a story of restoration and rebuilding against a backdrop of destruction and death under the Caliphate.

My arrival in the city came just as Kurdish troops with US backing were driving ISIS out of areas around a mountain called Sinjar, several hours west of Erbil near the Syrian border. The Yazidis who lived in the area considered it a sacred mountain; they called it Shengal.

I knew about this specific part of Iraq from the news, and from the Torah. When civilians fled ISIS to hide atop Mount Sinjar in 2014, the US airlifted food and water to keep them from starving. In my previous role as a White House correspondent, I had reported on some of President Obama's speeches about the humanitarian relief effort.

And at my synagogue as a kid, I had also heard about this place in the book of Jonah. A man with a deep, resonant voice read that story aloud every Yom Kippur in late afternoon, near the end of a twenty-four-hour fast. Long before the part of the story where the hero gets swallowed by a whale, the book of Jonah begins with God telling the protagonist to go to Nineveh. Rather than do the difficult thing, Jonah disobeys and flees, which sets the plot into motion. Mount Sinjar (the twenty-first-century road signs helpfully told me) is in Iraq's Nineveh province.

Driving there made me feel a bit like those tourists who go on *Game of Thrones* tours of Croatia, except I was touring the places I had heard about during the High Holidays every year. Watching miles of sand pass by the window, wearing my flak jacket and helmet, I understood Jonah's impulse to flee.

Dlovan Barwari, the local journalist working as my driver, fixer, and interpreter, pointed off to our right. "That's the Syrian border," he said. All I could see was more desert. If anything went wrong, from a car wreck to an ISIS attack, the nearest hospital was undoubtedly hours away. I tried not to think about it, which only made me think about it more. Of course I'd considered this in the abstract before we left, but back in the safety of my Erbil hotel room I mostly just felt eager to get out and find a good story. Now, my hunger for adventure struck me as naive, and the vast emptiness all around us made the risks feel uncomfortably real.

At checkpoints every few miles, Kurdish peshmerga fighters in uniform stopped our car to check our IDs. Dlovan had told them to expect us. Meanwhile, an app on my phone was pinging my location to NPR's security coordinator in London every ten minutes. If this reporting trip did go off the rails, they would have some idea of my last known location.

The road we were on was a narrow path of safety, with danger on either side. We were driving a long, indirect route to avoid the perimeter of Mosul, and the troops manning the checkpoints told us that there were still often skirmishes along this road, especially at night. *Skirmishes* sounds like such a milquetoast word to describe people shooting guns and rockets at one another. I clung more tightly to my safety gear, even as it felt bulkier and more suffocating after hours in the car.

Our destination was a town called Snuny, and we had a pretty straightforward plan. We had talked it all through with my editor and NPR's security coordinator before our departure from Erbil: we would meet with the mayor, interview a few townspeople, and then drive back to safety before dark, to file a piece telling the story of life returning to a town after ISIS.

As we pulled into the town, graffiti on the buildings offered a short-hand of Snuny's recent history. Black spray paint proclaiming *This is the Islamic State* had been scribbled out. In its place, paint in the red and green colors of Iraqi Kurdistan announced, *This is now the property of the Kurdish peshmerga.*

Before the war, about 150,000 people lived in Snuny. By the time I arrived in February 2015, only about 10,000 had returned. Most were single men; their families had for the most part decided it wasn't yet safe enough. We passed a few people with carts selling vegetables by the side of the road. A man on a small ladder tended to his olive trees, and another herded sheep. These didn't look to me like "war people in war places." They looked like struggling fathers and sons.

We did find one family, a mother with three young children standing outside a mud brick house with a few chickens and a lamb roaming the yard. Wedat Kasim told me that the animals were gifts, given to the family to encourage them to return to Snuny. Before coming back to this town, she had been on top of Mount Sinjar for nearly five months with her three-, five-, and six-year-old kids. "There was nothing to eat, no water to drink, no soap. We had maybe a little rice or cracked wheat each day," she said as Dlovan interpreted. Instead of bathing her kids, she would try to wipe down their faces with a little water. They didn't understand what was happening. "They would just cry and ask me to give them food."

Then she turned from Dlovan to me. "I have a question for you," she said in Kurdish, staring into my eyes. "As difficult as our lives are, thousands of women are still being held by ISIS, and their lives are worse. What about them?"

I didn't have an answer for her. I stammered out the only reply I could think of—that I hoped this story would make sure the world didn't forget about them. I told her that I was sorry for what she and her family had been through, and then we climbed back into the car and left them behind. Suddenly the flak jacket and helmet that had made me feel so secure an hour ago just made me feel inept, like a dumb Western interloper trying to inure himself against the reality he was witnessing.

At city hall, half a dozen armed soldiers escorted us in to meet the mayor. Nayef Sado Kasim was the first official I had seen all day who wasn't wearing a camouflage uniform. With a sharp gray suit and buzz-cut silver hair, he was clearly trying to project an air of normalcy in a city that was barely functioning.

Snuny had no reliable electricity, no water, no street cleaning, and no trash collection. Yet the mayor insisted on serving us lunch. We ate lablabi, a chickpea soup with a poached egg floating in the broth. There was fresh warm flatbread, and the ever-present sweet black tea. So many of my stories from that reporting trip feature the sound of stirring teaspoons clinking against the sides of small fluted glasses. I asked NPR's Middle East editor whether it was a regional audio cliché that I should avoid. "Not as cliché as starting a story with the Muslim call to prayer," he said.

When we finished our tea and our interview, the mayor told me that he wanted us to see something. Details were sparse, and we hadn't discussed this part of the plan with my bosses. Fearing that we would likely never be back here again, Dlovan and I climbed into a truck with a heavily armed driver and set back off into the desert.

In hindsight, I see that this could be a useful teaching moment for beginning journalists: what you should *not* do when reporting from a war zone is get into a car with an armed stranger and drive out into the desert, where you know there are ISIS fighters. That is the definition of a red flag situation. Fortunately the drive went without incident, and after twenty minutes we arrived at an ancient temple.

The eight-hundred-year-old shrine called Sharfadin is one of the holiest sites in the Yazidi religion. When ISIS swept through the area six months before my arrival, they razed ancient buildings and killed thousands of people. But a handful of peshmerga fighters decided that they would rather die than see Sharfadin fall. They had little food, and limited ammunition, but they stayed and fought.

Their commander was a man named Qasim Shesho. When Dlovan learned that this was the man we were going to see, he gasped. Shesho was famous in this part of the world. Dlovan told me that every Yazidi fighter knew his name. He had been part of every major Kurdish offensive since the 1970s and was considered a hero long before this siege.

Some of the younger fighters at the temple walked us into the meeting room where Shesho sat, a father figure in wire-rimmed glasses with a thick black mustache. One by one, they kissed the old man's hand and then sat against the wall. Once again, we were offered sweet tea in small fluted glasses. When I raised my glass to clink with Shesho's in a toast, he asked in English if I would rather have whiskey. At this, he gave a deep husky laugh and then began to tell me what had happened there.

He unfolded the kind of story you find in Hollywood, or ancient epic literature—a tale of a small number of vastly outnumbered men defending a sacred place. "We were alone," Shesho gestured around the room. "We were just eighteen peshmerga against ISIS." When the siege on Sharfadin began, he told me, they had so little food and so few weapons that four men would share one round of flatbread each day. "Every time we had to shoot, we wanted to save the bullet," said Shesho, "because we wanted each one to kill a person."

Word eventually reached Kurdish leaders in Erbil that the temple was standing and that fighters were defending it from ISIS. And so helicopters began to drop food and ammunition to the men. Shesho told me the attacks were relentless. There were car bombs, rockets, and snipers. One of his men was killed. "There were times we had no hope, so we said, *Let us die fighting*. That way we won't have to see our temple fall."

Weeks turned into months, and still the temple stood. Kurdish reinforcements arrived. Two hundred men at first, then more. Four of the commander's adult sons came from Germany to fight alongside their father. As Shesho spoke, I looked at the men standing against the back wall with their brothers-in-arms, and they nodded to me.

One of the sons took me outside to see the evidence of the fight. He pointed to a hole in the ground where a mortar fell, and then he removed a stone covering the hole. The mortar was still there, unexploded. As I leaned over to take a closer look, it struck me that this was another "what not to do" red flag training moment. I slowly backed away from the bomb.

I thought of the echoes between that unexploded weapon in remote northern Iraq and the World War II bomb unearthed in a Bethnal Green basement near the apartment I was calling home, thousands of miles away—this technology designed to kill, hurled at people who somehow escaped annihilation.

The entire story of these scrappy underresourced fighters holding back ISIS for months sounded so impossible to believe that part of me thought it couldn't really have happened. Their victory was the stuff of myth. But when I called representatives of the Kurdish government in Erbil, they confirmed the account. They told me about the airlifts of food, ammunition, and fighters. And perhaps the best testament to what happened was the temple itself. While ISIS smashed ancient, sacred buildings across Iraq and Syria, Sharfadin temple still stands, with barely any damage.

The men led me across a wide plaza to enter the eight-hundred-year-old shrine. Sunlight shined off the pale yellow stone, and two elegant cones crowned the building. At the tip of each cone, three gold balls and a crescent reached skyward.

We took off our shoes before passing through the first gate, and the men kissed the door frame as they walked under it. Inside the perimeter wall, we stood in a courtyard with a large tree where birds sang. It was so peaceful, I tried to imagine what it must have felt like as war raged there weeks ago.

At the center of the grounds, we entered a small, dark room where brightly colored knotted fabrics hung from the walls. A stone pillar at the heart of this chamber was where Yazidi worshippers brought their prayers. "During the siege, we came here every day and asked God to save us," a fighter named Shamwa Edo told me.

I asked Shesho to describe how he felt once Kurdish troops drove out ISIS, after four long months of fighting. That moment he realized the siege was over, "We didn't celebrate," he said, "we just cried."

Before Dlovan and I left Sinjar, our escort from the mayor's office had one more site to show us. We drove deeper into the desert and reached the small village of Harman, where even fewer people had returned than Snuny.

Our driver led us to a man patrolling a pile of dirt. The villager, Naif Brahem Khadir, explained what we were looking at. When Kurds brought an earthmover here to build a checkpoint, the machine dug into this mound at the side of the road and uncovered something awful—human bones and bloodstained clothing. Khadir was patrolling to make sure dogs didn't dig up the remains of his relatives and run away with the bones. He pulled a white headscarf out of the dried mud and showed me the bullet hole.

Some villagers who escaped ISIS at the start of the assault watched the massacre through binoculars from the top of Mount Sinjar. Khadir told us they estimate they watched seventy, perhaps one hundred, of their countrymen gunned down in this valley. No one had dug up this mass grave yet to give the people a proper burial, because they wanted the UN to document what happened before anything was touched. "The world must record this genocide," Khadir said.

My reporting trip came in the earliest days of the effort to turn back ISIS. It would take years more of grinding fighting on the ground, and bombs from the sky, before the group was driven out altogether. Only then was there something close to a full accounting of the destruction and death that the group caused.

In 2018, a UN report said that across Iraq, ISIS left behind at least two hundred mass graves like the one I saw. According to the report, they contained more than twelve thousand bodies. Iraqi scholars believe that the real number is much higher. The head of Iraq's Mass Graves Directorate estimates that one site alone held six thousand bodies. Each one of those corpses, someone's relative—a parent or child. Not "war people," but humans.

••

NEAR THE END OF MY time in Iraq, I visited an internally displaced persons' camp where Iraqis who'd been forced from their homes and towns lived in shabby tents. A little girl tied a string to the handles of a cheap plastic shopping bag and ran in circles in the dirt, going faster and faster so the wind would catch the bag and make it fly like a kite.

After seeing the acute pain of survivors around Mount Sinjar, I wanted to report a story from here that would take a wider perspective—to look at the longer-term psychological impacts of the relentless brutality that this conflict inflicted on civilians. Even compared to the baseline standards of war's inhumanity, the public beheadings and torture that ISIS routinely practiced were creating profound and lasting trauma for the people who lived through it. That was the story I went to tell from the IDP camp.

I spent a day with counselors and therapists at a clinic run by the International Medical Corps, as they tried to heal some of the less visible wounds of war. One man recounted to the therapist how he was forced to dig his own grave with a shovel and then survived the shot that was supposed to kill him. Another described watching his friend be doused in kerosene and set on fire.

And then I met a man I will always remember. He was a father who never gave me his name, whose seven-year-old son was killed in front of him. He told me that he was slowly trying to heal. "Last year I was 90 percent pain," he said. "Now I'm 50 percent." He pulled out his phone and showed me photos of his son as an infant and as a toddler. I asked if he could imagine a day when he would be 5 percent pain, or zero. "Insh'allah," he said. God willing.

Back at my hotel room, I wrote my first draft of the piece, recounting the stories of horror and introducing listeners to the therapists trying to offer some measure of healing. I ended on that "Insh'allah," the man's hope that someday he would be healed. I sent off the draft to my editor and filled the bathtub with water as hot as I could tolerate. After a long soak I emerged from the tub, walked over to my laptop, and saw that my editor had replied. Early in this reporting trip, he'd told me that the muezzin's call to prayer was the most cliché way to start a story from the Middle East. Well, he said, the word *insh'allah* is the most cliché way to end one. It's a shrug, he explained, a dodge. In newsrooms, the phrase "Only time will tell" is an inside joke—a way of saying, "I don't have a good way to wrap up this story, so I'll slap on an *only time will tell* and call it a day." I had landed on the Middle Eastern version of "Only time will tell." I needed a new ending.

I racked my brain and remembered something that I had described to my husband a few hours earlier—a moment that I hadn't included in my first draft. This is a rookie journalism mistake. One cardinal rule of reporting is that the anecdote you tell your spouse over the phone on your way back from a day of reporting should always be in the story you ultimately sit down to write.

This moment came after we had finished our last interview at the camp. We'd packed up our equipment and were trying to politely excuse ourselves while digesting all of the pain we'd witnessed. As we walked past the tents toward the main gate, we passed the man who'd told us about his seven-year-old son; the man who'd expressed a hope that one day he would be able let go of the pain, "Insh'allah." I waved goodbye to him as we walked by, but he didn't notice me. He was sitting by himself, scrolling through his phone, engrossed by the pictures of his child.

That became the last moment in the story. The image of him staring at his phone has always stayed with me. Not only because the moment is something anyone can identify with, whether or not we've endured tragedy. More than that, I think he was holding on to a sort of talisman. An object we can touch, and see, to ground ourselves in the inconceivable and unimaginable. The shining photograph on the glassy surface of his phone holds power, like an unexploded bomb outside an ancient temple; a white headscarf with a single bullet hole; a diary entry from a soldier who fought a century ago; or a red ceramic poppy, pounded into the dirt.

7

WAR PEOPLE IN OTHER PLACES

When I visited Iraq, the country had been a war zone for more than a decade. My assignment was to cover a fight that was churning toward a conclusion, and I had some idea of what I was flying into. Ukraine was different. I didn't travel there in 2014 intending to report on a war. Instead, I watched as the peaceful, modern city of Donetsk became a center of international conflict in real time—a foretaste of the destruction that would consume the country when Russia staged a full-scale invasion of Ukraine eight years later, in 2022.

At the buffet of the Hotel Ukraine in Kyiv, the label on the pitcher read, "MELTED WATER." I puzzled over what the translation could possibly be trying to say, until a local journalist friend explained that some people in Ukraine believe that water from melted ice is the healthiest. The food on offer was what I always thought of as Jewish cuisine: borscht, dumplings, pickles, stuffed cabbage. Thanks to the Hotel

Ukraine, I learned that my definition of "Jewish food" wasn't Jewish per se. This part of the world just happened to be where some of my ancestors came from, cities that had at various times been part of Poland, Ukraine, or the Soviet Union, as wars were fought, borders shifted, and Jews were forced to relocate from one city to another.

My hotel room came with a small balcony overlooking Independence Square, the *maidan*, where people still camped in tents, even months after demonstrations that had forced out a corrupt pro-Russian government. At night, I could smell the smoke wafting up from the camp stoves where people grilled meat.

The protests in that square began in November 2013, sparked by President Victor Yanukovych's refusal to sign an agreement to bring Ukraine closer to Europe. Tens of thousands of Ukrainians marched peacefully in that plaza, chanting "Ukraine is Europe." The government responded with tear gas, and as the protests swelled in 2014, authorities sent snipers to shoot live ammunition from the roof of the building where I was staying. Dozens of civilians were killed, and months later their photographs were still displayed in makeshift memorials.

The upshot of the violent crackdown was that Yanukovych was forced out of power, a pro-European government took his place, and Russia's president, Vladimir Putin, was furious. Putin seized Ukraine's Crimean Peninsula, and the West condemned him for it. So the tensions in Ukraine when I arrived in April 2014 were a microcosm of the larger push-pull between Russia to the east and the NATO alliance including the US and Europe to the west.

By the time I checked into my hotel on a crisp spring day, the country was at the center of a geopolitical tug-of-war, but it wasn't a fighting war. My assignment wasn't to file breaking news reports; I was there to find some bigger-picture stories about what had changed since the Euromaidan revolution.

I spent the first few days in Kyiv trying to tell stories that would answer my own questions about what was happening in the country. For a piece on corruption, I decided to look at the health care system. An AIDS activist arranged for me to meet a man whose wife was denied HIV medication and died at the age of thirty-eight. There was no medicine for her, because corrupt middlemen inflated the price of the drugs. "Nobody from the hospital showed any interest in treating her," the widower told me. He wouldn't let me use his name, since he had already been fired from one job when the boss learned that he had HIV.

For a story on Ukraine's economic crunch, I went to a park where old men played chess. The grandfathers ate cured pork fat and raw onions on dark brown bread as they downed shots of Ukrainian vodka called horilka in the middle of the day, anesthetizing them against the government's austerity measures. "Austerity won't affect us because we have no money anyway," a retired geology teacher named Sergei Kedun told me. "Our people are broke, so what difference does it make?"

The Jewish holiday of Passover arrived, and since I wouldn't be able to join my family for a Seder, I decided to report a piece on whether this holiday celebrating the exodus from slavery to freedom had new meaning for Ukrainian Jews in the context of the revolution. "We started our liberation three thousand years ago, and we still are in the process," a progressive Kyiv rabbi named Alexander Duchovny told me.

He offered to take me to Babyn Yar, the site of a notorious World War II massacre where Nazis killed more than thirty thousand Jews. Since part of my family was from this region, I was eager to go. I thought maybe after the pilgrimage to Babyn Yar, I would fly west to the city of Lviv to do some more reporting. I was sure that in a European-style city near the border with Poland, I'd find interesting stories about how people were responding to their new western-leaning government. But that was not how it went.

Instead, I started to hear reports from the other side of the country, near Ukraine's border with Russia in the east. Armed separatists in the cities of Donetsk and Luhansk went on local news stations to say that they had taken over city hall and other government buildings. The demonstrators announced that they wanted to become part of Russia, not Ukraine.

From Kyiv, I couldn't tell exactly what was happening or how significant it was. The only way to find out was to go there. I took a taxi to the airport and flew east.

··

THE CITY OF DONETSK HAD just hosted the European soccer championships, and the gleaming new airport reflected the international attention. Donbas Arena rivaled any soccer stadium in western Europe. Parks were freshly manicured, and fruit trees bloomed along my drive to the Holiday Inn in the center of town.

Occupiers had been in government buildings for less than a week, and Ukraine's government threatened that they would be out in forty-eight hours, whether by negotiation or by force. I left my bags in my room and walked along a lush greenway to a government building where a banner proclaimed the "People's Republic of Donetsk." It felt absurdly out of place, like the separatists barricaded inside had missed the memo that this was an idyllic spring day. Weren't hostile takeovers supposed to take place under ominous clouds or driving rain?

Razor wire and sandbags surrounded the concrete office building. Young men wearing face masks walked the perimeter holding metal pipes. Molotov cocktails sat unused behind stacks of tires. It was calm, but the activists seemed wound up. I didn't know if they were actually on something or just charged with a sense of mischief from the takeover.

A skinny young guy with a wispy mustache and a black stocking cap demanded to see my papers. He told me his name was Vadim, and he said that he wanted eastern Ukraine to be part of Russia—just like Crimea. He told me that if Ukraine's military attacked, the separatists were ready to fight back. But he wouldn't tell me what kinds of weapons they might have had inside.

Despite the gravity of the situation, I found myself stifling a chuckle. The whole operation felt so ad hoc, like these were posturing teenagers trying to look tough. Patriotic Russian folk tunes played over the loudspeakers. Every now and then someone grabbed a microphone to exhort the crowd with talk of Russian greatness. A group of old women made sausage sandwiches for the men behind the razor wire. As in Kyiv, some of the guys were downing shots of horilka in the middle of the day.

A few blocks away, the afternoon was completely serene. I found parents strolling with kids riding on their shoulders. Out of earshot from the Russian folk music, a duo with a guitar and a trumpet played covers of Adele as people passing by threw coins to the musicians. *We could've had it all, rolling in the deep . . .*

Sidewalk cafés served pizza and sushi while kids squealed in a playground. A man named Emir Gushinov was offering pony rides. He told me that business was slow, but not because of any revolution. "The main reason is that it's not a holiday, so all the kids are in school," he said. "This is a great business at vacation time."

A man who would only give me his first name, Michal, walked with a few of his friends, wearing the orange and black ribbon of the separatist demonstrators. He looked at the kids eating ice cream, the grandmothers sitting on benches, and told me most of the people in Donetsk were just "unconscious."

"Only about 10 percent of the people who live here really understand what's happening," he said.

"And do you think that 10 percent can change the fate of the country?" I asked him.

"The minority decides the fate of the majority," he said coolly, as if this had always been the way of the world.

I had a hard time believing him. A woman who introduced herself as Nadia exhaled cigarette smoke and backed me up. "What's actually happening is one hundred armed people are proclaiming a new republic. It's not the one million people who live in Donetsk," she said, rolling her eyes.

To her, war was something that happened to other people, in other parts of the world. Her home was a city of manicured parks, sushi restaurants, and a shiny new airport. I started to wonder about what happened when you could no longer assume that the democracy you had taken for granted would endure. When insurrectionists arrive in the hometown that you've always known as a peaceful, thriving city, how do you respond?

Years later, as I sat at home in Washington, DC, watching armed rioters storm the US Capitol, I thought of Michal and Nadia. The insurrectionists roaming the halls of Congress looked as absurd as the young men patrolling the razor wire outside buildings in eastern Ukraine. Was Michal right that people are just "unconscious," I wondered? Does a small minority actually decide the fate of the majority? I pictured Nadia with her cigarette, unaware of how profoundly her city was about to transform, and I wondered whether I was equally naive about the growing divisions in my own country.

..

ONE OF MY TASKS IN eastern Ukraine was to find out whether the protests really were an authentic uprising of local people, as Russia claimed, or whether they were being secretly organized by Moscow, as leaders in Washington and Kyiv insisted. In the beginning, nothing seemed organized by anyone. It felt like amateur hour, and I found it difficult to take the threat seriously. One demonstrator occupying the security services building in the city of Luhansk told me, "If we were funded by Russia, we would have food. We're starving in here."

Everything changed in one weekend. Organized militants took over government buildings across several cities in eastern Ukraine, all at once. They were professional, highly coordinated, and more heavily armed than the protesters whom I had met when I first arrived in the region.

I drove to one of those towns, called Horlivka, just after the weekend that everything shifted. Several new checkpoints seemed to have popped up overnight. At one checkpoint, a twentysomething man, swishing and twirling in short shorts and a neon vest, grandly directed traffic through the intersection. I'm sure he was aiming to come across as a tough and militaristic part of an occupying force, but instead he landed somewhere in the region of high camp. As he swept his traffic baton past our car window, I thought of go-go dancer friends in the US and imagined a parallel universe in which this guy was dancing on a box in a nightclub, strutting for tips, rather than fomenting an insurrection.

Locals in Horlivka told me that the militants were speaking with foreign accents and couldn't find their way around town. A video on YouTube showed a uniformed man introducing himself to Horlivka's local police as a lieutenant colonel in the Russian military. I went to that police station, where a spokesman for the rebels told me that the man in the YouTube video had disappeared. With a straight face, the spokesman explained that nobody knew who the guy was. "He probably escaped in back, through the fence," the rebels' representative declared as though it were the most normal thing in the world. After four years covering the White House, I was used to spokespeople spinning me, but that claim actually made me laugh out loud. The rebel didn't find it funny.

My interviews in eastern Ukraine had settled the question in my mind of whether Russians were involved in the uprising. They were clearly present, if hidden. And they were obviously helping to organize and arm the separatists. At the same time, I could see that Moscow was tapping into an organic sentiment, and a resentment, that had existed in this region for a very long time.

In Kyiv, all our interviews were in Ukrainian. But the local fixer I had hired, a Donetsk college student named Zhenya Afanasiev, told me that in eastern Ukraine we were more often speaking with civilians in Russian. The cities where separatists had taken over all had two names, depending on which language you were speaking: Donetsk or Danyetsk, Luhansk or Lugansk. Just opening your mouth told people which side you were on.

Many people living in those eastern Ukrainian cities had friends and relatives just over the border in Russia. Some Ukrainians in border towns couldn't understand why the government in Kyiv suddenly insisted that their Russian neighbors were their enemies. I met a police officer for a beer at my hotel bar, and he told me that his mother called him every day and told him not to attack the separatists, even if his commanders ordered it. Every day he reassured her, "I won't, Mom." Because of border tensions, he had to miss his sister-in-law's wedding in Russia. "These are our friends and family," he told me. "Why should there be border tensions?"

He explained that Ukrainian cops were paid about five dollars a day, which was why so many of them took bribes. In Russia, he said, the salary was around fifty dollars a day. From that angle, being part of Russia didn't seem so bad to him.

I could see that Russia wasn't creating a revolution from scratch. Unlike the full-scale assault of 2022, the operation in 2014 was part invasion, part civil war. Moscow was tapping into something real, exacerbating preexisting tensions, and inflaming divisions that were already bubbling under the surface.

When Russia later tried to run a similar playbook in the 2016 US elections, I felt a deep sense of déjà vu. The Facebook ads that Russian interests paid for in 2016, in many cases, were not about an American political candidate. They were about gun rights, LGBTQ equality, or racial justice. And in the US, the Russians played both sides of these debates.

The most successful Facebook ad that Russian trolls purchased in 2016 reached well over a million people. It was called "Back the Badge," described as a "Community of people who support our brave Police Officers." The Internet Research Agency, a troll farm in Saint Petersburg, Russia, paid eighteen hundred dollars for it. The most popular Texas secession page on Facebook, which had more followers than the official Texas Democratic and Republican Facebook pages combined, was a Russian front. It was called Heart of Texas, and by the time Facebook took it down, it had a quarter million followers.

Heart of Texas had a real-world impact too. The page organizers mobilized people in Houston to stage a protest called "Stop Islamization of Texas." At the same time, another account linked to Russia, "United Muslims of America," organized a counterprotest called "Save Islamic Knowledge." The two groups convened in the same place, on the same day. "What neither side could have known was that Russian trolls were encouraging both sides to battle in the streets and create division between real Americans," Senate Intelligence Committee Chairman Richard Burr later said. The senator added that to organize and promote these events, Russia paid about two hundred dollars.

After the 2016 presidential election, I interviewed a twenty-four-year old activist in North Carolina named Conrad James. He told me about being contacted by a website called BlackMattersUS. He checked them out—their Instagram feed, Twitter account, and Facebook page all looked legit. They asked him to organize a march in Charlotte for racial justice, and he did. It was peaceful, a few hundred people showed up, there were speakers. He even got a bank card to charge the cost of the equipment rental. This was all paid for, we now know, by Russia. Black-MattersUS was another page created by a troll factory, with the goal of exacerbating divisions in American society.

Russia ran these maneuvers in Ukraine before doing the same thing in the US: exploit existing tensions, inflame long-standing resentments, and undermine democracy by pitting citizens against one another. Of course, disinformation was part of the landscape too.

In eastern Ukraine in 2014, I started getting Facebook messages from my Jewish friends back in the US. They were alarmed by reports that separatists in Donetsk had instructed Ukrainian Jews to register with the new authorities. Since my friends knew that I was reporting in the region, they asked me to amplify and share the story. They should have asked me to fact-check it.

Their alarm stemmed from leaflets that had been distributed at an Orthodox synagogue in Donetsk. The flyers said that local Jews must come to occupied buildings with a passport, family history, a list of possessions, and a fifty-dollar registration fee—a huge sum of money in this region. According to the leaflet, the penalty for failing to register could be deportation, loss of citizenship, and confiscation of assets.

Now, this made no logical sense. And nobody who got the leaflets actually thought they were real. Part of the separatists' rhetoric, their whole narrative, was that Russia wanted to save Ukraine from Nazi-sympathizing leftists who were gaining power in Kyiv. "Bandera-ites" was the term they used—a reference to Stepan Bandera, a Ukrainian nationalist in World War II who fought for the country's independence and also aligned himself with the Nazis.

Putin often described himself as a defender of the Jews against the Bandera-ites. He would later describe his 2022 invasion as a "de-Nazification" effort (which was particularly absurd, since, at that point, Ukraine had a Jewish president). Logically, if the separatists had told

Jewish families in eastern Ukraine to register with authorities, it would have contradicted a big part of their whole sales pitch. To anyone with real knowledge of what was going on in Ukraine, the flyer telling Jews to report to the separatists was just obviously bogus.

"I didn't believe a word of it," Yaguda Kellerman, deputy chief of the Donetsk Jewish Community Center, told me. "You'd really have to be a fool to write anything like this."

Jews in Donetsk basically ignored the flyers when they landed. But then a small local story about them got picked up online and spread on social media. Suddenly, Jews around the world who weren't following the intricacies of the insurrection in eastern Ukraine became deeply concerned. And understandably so. From a distance, the story didn't seem so hard to believe. The leaflets had echoes of the Holocaust. When people in the West think of Jews in eastern Europe, pogroms and massacres are often the first things that come to mind. The disinformation played into people's worst fears about the political unrest in Ukraine.

"I got two hundred messages about it in one day," the rabbi in Kyiv whom I had interviewed about Passover (in what now seemed like another world) told me. "Letters from the United States of America, from the UK, from European countries, even from Australia."

And then the American secretary of state added fuel to the fire. "This is not just intolerable, it's grotesque," John Kerry said of the leaflets. "It is beyond unacceptable." I don't know whether Kerry understood the absurdity of the claim he was amplifying. But of course, America's top diplomat also had a political interest in portraying the Russia-backed separatists in Ukraine as Nazi sympathizers.

As a Jew, and as a western reporter in Donetsk who understood the intricacies of the growing conflict, I knew that I could help extinguish this disinformation wildfire. So I went to the synagogue where the leaflets were first handed out. Rabbi Pinchas Vyshetsky told me he knew that the Jews of his city were being used as pawns in a political game. "What I ask all the political leaders in Ukraine is: Leave us alone," he told me. "We are not a political organization. We're a religious community, and the people that are coming to the synagogue, they didn't come to the synagogue to take part in a political meeting."

He said that the flyer was intended solely as a provocation. Nobody ever identified the culprits—most likely someone trying to make the separatists and Russians look bad. In a way, the fact that the flyers got so much attention meant the provocation worked. By reporting out a story explaining the truth of the situation, I was at least able to cut through some of the fog of war. After that, every time someone sent me a worried Facebook message about the leaflet, I replied with a link to my reporting.

The most desolate place I visited during my time in Ukraine also gave me a ray of hope. The city of Perevalsk sat just over the border from Russia. It was a hub of manufacturing and mining under the Soviet Union that nearly became a ghost town after the USSR collapsed in 1991. I wandered through potholed streets with abandoned factories, crumbling houses, and empty windowless shops. One local told me that the only factory still in operation was giving everybody lung disease.

And then I saw Lida Vasilivna. Amid the gray and brown, her bright purple coat and babushka jumped out of the landscape. I asked her what happened to Perevalsk, and she shrugged. "What happened here in our Ukraine is what happened in the whole world. Industry, coal mines, everywhere you look, it's all in decline. Business just went belly up."

She held a large glass jar of seeds in one hand and a shovel in the other, black rubber boots on her feet. "I'm in a great mood today, because I planted onions and tomatoes," she told me. In the photo that I took of her, she has a wide grin and her hand in the air, "Waving to everyone in America," she said.

Within a year of my visit to eastern Ukraine, the sparkling new Donetsk airport was rubble, a bombed and burned-out shell. The soccer team abandoned the city's fancy arena and relocated to a place outside the war zone. To enter the region required special military permission.

My interpreter, Zhenya, had to flee his dorm and transfer to a different school when armed fighters in 2014 decided to use his college campus as barracks. He moved to Lviv, in the west, and landed a job with a big multinational company. I lost touch with him for eight years until NPR hired him again, to help cover the Russian invasion in 2022. The man I had met as a college student was now nearly thirty. He had returned to the occupied territories in the east a few times since he fled to Lviv. A "horrible experience," he told me. Zhenya was "a blank sheet of paper" when I first met him, he said. "Now, we have so much more to lose."

..

AS RUSSIA TRIED TO ENGULF Ukraine with soldiers and rockets, I was reminded of Lida Vasilivna and her jar of seeds. In the earliest days of the 2022 war, a cell phone video showed a Ukrainian woman approaching an armed Russian soldier. She extends her hand to the man in his camouflage uniform. "Take these seeds and put them in your pockets," the woman in the video says. "So at least sunflowers will grow when you all lie down here."

A few weeks after Russia began its invasion, I arrived just forty miles west of Lviv, on the eastern border of Poland. Millions of Ukrainians were pouring out of their country, almost all of them women and children. Under martial law, men of military age were conscripted to fight and forbidden from leaving. The scale of the exodus was almost unprecedented; more people left Ukraine in the first month of that war than left Syria, Iraq, or Afghanistan in an entire year of those conflicts.

In a small Polish mountain village near the border, I stood on a nineteenth-century railroad line as crews of men in orange jumpsuits slowly rebuilt the tracks by hand, working in freezing temperatures. They used pickaxes and rakes to dig out rocks, then they hauled rotten old wooden railroad ties out from under the metal rails and slid new ones in to replace them. This was the clearest sign I had seen that officials did not expect the war to end any time soon. Nobody would put that kind of grueling work into replacing an ancient railroad from the Ukrainian border into Poland if they expected the conflict to be over in weeks, or even months.

I was shocked to see how the conflict had transformed Europe in a matter of weeks. In Poland's largest border town, up to fifteen hundred people were passing through every hour, the mayor told me. I met him in the café of an opulent train station in the town of Przemyśl. The juxtaposition was stark: frescoes on the ceiling, lush curtains draping the windows, and walls painted in shades of cream and peach with decorative flourishes contrasted with desperate women who poured out of crowded trains from Lviv, looking dazed, lost, and desperate. They wore winter coats and carried suitcases, children, or dogs. Many had been traveling for days and didn't know where they were going to spend the night or what their destination would be.

An entire ecosystem had sprung up to support them, from big international organizations like the UN and the Red Cross to ad hoc groups of volunteers. A taxi driver told me that on his one day off every week, he made the five-hour drive from Warsaw to the border and gave Ukrainians a free ride west.

This was, to put it mildly, not the approach to refugees that Poland had been known for. The Przemyśl mayor himself, Wojciech Bakun, had once belonged to a political movement that advocated building a wall on the border to keep Ukrainian immigrants out (inspired by Trump's Mexico border wall). In the past, conservative Polish politicians had talked about Ukrainian immigrants in ways that echoed anti-immigrant talking points in the US, claiming that Ukrainians would steal jobs from Polish citizens and change the fabric of Polish society. Now those views were suddenly unpopular, and Bakun was at the leading edge of the largest refugee resettlement effort in Europe since World War II.

I asked a professor who tracks far-right groups in Poland how he explained that transformation. "People change," Rafal Pankowski told me. "Faced with a big challenge, a change of heart is possible."

All over the country, I saw people marvel at that change. Poland's head rabbi, Michael Schudrich, told me about a building that had been established a century ago as a center of Jewish learning and returned to Poland's Jews early in the twenty-first century as Holocaust restitution. Since the war began, the building was being used to house Ukrainian refugees. "Sometimes I have a feeling that maybe it's for this one moment that the building was built," the rabbi told me.

As I asked him about that history, I misspoke and accidentally referred to Jews "fleeing Poland" instead of Ukraine. He caught that slip of the tongue. "This is one of the great historical ironies that for hundreds of years, we are used to the stories of Jews fleeing Poland," he said. "Now Jews are fleeing into Poland, and they're safe."

"How do you think about that?" I asked.

"I try not to," Rabbi Schudrich said. "It's too overwhelming. But it does show the human capacity for change. History is important, but it does not dictate the future. We dictate the future."

8

THE OTHER MAN I MARRIED

We've got a pretty good meet-cute story. On his way to meet me for the first time, an older woman on his train went into cardiac arrest. He knew CPR, from back when he was a police officer. So he rushed to her side and administered first aid until the medics arrived.

We both showed up early to our meeting, and to break the ice I asked him how his ride down was. When he told me that he'd saved somebody's life on the train, I knew he was the one. That we were destined to work together, as correspondent and producer. Then my colleagues showed up, and we started Rich Preston's job interview.

At NPR, each international correspondent works with a local producer. Some of these journalists have been at the NPR bureau for years, through several rotations of correspondents. They speak the languages and have local contacts. As foreign correspondents, we wouldn't be able to do our jobs without them. They can simultaneously be an interpreter, driver, office manager, and even another reporter. They can also be a gut check on whether a situation is safe, and on how to get things done in a country.

But the situation at the London bureau is different from the others. NPR rents desks and studio space from the BBC, at the network's headquarters just off Oxford Street in central London. Part of the arrangement is that NPR pays the BBC a producer's salary, and a BBC employee does a rotation with NPR's London correspondent for a couple of years.

When I moved to London, I inherited a very sweet and slightly spacey producer who always seemed a bit frazzled by the world. A few months later, her term had expired and we lined up a slate of interested candidates. But the producer whose term was expiring had applied for a renewal.

The BBC's HR regulations required us to ask each job applicant the same questions. We could choose at the start of the day what those questions would be, but we couldn't vary them from one interview to the next. One of the questions I decided to ask was, "What's a website where you find interesting story ideas?"

At that question, she paused for an uncomfortably long stretch. Our panel of interviewers all looked at one another, wondering whether we should offer her some guidance, or just put her out of her misery. She took a slow drink from a glass of water. Another long pause. Finally, she said, "Ask Jeeves?" with an inflection that suggested she was asking us. Not that it would have made a difference, but by that point Ask Jeeves had dropped the Jeeves and gone by Ask.com for about a decade.

Another applicant clearly saw producing as an inconvenient but necessary stepping-stone to becoming a foreign correspondent himself. When we offered to answer any questions he had about the job, he asked how often he would be allowed to file on-air reports for NPR. I was a little nervous that if he was chosen to be my producer, he would smother me with a pillow while I slept and offer to step in for me when I didn't show up for work the next morning.

Rich had come down from Scotland for his interview, which is how he wound up saving that woman's life on the train. By the time he walked into the room after a long morning full of interviews, I had nearly given up hope of finding anybody great to work with. He told us he liked to find stories from *Wired*'s website, which reflected his interest in technology. He also produced a BBC arts program in Scotland (which is how he met Alan Cumming, years before Alan and I created a stage show together). In short, he liked to consider all the things.

Rich exuded competence. Nothing fancy or excessive; his suit was from Zara. I didn't know then, but I would soon learn that his most treasured belongings were his label maker and rolls of electrical tape in various colors—to easily identify at a glance which cable connects to which plug, of course: orange to orange, green to green. I could tell from our first conversation that he'd be able to handle deadlines and crises without breaking a sweat.

From day one, our setup felt like a happy arranged marriage, and we quickly fell into a rhythm working together. First thing each morning, Rich and I would text each other to figure out the day's plan. Should we work from our desks at the BBC, or at the dining table in my apartment, or in the lobby of the Ace Hotel? Since my editor was based in Washington and didn't get to the office until 2 p.m. London time, nobody at headquarters cared where we were hour by hour, as long as we stayed productive. Each day was ours to spend more or less however we wanted. It was the ultimate flexible work schedule.

In the middle of the workday, we would go for long runs together along the River Thames or walk to an underground Victorian men's room that had been converted into a coffee shop called Attendant. We sat at stools nestled into the old urinals, having a cappuccino and banana bread. Rich often ordered flapjacks, which in the UK is a bit like a dense granola bar, sticky with oats and dried fruit. I could never figure out the appeal and sternly told him that I was disappointed in his life choices. About once a week I would off-handedly tell him that he was fired, and he would remind me that as an NPR employee I had no authority to fire him from the BBC. Then we would make dinner plans together.

Rich's sense of humor was as tone-deaf as his singing. He would tune-lessly belt out the theme song to *Jurassic Park* with the lyrics "Dinosaurs are here, and they're getting near." In anticipation of April Fools' Day, he actually tried to persuade the composer John Williams to record an NPR interview "revealing" that those were the original lyrics, nixed by Steven Spielberg. The composer declined to participate.

We livestreamed our antics on social media, trying to nod at something vaguely journalistic in the process. On the night of the British general election in 2015, we bought a rainbow sock puppet from a children's toy shop, named her Daisy, and had her explain the significance of the results in streaming videos between our radio hits. I can't imagine what made us think Daisy was a good idea. Sock puppets were not then, and are not now, part of NPR's social media strategy. I think we came across as more Lucy-Desi than MacNeil-Lehrer.

Rich and I learned to play up the whole "dynamic duo" thing for our social media followers, who ate it up. On Twitter and Instagram, people tracked our travels around the world and called us Batman and Robin, Holmes and Watson, 007 and Q. There were hashtags. There was even fan fiction. Rich learned what "stans" were from working with me.

Since my husband has no social media presence, lots of people assumed Rich and I were a couple. Even some of my friends who know my husband suspected that perhaps Rich and I were a couple. (To be clear, we were not.) Mike was still living in DC while I was in London, so a few months passed before my work husband and my real husband finally met in person. They hit it off as only two people who've spent way too much time around me can.

"Well, he's obviously in love with you," Mike told me later.

"Well, we're in love with each other," I snapped. "But not romantically!"

The truth was that there was something about the buddy movie Rich and I were living out together that had a touch of romanticism. Although our friendship was entirely platonic, our ease with each other, our travels all over the globe, and our general shenanigans felt like the kind of bond you forge during the long days of summer camp or a year abroad—someplace that exists outside of ordinary time, where unexpected adventures await around every corner. I thought I'd left that feeling behind in my teens. It certainly wasn't the kind of friendship I expected to find in my thirties.

I had been a reporter for years and never had so much fun doing it. I thought of Rich as equal parts little brother, sidekick, and best friend. Our first reporting trip outside London brought us to Scotland, where he grew up. His girlfriend happened to have booked the same train as us for a trip of her own. She was younger than he was, blond, and didn't stop talking the entire train ride. I didn't tell Rich that I was disappointed in his life choices at that point. It's one thing to say it about a flapjack, another about a girlfriend. But they broke up a few weeks later, and I was quietly relieved. Not that it was any of my business, but I felt protective of him and thought he deserved better.

On that trip up north, in and among serious stories about the Scottish independence referendum and other weighty issues, we reported a light feature about distillery cats. Distilleries originally brought these cats in to hunt rodents drawn to the grain used in whisky. These days they're more likely to be brand ambassadors on Instagram.

Rich and I drove along winding roads to the oldest distillery in Scotland. Glenturret has produced whisky since 1775, and a bronze statue of a cat proudly memorializes Towser the Mouser, the greatest distillery cat of them all. She patrolled Glenturret from the 1960s to the 1980s and holds a place in *The Guinness Book of World Records* for catching mice. Lifetime kills: 28,899.

The star of our story was a new kitten at Glenturret, named Peat, who had just inherited Towser's proud station. Rich held the big bushy microphone up to Peat, who obligingly pounced on it as if it were a mouse. The adorable fluffball did exactly what we needed for the radio, meowing and purring as if on cue.

I regret to tell you that this story ended in feline tragedy. After we filed our report, it sat unaired for several weeks before finally running on *All Things Considered*. Almost immediately after the broadcast, Rich's phone pinged with an email from the folks at Glenturret. He and I were on the train together, and I saw his face go white as he swallowed hard. Rich put his hand over his mouth and looked up at me. Peat, the six-month-old kitten, had been fatally hit by a car the day before our story ran. The distillery wanted to give the staff a day to process the news before they announced it publicly. In that twenty-four-hour window between the kitten's death and the public announcement, our story featuring Peat was broadcast to the world.

I believe that this is the only time in the half century of *All Things Considered* that the program has ever aired an obituary for a kitten. The day after our distillery cats piece ran, Robert Siegel began a segment with, "And now, a sad update to yesterday's story . . ." The remembrance for the late Peat noted that people were already suggesting names for his successor. One popular idea: Repeat.

..

FOR MOST OF MY LIFE, my friendships have been big in numbers, small in depth. That's not necessarily by choice. Washington, DC, is a transient city; people move away, and I wind up spending a little bit of time with a lot of different people. With Rich, I had a best friend for the first time since childhood. He was someone I talked to every day, worked with under extreme stress, and still wanted to spend time with on the weekends. We knew that our time in each other's company had an end date, which made us both appreciate the experience more. The two years he and I spent working together in London are a patchwork quilt of memories stitched together from across the European continent, forged in crises and scenes that I will never experience again.

In the summer, we took the train from London down to Calais, France, to interview refugees at the migrant camp known as the Jungle. We met people from the Middle East and Africa who were waiting to hitch rides across the English Channel to the UK. Some had lived there for months already. One Afghan man had opened a restaurant in the camp; an Ethiopian man had built a church. When they decided it was time for them to leave, they would pass these handmade buildings on to a newcomer at the Jungle.

Alpha Jaigne, of West Africa's Fulani people, had built an entire compound full of art in the middle of this informal camp. He had a traditional Fulani home with a thatched conical roof, surrounded by tomato plants, an herb garden, and a chicken coop. He'd painted messages on the walls. One read in French, "Here we sell immunization shots against racism." Another, "I am not afraid of death. You can kill me, but you will not dishonor me." Jaigne told us, "This is my way of reminding everyone who passes by that people need more than money. They need humanity."

As an experienced reporter, I was familiar with these kinds of interactions. But I was used to being a solo operator, cradling memories of reporting trips in private and maybe one day sharing them over a meal with family or friends. Now, Rich and I could process them in real time. As we worked our way through a bowl of mussels and a bottle of white wine that night, we talked about whether our presence in Calais would do any good; whether "raising awareness" was just an empty phrase we used to make ourselves feel better; whether we should feel guilty for having a decadent meal after a day spent with people who were fighting to survive; and whether Jaigne's mission of "immunizing people against racism" was noble, futile, or both. These were the sorts of questions I had always asked myself on reporting trips to places where people were struggling. It felt good to be able to chew them over with someone else for a change.

Months after those stories aired, French authorities tore down the camp and forcibly dispersed the people living there. According to local reports, today when police in the area find tents and sleeping bags, the authorities douse the camping supplies with pepper spray to make them unusable. I don't know where they imagine those people will go.

In the dead of winter we took a trip to Sweden, where Rich and I reported on a growing extremist anti-refugee movement. And then we flew north from Stockholm to Kiruna, up above the arctic circle, to squeeze in a feature story on the Icehotel. Artists from around the world travel to Kiruna every fall to carve rooms out of snow and ice, designing chambers that look like forests, chessboards, or cathedrals.

As we toured the grounds, Rich's long eyelashes turned into icicles. We ate reindeer stew, drank Swedish vodka from glasses made of ice, and used kick sleds to race along the frozen Torne River. We spent the night under reindeer blankets in one of the ice rooms and awoke before dawn to cups of warm lingonberry juice. After an early flight back to Stockholm, we put together a sound-rich story about this arctic work of art that disappears into the river every spring.

In Rich's home country, at a small Scottish town on the North Sea called Fraserburgh, we reported an environmental comeback story on rebounding cod fisheries. Our interviews took place at the water's edge as the sun rose on a fish auction, then we sat down to eat breakfast at a working-class diner near the docks. The fishermen around us were talking about us, using the thick local dialect that they assumed we couldn't make sense of. They didn't know that Rich grew up in Aberdeen and understood every word.

We grew accustomed to people assuming that we were a couple any time we went out together. The fact that we were not felt like an inside joke that we shared, and we took people's assumptions in stride. In London, Rich started dating a smart, stylish architect named Farida Farooqi—a much better fit than the girlfriend I met on our first reporting trip. Even before their relationship got serious, Farida would refer to me as Rich's boyfriend and herself as "the other woman."

If Rich and I publicly gave off the vibe of boyfriends, our private dynamic was that of old married people who pushed each other's buttons. Sometimes we would trigger and exacerbate each other's worst tendencies, like his obsession with order and neatness or my insistence on always doing more. Occasionally that habit of egging each other on had larger consequences, like the time we created an international incident in Ireland.

We had planned a December reporting trip from Belfast down to Dublin, with a stupidly ambitious schedule—reporting on everything from wearable tech for cows (collars called moo monitors) to zinc mining and tax havens for American corporations like Apple.

Our schedule was already going off-track by the time we arrived in Dublin, where we'd lined up three back-to-back interviews with government ministers in one afternoon. One by one, each of them canceled. Or, actually, one didn't cancel; he just failed to appear, and his press secretary didn't pick up the phone.

I got the ball rolling with a tweet that I would come to regret.

Incredibly, 3 Irish government ministers have canceled interviews with us at the last minute today, for 3 separate stories. Slainte, dudes.

Rich went a bit further, tweeting:

I can't stand incompetence. I've experienced that in abundance today. Ireland: your professional politicians ain't so professional.

And then he added:

I've interviewed prime/first ministers, ministers, mayors & councilors from Europe to the US to Africa. Worst experiences to date: Ireland.

We thought we were just letting off steam. Then our phones started ringing. Irish journalists were calling, asking us to name the ministers.

We declined, thinking that would be the end of it. Then the Google alerts started popping up.

The headline in the *Journal* read: "America's Main Public Broadcaster Is Not Happy with Our Ministers."

IRELAND'S POLITICIANS ARE some of the most incompetent in the world, according to reporters from America's National Public Radio.

The broadcaster's International Bureau Producer Rich Preston yesterday tweeted that, having covered current affairs across Europe, the US and Africa—Irish politicians topped the list as most unprofessional.

The story added, "It seemed that our affection for fluid engagement times doesn't travel well internationally."

This came at a moment when Irish people were angry at their government for unrelated reasons—some domestic political fracas. So our tweets became pitchforks and torches that people wielded in their march on the castle of their elected representatives. The hashtag #NameAndShame started trending in Ireland. My editor back at NPR headquarters got a call from an angry and confused press officer at the Irish embassy in Washington.

"What the hell is going on over there?" my editor asked me.

In Dublin, a press secretary for one of the ministers eventually called me back, asking if there was anything she could do to rectify the situation. Our reporting trip was almost over and we were about to fly back to London, so Rich and I suggested they meet us at an airport hotel.

Simon Coveney was the agriculture minister at the time. Europe was lifting a quota on milk production, which meant Ireland anticipated a booming market for Irish dairy products. (I never claimed this was a groundbreaking story.) "We are planning to grow the volume of milk production in Ireland by 50 percent in the next five years," Coveney told me in the hotel lobby, before we ran off to catch our flight. An international incident, just for that forgettable quote.

Years later, Coveney became Ireland's minister for foreign affairs, equivalent to the US secretary of state, in charge of international diplomacy. As host of *All Things Considered*, I frequently interviewed him about Brexit . . . never mentioning the drama that the two of us were involved in years earlier. I don't know whether he had forgotten about it or was simply polite enough not to bring it up. Either way, as the incident was not my proudest journalistic moment, I was not about to jog his memory.

In the final days of my tenure in London, Rich and I both felt like we were headed toward a cliff. I would happily have remained NPR's London correspondent for another year or more, but I had unexpectedly been offered the opportunity to host *All Things Considered*, a show that I'd listened to practically since birth. As I told the newsroom executive who first raised the possibility with me, "There are not many jobs that I'd be willing to leave London for right now; hosting *ATC* is the only job that I can imagine being *excited* to leave London for right now."

Rich created a cavalcade of going-away celebrations. As a surprise, he arranged for me to raise the drawbridge on the Tower Bridge, which we had passed hundreds of times on our runs. On Sound-Cloud, he created an audio retrospective of my time in the UK. As yet another parting gift, he gave me a handsome, wide, black umbrella with a curved wooden handle and a leather clasp embossed with my initials. (I always lose umbrellas. I vowed not to lose this one. I lost it anyway. I'm sorry, Rich.)

On the morning of my flight back to the United States, we met at my apartment one last time to have a meal together. We walked to a twenty-four-hour restaurant in my neighborhood called Duck & Waffle. It sat at the top of a skyscraper, with panoramic views of the sun rising over the city of London. Neither of us felt like eating much. When I climbed into a black taxi for the drive to Heathrow, we were both trying not to show the other that we were crying.

Rich sent a multipage memo to my new producers in Washington, providing care and feeding instructions for Ari Shapiro. It included pointers like, "If Ari doesn't get to exercise during the day, he'll become fidgety." And, "For snacks, he prefers savory over sweet. The peanut butter filled pretzels from Trader Joe's are a good bet. Make sure not to get the salt-free kind."

..

THIS WAS NOT THE END of our story. My first international assignment as host of *All Things Considered* was to cover the UN climate summit in Paris. Rich, who was still working for NPR's London bureau, caught the train down to France to produce our coverage. The team was reunited!

Our hotel was in the center of town, and the summit was in a distant suburb. One morning before we caught the train, Rich looked a bit green at breakfast. He thought it was the pâté he'd eaten the night before, but he was confident it would pass.

It did not pass. When we got to the summit, I walked him to the medical tent. The nurses there whisked him off to a nearby hospital, while I had to spend the day covering the news.

That evening, after I had filed my stories, I asked at the medical tent which hospital they had sent Rich to. They gave me the address, and I took a taxi to a dark and mostly empty clinic in a glum Paris suburb. Through my broken French, I asked the people at the front desk where I could find a patient named Rich Preston. They told me he wasn't listed. I assured them that he was on a gurney in one of their hallways, as he and I had been texting about his location. I texted and told him to shout, to see if I could hear him. He shouted, but I heard nothing. I wandered the halls, calling his name.

With 3 percent battery left on my phone, Rich dropped me a pin. That was when I saw that I was in the wrong hospital, in the wrong suburb. I took another taxi and finally found him. He was on a gurney in the hall, just as he had described, hooked up to an IV drip. He looked pale, weak, and miserable.

It was just food poisoning, but he was still dehydrated and woozy. The doctors didn't want to release him until some test results came back. So I pulled up a chair and read him fiction by Martin Amis from a recent *New Yorker* that happened to be in my backpack. He was released a little before midnight, and I piled him into a taxi for the long ride back into Paris. I kept Farida up to date on the entire odyssey, and she told me she was glad I was there to look after him.

Mike thought our bromance was adorable. For my fortieth birthday, he knew exactly what kind of a gift to give me. Mike commissioned Rich to create a *This Is Your Life*-style audio documentary, weaving together the voices of my parents, friends, colleagues, and more. Then Mike flew Rich and Farida to the US to surprise me with the montage. They met me with champagne, and later that afternoon Rich confided that he was planning on proposing to Farida during that trip. They had been together almost three years by then. After she said yes, he asked if I would be his best man, and I was honored to accept.

Neither of us was the bachelor party type, but I figured as the best man I should at least offer to throw him one. Rich said, "Oh no, I don't need a stag do" (as they're called in the UK). I breathed a sigh of relief. "Just an outdoor weekend in the wilds of Scotland or something like that would be nice."

Excuse me? Couldn't we just do a pub crawl in London? I didn't know how to plan an outdoor weekend in the wilds of Scotland. I wasn't even sure which part of Scotland the wilds were.

I didn't express any of that to Rich. Instead, with some help from his London lads, I pulled it together. Six of us spent a long weekend in September at an inn in the Scottish countryside. The notoriously chaotic Scottish weather even cooperated. We went kayaking on a loch, ate fish and chips and deep-fried Mars bars, and bicycled through the rolling hills. On Friday night we took him to a small-town pub, where one member of our crew ordered far too many rounds of shots. While the rest of the guys passed out quietly in their rooms, Rich spent the night curled up and moaning, "I don't like it." I stayed by his side, thinking that after he'd ensured my well-being for so many years as a producer, it was appropriate for me look after him for a change.

One month later, Mike and I flew to the south of France. At a chateau overlooking a wide manicured lawn, I strapped on a kilt with the rest of the wedding party. In addition to being his best man, the bride and groom had asked me to officiate. In my remarks at the ceremony, I quoted the writer Raphael Bob-Waksberg on finding "someone who will love you in all your damaged glory." I talked about my friend Hector Black, then ninety-four years old, who came out at age seventy and urged us all to simply love one another. I led them through the exchange of rings, and vows.

That evening, after dinner, I delivered my best man toast. It was, in fact, a gentle roast, revisiting some of the highlights and lowlights of the years Rich and I had spent traipsing around the world together. Seeing Rich's and Farida's parents and relatives in the crowd, I decided in the moment to cut my best line.

Later, I told Rich what I had planned to say: "For years, friends and strangers on social media have been asking when I was going to marry Rich Preston. Well today, I finally did." I had thought the double entendre would be a lighthearted way of staking a claim to Rich even as I sealed his bond with Farida. But I understood that I didn't need to assert our special connection in front of everybody at the wedding. Like so many other inside jokes and memories we had formed together, this could be something the two of us just quietly understood.

9

THE THIRD RAIL OF JOURNALISM

I couldn't figure out why the TV show seemed so familiar. It was a ten-part miniseries on HBO called *Our Boys*. The drama was subtitled in Hebrew and Arabic, one of the first programs that HBO picked up in a foreign language. I watched it before bed night after night in Washington, DC, in the summer of 2019, feeling a strange sense that I had heard the story before.

The series begins with three Israeli teenagers being kidnapped and murdered by Palestinian militants. In retaliation, Jewish extremists kidnap and murder a Palestinian teenager. By the time the show took us into the Palestinian family's mourning tent, it hit me. I'd been in that tent. I hadn't known the show was based on a true story—one that I'd covered.

In 2014, the death of sixteen-year-old Mohammed Abu Khdeir was one of the sparks that ignited a war between Israel and Gaza. My colleague Emily Harris covered the conflict from Gaza, while I flew from my base in London to report from the Israeli side of the border.

I went to the Abu Khdeir family's mourning tent in East Jerusalem, because I'd heard that a bus full of sympathetic Jews was planning to show up, sit with the family, and offer condolences. I wondered how the encounter would go and wanted to see whether people would be able to build a bridge across this canyon of religion, identity, and mutual suspicion. When I arrived, I was surprised to find there weren't many other reporters there. To me, this seemed like an obvious draw for journalists looking for a break from the dark chronicle of rocks thrown and rockets fired.

Mohammed's uncle, Walid, told me he didn't want the visitors' sympathy. "We have decided not to receive any Israelis," he said. He felt like people were trying to distort his family's image, to use their story for politics, and he didn't want to be a part of their game.

I recognized that he was talking about me, the American journalist, as much as the Israeli visitors. I was there searching for a ray of hope on the eve of war—a moment that could demonstrate something other than fear, resentment, and pain. But the family was feeling more angry than hopeful. The narrative I had in mind wasn't a story Walid was looking to tell.

I often tell journalism students that if they finish a reporting project with exactly the story they had set out to find, something has gone wrong. The best stories should surprise us; they should defy our expectations and veer in directions we weren't expecting. Part of our challenge in life—and all the more so in journalism—is to let go of our preconceived narratives, remove our blinders, and see what's actually in front of us. As a reporter, I do my research, make a plan, then throw the plan out the window to adapt to the reality of a situation.

The reality of this situation was that the bus wasn't showing up. Not good for my story, but the Abu Khdeir family was relieved. Half an hour after the Jewish group was scheduled to arrive, there was no sign of them. I started putting away my gear, resigned to leaving without what I'd come for. Then the bus pulled up with a wheeze, stopped across the road from the tent, and dozens of people started pouring out. I could see the family tense up.

At that point I'd been in Israel for less than two full days, and it had already been an eventful trip.

..

WHEN I LANDED IN TEL AVIV the previous morning on an overnight flight from the UK, Israel's notoriously tough immigration officials asked my reasons for entering the country and what I was planning to do there.

"Are you Jewish?" the immigration officer asked.

"Yes."

"Do you belong to a synagogue?"

"No, but I celebrate the holidays."

"Did you go to services for Hanukkah?"

I rolled my eyes. "Jews don't go to services for Hanukkah."

That was enough to pass. They let me enter.

To work in Israel, foreign reporters have to get an ID from the Government Press Office, so that was my first stop. I tried to charm the guy behind the desk with my broken Hebrew as he handed me a thumb drive. "This is full of useful information," he said in flawless English. "Maps of the country, profiles of government leaders, background information."

"And the Israeli spyware you've put on the thumb drive, that's just a bonus?" I asked, giving up on my attempt to unearth Hebrew vocabulary from the recesses of my brain. I had never learned the word for spyware.

He chuckled. Israel is known as a world leader in cyber-espionage, so I figured if the device did have malware, that might make an interesting little story about the Israeli government's efforts to keep tabs on foreign journalists. I pocketed my new foreign press pass along with the thumb drive, which I had no intention of ever plugging into my laptop.

I always like to frontload a reporting trip. Every field producer I've worked with knows that I prefer to hit the ground running and get something on the air right away. If you wear yourself out at the front end, you can spend time writing in your hotel room on the back end, or even go catch a movie if you're way ahead of schedule. (That's how I wound up seeing *Mamma Mia! Here We Go Again* in a US-Mexico border town.) It's satisfying to get on the air and establish your presence in a new place right out of the gate. Plus, one story tends to open doors to the next one, and if things fall apart in the first couple days, you've still left yourself enough time to regroup and try a different approach.

For all of those reasons I decided to power through my jet lag, press pass in hand, and report a simple, short piece my first day in Israel. The war with Gaza hadn't really started, but skirmishes were getting more intense by the day. I told my editor in Washington that I would go conduct some interviews in Jerusalem's Old City, take the temperature of the place, see how locals were feeling, and weave in those person-on-the-street quotes with updates on the latest news. It was a low-key plan, but it turned out not to be a low-key day.

NPR's local producer, Nuha Musleh, has worked with foreign correspondents in Israel for years. She has a voice like a chain-smoker and a zeal to get a good story. She took me to the Arab part of the Old City, where we began interviewing Palestinians shopping in the marketplace. An old man described his anger over the death of the Palestinian teenager, and Nuha interpreted as though she were delivering an audition monologue.

"I am blinded by bitterness!" she growled.

I turned from the old man to Nuha. "Did he really say he's blinded by bitterness?"

"Well, I'm making it poetic," she shrugged. "This isn't word for word."

We started to interview a young woman named Haneen Ashhab, who told us she was thinking of buying pepper spray to defend herself. As she was saying, "I've never been so frightened in my life," chaos erupted. Nuha clutched her shoulder, screaming. Everyone hit the ground.

My mind flashed to the hostile environment training course that NPR sends reporters to every few years. It's an intensive three days in the countryside, where we're taught everything from how to dodge bullets to what to do if you're being kidnapped. While cowering in the Old City, I ran through a checklist: *When did I last check in with head-quarters? Do I have anything that I could use as a tourniquet? If I have to record a hostage video, is the word* cat *code for "I'm fine" and* dog *code for "I'm in danger"—or vice versa?*

In a few seconds, I realized that this situation would not involve a tourniquet or a hostage video. As everyone picked themselves up, Nuha pointed to fat chunks of concrete on the ground. Someone had thrown them at us. One hit Haneen, another scraped Nuha's shoulder. We made sure nobody's injuries were serious, as a merchant pulled another rock out of his toppled display of cigarette lighters.

I was still recording as everyone shouted in Arabic, "Who did it? Where did they go?" A young Palestinian boy stepped forward. "I chased them! They're religious Jews," the boy said as Nuha interpreted. "They're wearing black."

At first, I was dubious. Of course this Palestinian kid was going to say that an Orthodox Jew threw the rocks. I expected that we'd never find out who really did it, but then we heard that the police had some-one in custody. So we found two uniformed officers outside the gates of the Old City and asked them what had happened. They directed us to the police station.

When we arrived, officers confirmed that they had arrested an ultra-Orthodox man. The kid was right. On the one hand, I was embarrassed to have doubted him. On the other hand, there's an old line in journalism: if your mother says she loves you, get a second source. There are worse traits for a reporter than skepticism.

The waiting room at the police station was tense. Haneen was already there with her grandfather, and I could see how upset he was. "Don't stir up the situation," the Jewish police officer said in Arabic to pacify the Palestinian grandfather. His words had the opposite effect. "I will stir it up as much as I have to!" the old man shouted. "My granddaughter was hit!"

When Nuha told the officer that she was also attacked, the man in uniform started asking her pointed questions and began to escort her to another room. Another flashback to hostile environment training: *Don't let the team get separated!* The British instructors drilled that lesson into our heads. Never mind that on our return to London, after three days dodging imagined sniper fire and staunching fake blood in the British countryside, most of our team boarded the train and then saw through the window of the train car, as we were pulling out of the station, that one of our colleagues was still standing on the platform looking for us. Never mind that—keep *this* team together!

I resolved to do everything in my power to stand with Nuha, to protect her. I towered over her compact frame. I made sure my foreign press pass hung boldly around my neck. I extended my microphone, so the Israeli police officer would understand that he was on the hook for every word. The officer grabbed my arm, shoved me into a stairwell, and took Nuha into a different room. So much for my resolve.

We were reunited in the police station lobby after she'd given her witness statement, and Nuha told me that her conversation with the police officer felt like a microcosm of the larger conflict. The officer told her, "I'm used to people being hit by stones. I know how it feels to be hit by stones. Because we have many people who come here reporting being hit by stones. And they are all Jews." The officer couldn't see Nuha as a victim, only as someone from the other side.

I called an Israeli police spokesman to ask for an on-the-record explanation of what the officer meant. "He was just giving information," the press guy said nonchalantly. "Most of the people who are injured in these incidents are Jews."

At first I saw his response as appallingly insufficient. Then I had to admit that this police spokesman's reaction was not so different from my own first instinct. I doubted the Palestinian kid when he said the attacker was Jewish.

Thinking about the spokesman's knee-jerk defensiveness, I scrutinized my own biases more closely. After all, I was bar mitzvahed. I can speak Hebrew (poorly). I even know the words to Hatikvah, the Israeli national anthem. Of course I knew all of this when I accepted the assignment to cover the war in Israel. But after my first day in the country, I started to question whether my life experiences and instincts were tilting my journalism in ways that I couldn't perceive. I tried to reassure myself that I had done the reporting work to find out what had actually happened and shared that story with listeners, even when it proved my hunch to be wrong. But the misguided hunch itself was making me start to second-guess myself.

··

OBJECTIVITY IS RELEVANT TO ANY conversation about journalism, but the stakes during the war in Israel felt higher than any other story I've covered. A Middle East expert edited every short spot that I filed for NPR's hourly newscast, because the careless use of a word like *occupied* or *terrorist* could fuel a media outrage cycle for days. (News reports on Brexit or North Korea didn't receive nearly the same level of scrutiny.)

Activist organizations on both sides of the Palestinian-Israeli conflict spent every day looking for ways to inflame their supporters, often in order to solicit donations, and journalists provided convenient fuel for their indignation bonfires.

Early in my career, protesters marched outside NPR headquarters, calling the network "National Palestinian Radio" and other names. Over the years, there have been boycott threats and letter-writing campaigns from pro-Palestinian and pro-Israeli advocacy groups. For more than a decade, NPR actually paid an independent auditor to review the network's coverage of the Israeli-Palestinian conflict and issue quarterly reports that included the number of Israeli and Palestinian voices heard on the air.

I felt that if I made any on-air misstep, it could spark a partisan feeding frenzy, undermine my credibility, and possibly derail my career. To some extent, that's true for any journalist covering the news. We may all be one dumb mistake away from getting doxxed or canceled. But the intense scrutiny of NPR's Israel coverage made it an even more precarious ledge than other wars and domestic political debates. Of course for me, there was an added wrinkle. The name Ari Shapiro doesn't exactly scream, "I was born in North Dakota."

The conflict has provided fodder for more NPR ombudsman columns than perhaps any topic but Trump. One of those columns included an assessment of my work in the country in 2014. "Is NPR Biased in Its Gaza Coverage?" the headline asked. Ombudsman Edward Schumacher-Matos quoted one listener who wrote, "I'd like to expect better from NPR than Ari Shapiro's report yesterday. To begin, your only correspondent in the report was Jewish. What would your pro-Israel listeners say if your only correspondent was an Arab?"

"I have no idea what Shapiro's religious conviction is," Schumacher-Matos wrote. "I see nothing in his reporting that reflects a religious bias, and so see no reason to ask him."

I guess I should have been thankful that he hadn't sided with the letter writer, but it also felt a bit like "Don't Ask, Don't Tell" for Jews. I wish that he'd confronted the question head-on. Should newsrooms bar Jews from covering certain stories? Should managing editors exclude women from covering debates over reproductive rights, or take Black reporters off racial justice beats? Since all Americans pay taxes, maybe stories about tax reform should be assigned only to noncitizens. Ah, but immigrants in the US pay taxes too, so I guess we'll have to outsource those stories to the BBC.

My point is not that objectivity is an unworthy goal, or that every journalist has an axe to grind. It's that there's no such thing as an absence of identity. We are all shaped by the lives we've lived. We all have a stake in our government, in our economy, in the quality of our air and water, and in the shape of our society. When journalists pretend otherwise, it just entrenches existing power structures. The "view from nowhere" that earlier generations of journalists aspired to was never actually from nowhere. It was from a straight, white, Christian, male perspective—not coincidentally, the perspective of people whose power is built into existing systems. Sometimes fish don't recognize the water they're swimming in, but I don't think the status quo is ever neutral.

If I had wanted to pursue a career in activism, I could have. I understand why politicians make bad faith arguments that journalists are just partisans in disguise. Those arguments help them to undermine public confidence in the work of the free press and to sow doubts about fact-based reality. Then, when journalists publish unflattering stories about those politicians, elected officials and their cheerleaders can dismiss the evidence of corruption or hypocrisy as "fake news." I welcome thoughtful criticism of my actual work. But please don't argue that my reporting is tainted just because of who I am.

The pressure campaigns around NPR's Israel coverage didn't make me want to opt out of covering the war. But they did raise the stakes and had me second-guessing every journalistic decision I made in the country. I suppose that's another goal of the critics—to make covering these stories so fraught and unpleasant that reporters decide to do something else instead. I wasn't going to give them that satisfaction.

..

AFTER BEING WELCOMED TO ISRAEL with thrown rocks, I hoped to find a more uplifting story in the Abu Khdeir family's mourning tent the next day. Standing in the shade of the canopy, I watched a stream of Jews make their way from the bus to the white plastic chairs where family members sat. Banners on the surrounding fences showed the face of a slight boy with big eyes. This was Mohammed, the sixteen-year-old murder victim—the martyr, as the signs described him.

Some of the Jewish visitors were clearly observant, wearing yarmulkes or headscarves. Others were in flip-flops and sunglasses. Walid, the uncle, stood to greet them. He told me his culture of hospitality compelled him to greet these guests warmly. "I am an Arab," he said. "As long as they are in my house, I cannot turn them back. They are welcome in my house."

A cousin, Nihaya Abu Khdeir, stood at the edge of the tent with mixed emotions. "We have our culture and our respect," she told me. "We can't just tell them to go, even if we want them to."

So the Israelis sat awkwardly in the plastic chairs. "I'm just here basically to say sorry in front of the family," a man named Matan Ben-Or told me.

"I personally think that any time one person does something good for another person, this world is a little better," said Neina Leibel, a teacher.

"Do you ever feel like you're just shouting into the wind?" I asked her.

"No," she said. "I think that nothing gets lost."

She showed me dates and coffee that she'd brought as gifts for the family. She tried to offer them, but one of the aunts rejected her. "I don't want anything from you," the woman spat. So Neina just sat with the gifts in her lap. "I don't feel insulted or anything," Neina told me. "I understand very well how she feels. You know, I cannot put myself into this family's situation."

It was uncomfortable for everyone. The Abu Khdeir family felt grief and resentment, now with the added layer of a sense of duty to perform an act of hospitality that they would rather skip. And the Jews in the mourning tent could see that their presence wasn't wanted, so they didn't know what to do next. Should they sit? Or leave? And then there was me—the scavenger with the microphone.

The sound of shouting snapped me out of my self-doubt. Nuha grabbed my wrist and dragged me through a gate at the side of the house. On the other side of the fence, I found the women of the family sitting in the shade of a grape arbor.

The screaming was coming from inside the house. "Don't let them in!" Nuha interpreted for me. "I told you not to let them in!" One of the female relatives was furious that the Jewish mourners were allowed into the family's presence. Even the deeply ingrained culture of hospitality wasn't powerful enough to override her rage at these intruders. But under the grape arbor, the Palestinian and Israeli women sat together.

A Jewish woman named Ruth Danziger told me she just wanted the family to know that the men who killed Mohammed "are extreme people who do not represent us." I asked her if it was difficult to extend a hand like this while people on the other side of the country were firing rockets at one another. "Maybe, maybe," she said. "But I think the peace will come from the people, and not from our leaders."

Nuha shoved me to the front of the line of women. I felt grossly out of place—the only man in this space, the only American, the only journalist. And in a chair at the center of the grape arbor, Nuha introduced me to Mohammed's mother, Suha. She was weeping over the loss of her son. Many of the Israeli women were crying with her, offering hugs and placing hands on her shoulders.

"Ask her how she feels about this!" barked Nuha. Then, with barely a pause, "I'll do it!" Nuha posed the question in Arabic, as I held my microphone out to the grieving mother.

"I want them to support me," Suha said through her tears. "I want them here."

After the hours that I had spent in the company of this family, that was not what I expected to hear. At the innermost ring of this circle, the woman who felt Mohammed's death the most acutely told me that she felt consoled by the presence of these other women. I took her reply as an affirmation, reminding me to push through discomfort, friction, and conflict, to find what lay underneath those layers.

As I left the mourners, Neina Leibel ran up and grabbed my elbow. She wanted me to know that a member of the family accepted the dates and coffee that she brought as a gift. "And I was even hugged and kissed."

"Really?" I asked.

She nodded, laughing and also crying.

After a couple of weeks in Israel, I returned to London. I had attended funerals and visited bomb shelters, broken the Ramadan fast in Ramallah and watched the iron dome missile defense system intercept Hamas rockets over Tel Aviv. But I still had one final story to tell—one that I'd brought back in my pocket with me.

I was already writing the piece in my head, about the subterfuge and espionage tactics the Israeli government used against foreign journalists working in the country. A top British cybersecurity firm agreed to collaborate with me on the project. I handed them the thumb drive that I had been given by the Government Press Office on my first day in Jerusalem. I hadn't let it anywhere near my computer.

The firm did an exhaustive analysis, searching for what I just knew would be there. Two days later, an analyst called me with his findings. There was nothing. No malware, no spyware, not even a virus. The thumb drive contained maps, profiles of government leaders, and background information, exactly as the press officer had said. The narrative of espionage was all in my head. Another good story, ruined by the facts.

10

THE BEST STRANGERS IN THE WORLD

The menu at Ali Demir's café in Izmir, Turkey, was nothing special. The crowd outside wasn't there for the kebabs. Nobody was posting photos of his fries to social media. Everybody at Ali's place wanted the same thing: the Wi-Fi.

Instead of sidewalk seating, Ali had set up long folding tables outside his restaurant. Those tables were lined with power strips, and every plug was full. Pieces of paper taped to the windows gave the Wi-Fi login and password. People sat on chairs and on the sidewalk, their phone chargers connecting them to the power. On small glowing screens, they talked with their spouse, their parents, or their children in Syria.

It was 2015, the height of the Syrian refugee crisis, and I had come to coastal Turkey to tell the story of the largest human migration since World War II. Syrians had told me about their experiences with human smugglers, outrageous prices for life vests, near-death experiences, and families torn apart.

Ali Demir offered a different kind of story. He told me that he let people wash up in his bathrooms. Even though it was technically illegal, he let mothers with young children sleep upstairs in his office. This was small-scale philanthropy. Most of the Syrians didn't have money to buy a meal, and they wouldn't stay in Izmir long enough to become loyal customers.

"So why do you do it?" I asked.

"These are people who are running away from war," he said. "And if I put myself in their shoes, I would appreciate it if someone would do the same for me."

It was a subtle but revolutionary act, to try to see the world through their eyes. When someone's desperate journey intersected with his small business, his bubble of safety, he could have looked away. But he opened his doors instead.

Of course, I loved his story for that reason. It's the whole Mister Rogers "Look for the helpers" thing. But even more than Ali Demir's generosity, I was excited to have stumbled onto this scene for what it said about the migrants themselves. Because I was looking for a way to break through the background noise. To help people in the US see these Syrians as three-dimensional humans, not just some faceless mass. And what could be more relatable than looking for a Wi-Fi hotspot or a place to charge your phone?

Izmir is a sunbaked resort city by the Aegean Sea built on the ruins of ancient Smyrna. For a summer tourist, the Greek islands are a day trip. For a Syrian refugee, the same journey could be fatal. So there was a weird split-screen effect to my experience there—wealthy vacationers enjoying their luxury hotels, alongside desperate migrants fleeing war.

I left my London apartment before dawn and dropped my bags in the Izmir hotel room by midafternoon, with three days to file a story and no real leads on how to find one. So I started at the hotel's front desk. "Excuse me?" The receptionist looked up from his phone. "Do you know where I might find some Syrians?" He shrugged and gestured vaguely toward the door.

I recognized that I was embodying an ugly stereotype—the foreign correspondent parachuting into a place I had never been before, pretending to be qualified. I'd always been proud that NPR had more than a dozen international bureaus, including a full-time correspondent in Istanbul who understood Turkey. When news broke in Cairo or Mumbai, NPR had people who lived there and knew those places.

I didn't know this place. But the story was in Izmir, and the only person who could get there just then was the correspondent from London. Our Istanbul correspondent was otherwise occupied, so I had little choice but to lean into the cliché.

When aspiring journalists ask me where to begin finding sources for a story, I tell them it doesn't matter where you start. Just start. The breakthrough might come from a hotel receptionist or a local journalist. Or, in this case, from Instagram.

My first task was to find a fixer, or at least an interpreter. I looked up the offices of the local newspaper and wandered in that direction along the waterfront, thinking maybe I could hire a local print reporter to work with me. Sidewalk vendors stood over wide platters of mussels stuffed with rice, slices of lemon perched on top. Old men dropped fishing lines into the water. As the sun dipped into the sea, I posted a photo of the boardwalk with the caption "Welcome to Izmir, Turkey. Departure point and waiting area for many of the Syrians hoping to reach Greece and the rest of Europe." It wasn't a great photo. I wasn't even thinking of it as a way of fishing for leads in my reporting. But I got a bite.

Someone named Dicle wrote in the comments, "Ari, you're in my hometown and I am not there to come across to you! Oh, who am I? Just a big fan."

Sometimes, journalism demands shamelessness. I replied, "Do you know any local Arabic/English speakers who I could hire to work with me for a few days?"

A woman named Lindsey Leger jumped into the replies. "I just left Izmir a couple days ago, my flat mate there is Palestinian and could probably translate if you need it."

A few DMs later, I gave her roommate a call. Bara Wahbeh was an engineer working on a renewable energy project in Izmir. He spoke Turkish, Arabic, and English. Perfect! Also, he had no journalism experience. No problem!

We met for coffee the next morning, and Bara told me the best place to interview Syrian refugees would be a neighborhood called Basmane. It was a hilly warren of narrow streets and improvised shacks. The Turkish word for them was *gecekondu*—literally, "set up overnight."

When we reached Basmane, I found a slice of Syria in the middle of Izmir. In an open square, women were drying laundry on clotheslines. Syrians who had been there a bit longer than the others had set up shops selling bread and tea.

The refugee economy was extortionate. A dirty, cramped room was going for one hundred dollars a night. A shower cost extra. A man named Mohammed Elwan told me he and his family had sold their home and all their belongings to get to Izmir. Now, they were sleeping on the ground.

Nearly everyone was waiting for the same thing. A phone call from a human smuggler saying, "Time to go to Greece!" The trip cost twelve hundred dollars per person, half that for kids under ten. So an overcrowded raft could make as much as fifty thousand dollars for the smugglers. And word was they would kill anyone who tried to buy their own raft. In the windows of casual clothing stores, mannequins sported life vests in bright colors—the better to identify people floating in the Aegean.

I bought breakfast for a young man named Hussein Ramadan. He was wearing a blue and gray long-sleeved athletic shirt, and his eyes looked heavy. With Bara interpreting, Hussein told me he had gotten the call just hours ago—at 2 a.m. He showed up at the meeting point with his life jacket, where the smugglers crammed forty people into vans. They got to the beach a couple of hours before dawn, and the forty migrants all piled onto a raft built for ten.

"We put the women and children in the center of the boat, the men all sat on the edge," he told me. "We'd only just started when the boat hit the rocks. It started to take on water."

The raft deflated and sank. Hussein was lucky to have a life vest to get back to shore. The experience was so traumatic, he told me, he abandoned his plan to go to Europe. Instead, he intended to return to Syria—having spent all his money on this aborted mission. "War is better than dying at sea."

There were stories like that nearly every day, of rafts sinking in the Mediterranean. Months later, a photo of a drowned three-year-old named Alan Kurdi seemed to clear the global fog and wake people up to the reality of what was happening. But that day in Izmir, I didn't know how to tell a story that would connect.

I thought back to all the ways people in my own life had tried to show me the reality of global migration. The phrase *nation of immigrants* was such a constant in my childhood that it became the kind of persistent background drone you stop noticing. I guess I took it for granted that everyone came from someplace else. I knew my own family's story of fleeing pogroms and the Holocaust. And every year at Passover, my religion reminded me to welcome the stranger, since we Jews were once strangers in the land of Egypt. Maybe we had to hear the refrain every year because the reality of it slipped so easily through our fingers.

I decided it wasn't enough to parachute in for a few days. I needed to find someone whose story I could tell in its entirety, through to its conclusion—no matter the ending. Someone whose journey I could follow for as long as it lasted. Listeners could get to know them over time, as more than a few short quotes. Maybe that would help cut through the noise and get people to see migrants as more than just a symbol or a story, but as fully human.

I got buy-in from my editor, and from my colleagues in other parts of Europe. They agreed to help me tell this story. Now I just needed to find my protagonist.

..

IT WAS NEARLY ONE HUNDRED degrees in the middle of the day, and Syrian families slept on flattened cardboard boxes in whatever shade they could find. Monzer Omar was awake. He had a gentle, easy smile and was eager to practice his English with me.

Monzer was thirty-three and traveling alone. He decided that it wasn't safe enough to bring his pregnant wife and two daughters on this journey. The girls were just one and three years old.

He told me he was an English teacher in Syria. Then the war started, and the military's barrel bombs destroyed his village near the city of Hama. When the government tried to force him to join the army, he moved his wife and daughters to his parents' house and paid a smuggler to bring him here to the edge of the Aegean.

He had been waiting days for another smuggler to send him across the water. But the only call he got was from a panicked friend whose nephew was on a sinking, overcrowded raft. Monzer tried to call the nephew to get the raft's GPS coordinates and send help, but nobody picked up the phone.

When he would use the café Wi-Fi to call his wife and kids, his three-year-old would say, "Papa, come home." He told me he was afraid that his one-year-old wouldn't remember him.

He didn't know this, but our chat felt to me like some twisted kind of audition. There were thousands of Syrians in Izmir at that moment. Was Monzer the person whose story I should follow? Would his journey be the one I'd latch on to? What if he gave up and returned to Syria—or worse, died in the crossing to Greece? Maybe instead, I thought to myself, I should use this conversation for a brief quote in a news spot at the top of the hour. Maybe I should keep looking.

Asking myself these questions felt like a cold and inhuman calculation, especially as the person I was talking to was risking his life. I tried to reconcile humanity with strategy, emotion with professionalism: I decided to commit to Monzer.

I asked him to let us follow his story, wherever it led. I told him that I wouldn't be able to pull strings or fund his travels, but I'd share his journey with the world so that people might get a better understanding of what he and millions of others were going through. He agreed. Neither of us could have imagined that this narrative would unfold over years, across half a dozen countries, even involving the US ambassador to the United Nations.

..

WHILE MONZER WAITED ON THE sidewalk, I filed daily news stories from Izmir about the refugee crisis. After he had waited a week, slowly burning through his savings, Monzer decided to try a different route. He took a bus three hours south to the beach town of Bodrum, and I followed in my rental car.

The ancient city of Ephesus was just off the highway, but I didn't have time to stop. As I passed men selling flats of figs by the side of the road, I wondered whether I should have offered to drive Monzer.

It wouldn't be the last time I'd ask myself where the line was between journalistic noninterference and cruelty.

Bodrum's shore was packed with fancy resorts, and luxury yachts crowded the harbor. My beach hotel advertised excursions, and one of the most popular was a catamaran ride to the Greek island of Kos, less than three miles away. This was the closest point by sea between Turkey and Greece. You could see the European Union from Bodrum's beaches.

A tourist named Miriam told me she had a great time visiting Kos. "Twenty minutes by boat, so it's not that far." But of course, when she reached her destination, the humanitarian crisis was unmissable. "It was quite shocking, because it was literally just people lying down on the beach with their children."

"Isn't it a pity when a global human tragedy spoils one's summer holiday?" I wanted to reply. But of course I also understood where she was coming from. Who doesn't want to shut out the world's misery for a little while?

A few people warned me about the Turkish organized crime syndicates that ran this human trafficking operation. They didn't like reporters digging into their business. So I abandoned my earphones and boom microphone when I went out to do interviews. I just carried a small recorder in the palm of my hand. As I talked to refugees, I constantly glanced down at the audio levels, hoping the recorder's internal microphone was doing its job. Each evening when I returned to my hotel room, I frantically uploaded the audio to my laptop and listened back to make sure that everything had actually been recorded.

At the Bodrum bus station, I met a structural engineer from Syria named Ahmad Akkad. He was in his early twenties, fluent in English, confident bordering on cocky. At first he asked me not to use his last name, because he hadn't told his family that he was planning to cross the Mediterranean in a raft. (Once he landed in Germany he told them, and then gave me permission to use his full name.)

Over tea, he told me he had been designing hotels in UAE. But he didn't see a future there, so he decided to apply for a master's program in Berlin. When the waitress brought us a bill, I tried to pay it. He bristled, "Do you think we're all poor?"

"No, but I have an expense account," I tried to explain. "I'm not the one paying for this, my company is!"

He didn't want to be a charity case. I finally convinced him to split the bill with me.

That night, my phone started buzzing at 1 a.m. with WhatsApp messages from Monzer:

There is a big problem.
Two smugglers are conflicting on the same starting point.
The first one is Turkish; the other is Pakistani.
Pray for me please.

A few hours later, more messages:

Our group didn't go to Greece from Bodrum.
There was a crime as a result of the conflict between the smugglers.
We saw dead bodies on the seaside.
We have to go back to Izmir.

Monzer returned to the same sidewalk where I first met him, sitting on that cardboard box. And my reporting trip in coastal Turkey was over. I had to fly back to London.

Two days later, I was packing up my London apartment to move back to the US for a new job hosting *All Things Considered* when a voice memo arrived from Monzer. I could hear his relief.

"I'm on Mytilene Island." Mytilene is a city on the Greek island of Lesbos. He had made the crossing. "I'm waiting to go out of Greece to Macedonia."

This leg of his journey was complete. But he had many more to go. My colleagues Joanna Kakissis, Eleanor Beardsley, and Soraya Sarhaddi Nelson met up with him on the next stages of his journey—from Greece to Macedonia, to Serbia, Hungary, Austria, and Germany. Many of the details of those legs of the trip came from their reporting, as NPR listeners followed his journey across Europe in real time.

Monzer was grateful that his daughters didn't join him on the crossing. "You could die any minute, any second," he told Joanna. The engine failed halfway through the journey, and the raft started to fill with seawater. They bailed it out with plastic bottles. "Some babies were crying all of the way."

He lost his glasses in the crossing, so he was squinting. He had grown a beard and carried a backpack with a change of clothes, some toiletries, a phone charger, and a yellow teacup that a pizzeria owner on Lesbos gave him.

Nobody could tell him how to find the bus. A man on a motorbike tried to scam him into buying fake bus tickets. Finally, his group found their way north to the Greece-Macedonia border.

They walked for six hours to a train, then a taxi, and reached the border between Macedonia and Serbia, where another bus took them to the capital, Belgrade. The next day, onward to Hungary. A knife fight broke out when too many people tried to board a bus there.

Monzer was exhausted and confused. "I just want to arrive to Germany and take a rest," he said. He called Chancellor Angela Merkel "Mama Merkel, the mother of Syrian people."

Monzer was lucky. Later that year, Serbia, Hungary, and other European countries would put up fortified border fences to keep other refugees from following this path.

His wife and two small daughters were his virtual companions on this journey. He sent them voice memos any time he could find Wi-Fi. "I tell my wife everywhere I go," he said. "I tell her I am in Serbia, I am on the border with Hungary. She lives this with me."

In turn, she would send him updates from his parents and daughters. "I remember my mother and father," he said, tears welling up. He knew that if he received asylum in Germany, it wouldn't be easy to bring them. "Maybe I will never see them again. But my wife and daughters, I hope I will see them in the near future."

In Hungary, Monzer tried to find his way by foot using the GPS on his phone, but he struggled with the Hungarian names on the map. Smugglers tried to rob his small group, and Monzer considered taking out his pocketknife to defend himself. He decided against it. He had only ever used it for cutting fruit.

They hid from Hungarian border police in cornfields, then ran to find a road, where taxis took them to Budapest. Hungary didn't allow migrants to rent rooms in hotels or hostels. A rundown inn charged migrants twenty dollars just to sit in the courtyard. So along with at least a thousand other Syrians, he camped in a park, washing his blistered feet in a tap and filling his plastic bottle with water. Three elderly Hungarian men, fishing at the park's pond, watched without smiling. "You really feel less than human," Monzer said. "But I am so tired, I don't care."

The next day, he shaved his beard and put on his favorite aftershave— he had carried a bottle of it from Syria. As he shared dates with other Syrians at the park, they heard a rumor that Hungary was letting migrants travel by train to Austria. They rushed to the station and spent all day waiting in line. By the time they reached the front, ticket sales to migrants had been canceled.

"Now we must find a smuggler," he said, deflated. "I'm so tired that I'm worried I cannot make a good decision. Oh, just to close my eyes and to have a shower."

He camped for three nights in the park. And then, Hungary decided to bus migrants to Austria. There was nowhere for him to sit on the bus, but he didn't care. "I am on the border of Hungary and Austria!" he said in a voice memo. "And really, really joyful."

The next day, he arrived in Germany. At a camp in Dortmund, he finally showered and slept soundly. He told his wife, "I made it, my love." The journey from Syria to Germany took twenty-five days.

A month after his arrival, my colleague Eleanor Beardsley met Monzer in the northern German town of Warendorf. He told her he was still getting used to some things, like adults riding bicycles. "You are a big man. Why drive a bike?" he laughed. "It's for kids!"

He was relieved that he no longer had to worry about where to find food or a place to sleep. But landing in Germany brought new worries. He was waiting for his residency papers. His wife was six months pregnant with their third child. They had hoped the baby would be born in Germany, but at this point it didn't seem likely she would be allowed to come in time.

··

AS MONZER WAS FIGHTING THROUGH that exhausting journey mile by mile, I scanned my American passport at Heathrow airport and jetted across an ocean in an afternoon. While Monzer was traveling a world away from his spouse, I reunited with mine. Mike stayed in DC for the nearly two years that I was overseas, tied to a job at the White House. It was September 2015 when I arrived back in Washington to start hosting *All Things Considered*.

I walked into my house, took off my shoes, and dragged my suitcase upstairs. As I set it down, my eyes landed on a framed work of art that a photographer friend created years ago. The piece consists of large block letters against a white backdrop. The text says: THE BEST STRANGERS IN THE WORLD LIVE HERE, and hidden in the letters is a blurry black-and-white silhouette of a human figure. Mike and I had owned the piece for years, but with my move back from London, it hit me differently. I thought of the time I had spent overseas and the thousands of people I'd met who had trusted me to tell their stories—indeed, the best strangers in the world. As I looked at the artwork, I resolved to explore the US with the same curiosity that I had approached other countries during my time abroad. Even if our highway signs and fast-food restaurants all looked identical, I wanted to see if it was possible to view the United States with the same fresh eyes that I had brought to international reporting.

The first time I had a pause from hosting the daily news show to work on a larger project, I decided to take a different angle on the same global story I'd been following with Monzer. My producer Matt Ozug and I flew to Toledo, Ohio, to spend some time with Syrian refugees in the US.

Toledo is 470 miles from Washington. Out of a perverse curiosity I looked up where I would be if I traveled the same distance from London. Zurich, Frankfurt, or Lyon all sounded nice.

At the entrance to our Toledo hotel, a sign had a big black image of a gun with a red line through it. *NOTICE: It is illegal to carry a firearm, deadly weapon, or dangerous ordnance anywhere on these premises.* I was definitely back in America.

This country only ever admitted a tiny fraction of Syrian refugees. Out of nearly twelve million displaced Syrians, the US took in eighteen thousand total during the entire Obama administration. Some European cities accepted twice that many in a given week.

So Mohammed al-Refai knew that he was one of the lucky ones. He had big dark eyes and a shy smile. The twenty-two-year-old butcher arrived in Toledo in May 2015, a few months before Monzer decided to flee Syria for Europe. Mohammed had been living with his family in a Jordanian refugee camp. But his good luck came with a catch. For reasons that nobody I found could explain, his siblings and parents were not given visas. He had come to the US alone.

The State Department told me that families are usually kept together in these situations. When I tried to figure out why Mohammed's case was different, they said they couldn't give me any information about individual cases. And when Mohammed arrived in Toledo by himself, the local agency that helped resettle refugees wasn't sure what to do with him. He had no American friends, no local relatives, nobody to help ease his arrival in a new country.

That was how four white guys who had recently graduated from the University of Toledo wound up taking in a Syrian refugee who didn't speak much English.

When I showed up at their home near the UT campus, it was shockingly clean for a place where dudes in their twenties lived. They had art on the walls, and they'd vacuumed the rugs. The guys called their new roommate "Moh." Doug Walton was sort of the ringleader of the bunch; he worked at a church on campus. When he heard about Mohammed, he saw an opportunity to put the principles of his faith into action.

Why did he do it? "My immediate answer just sounds so cliché," Doug said, "but I think the motive is love. I was told he was coming, and that I had an opportunity to help him out. And I was like, yeah, why wouldn't I do that?"

I thought about Ali Demir, the Turkish café owner in Izmir who set out power strips and Wi-Fi for refugees. The man who said, "If I put myself in their shoes, I would appreciate it if someone would do the same for me." And I wondered what made people like Doug and Ali different from the rest of us.

When Mohammed got to town, he could say hello and count to ten, and that was the extent of his English. But Toledo had a big Middle Eastern population that had been in the city for generations, so Doug and the other guys took their new roommate to a Middle Eastern supermarket.

"And he just runs up to the counter and starts speaking in Arabic,"

Doug remembered. "And the guy's talking back to him in Arabic. And his whole countenance just changed. Like—*Oh my gosh, what a relief.*"

That guy speaking Arabic was Hussein Mroueh. When Mohammed told his story to Hussein, "It kind of broke my heart," the older butcher told me. Hussein saw his own twenty-one-year-old son in twenty-two-year-old Mohammed. "So whatever money I had in my pocket that day, I did give it," Hussein laughed. "Plus, you know, the second day, I gave him more."

He also gave Mohammed a job. Everyone else working at the market was fluent in English and Arabic, but they made an exception for him. After a few months working at the butcher counter, he had mastered the words he needed to take orders. "Chicken legs, chicken breast, goat, steak, lamb, beef, turkey," Mohammed rattled them off.

This place couldn't have been more different from the butcher shop he had worked at in Syria. It was bright, clean, and air-conditioned. Back home, Mohammed explained, they didn't refrigerate the meat. They sold it in the same spot where they killed the animals. And, he said, it tasted better over there.

Doug ordered some chickens, cut up, skin on. Mohammed rang up the order. And then the roommates invited us over for dinner. When Matt and I returned to the group house that evening, it smelled like saffron and cardamom. Doug had made kabsa, a Middle Eastern dish of chicken and rice. We sat around the platter of food, and Doug said grace. "God, thanks for bringing all these interesting people together from all parts of the world and all parts of the country . . ." Afterward, there was baklava and tea. The roommates arm wrestled.

A year later, I would return to Toledo after the 2016 election that dashed Mohammed's hopes of bringing his parents and siblings to the US.

··

SO NOW I WAS FOLLOWING the stories of two Syrian refugees—Monzer in Germany and Mohammed in the US. Plus occasional updates from Ahmad Akkad, the structural engineer who'd insisted on paying for his own tea in Bodrum.

Ahmad got the most straightforward happy ending: he earned his master's degree in Germany, went to work for a German engineering firm, and became part of the cosmopolitan, international fabric of Berlin. In 2019, I caught up with him on the thirtieth anniversary of the fall of the Berlin Wall. He told me, "I hope that in the future, all walls fall down."

To what end was I tracing all these threads, though? Journalists often tell the same kinds of stories as advocacy groups, but for different reasons. Refugees International could just as easily have told the story of Monzer or Mohammed, with a link at the end to donate or call your elected official. Every time I put another installment of Monzer's story on the air, listeners asked how they could help. And I felt conflicted about it. I was glad that his story moved them. But there were millions of displaced Syrians in need. Should Monzer, or Mohammed, have gotten cash from a concerned NPR listener just because I happened to tell their stories and not others? And if they shouldn't have, then why exactly was I asking these guys to narrate their most traumatic experiences for the world to witness? Was this just vampirism, where people poured their pain into my microphone, and I walked away with a paycheck?

It is a central tenet of journalism that one of the best ways to tell a big story is by telling a small one. But I wondered whether zeroing in on an individual's story actually was a way of clearing the path to real change. Perhaps I was just narrowing the aperture, cutting global upheaval into bite-sized morsels for our audience.

A call I received in June 2016 put some of those questions to rest. It was from the office of Samantha Power. At the time she was President Obama's ambassador to the UN, and she was traveling to Germany for a roundtable event with Syrian refugees in Berlin. Her staff wanted to let me know that she had invited Monzer Omar to be part of it. So my reporting did get through to someone who could make a difference.

After the event in Germany, I called Ambassador Power from an NPR studio and asked how Monzer seemed to her. "On the one hand, he's getting settled in Germany," she said. "On the other hand, he's away from his three kids, and I think his heart is breaking." He hadn't even met his youngest child.

It had been almost a year since I met Monzer in Turkey. When I called him after his meeting with Ambassador Power, he told me he didn't have a work permit yet. He was sharing an apartment with several other Syrian refugees, where he spent his days studying German and trying to work through the overwhelming bureaucracy. When he would speak English or Arabic in public, people would tell him, "You are in Germany. You should learn German."

"Of course I know that," he would say. "I'm doing my best."

Monzer's wife and three girls were still living with his parents in Syria. When they talked on the phone, his oldest, now four, would say, "Baba, I miss you."

"It's difficult for me to be here and them there," he told me. "You can't hug them. You can't see them. You can't kiss them."

He had hoped that it would be maybe six months until his family was reunited. Nearly twice that much time had passed, and he still couldn't see a good way to get them out of the war. His hope was flagging.

"Maybe my family will die. Maybe my children will die, okay? What's the use of coming here? I came here just to help them. What's the use if I come here and I lose my family?"

Back in Toledo, Mohammed's roommates were feeling the pressure of living in a swing state during a presidential election. A Trump campaign flyer landed on their doorstep, promising that the Republican candidate would "Stop the Influx of Dangerous Refugees from Syria" if elected president.

For the roommates, it was surreal to see this national debate literally show up at their front door. "We want more of them," Johnny Zellers told me. "Like, we have one. I have one in my house right now. Like, I could go say hi to him."

The guys in the house leaned conservative and took their Christian faith seriously. But in November 2016, they cast a mix of votes for Clinton and third-party candidates. None of them voted for Trump.

They didn't own a TV, so on election night they all went into Doug's room and huddled around their phones with Mohammed to watch the results come in. They sat together, hugging him as the outcome became clear.

The first time they ever really talked about it with one another was when I went back to visit them in January 2017, a couple of weeks before Trump's inauguration, to ask what the experience of watching the election had felt like.

"We didn't really know how to respond," Johnny said. Mohammed "definitely got sad thinking maybe his family may not be able to ever come here. That's the biggest hope that he's had this past year. Just like—*I hope my family comes*. Now with Trump elected, those chances go down a lot."

Mohammed didn't want to talk about politics. The shock of what Trump's victory meant for his family was still too new. But the other guys agreed to get into it with me while he was at work.

"It was weird to have a vote in a situation that felt like we were voting for people who were helpless," Andrew Trumbull told me. "Usually we vote on, like, jobs or whatever. And so for me, that's not a big deal. I'll find a job. I'll make things work. Whoever gets elected—they're not going to change things that drastically." This time the stakes were higher. It felt personal.

When I visited the Middle Eastern supermarket where Mohammed was working as a butcher, he seemed like a different person from the recent arrival I had met a year earlier—more confident, easily answering my questions in English without an interpreter.

He told me he would video chat with his family at least once a week. They would drink tea together. He'd show them the snow on the ground in Ohio, and they'd tell him how proud they were that he was learning English and working. The roommates taught Mohammed some of their favorite pop songs, and he taught them some Syrian tunes. They sat around the living room with guitars, belting out Carly Rae Jepsen: *Boy problems, who's got 'em . . .*

They didn't talk about his family's future. Mohammed was anxious about the days ticking down to Trump's inauguration. The office that issues green cards told him to stop calling. And his uncertainty also changed the other roommates' thinking about their own future.

Before, the assumption was, "Moh's here, his family will come, and then we'll all move on with our lives," Johnny said. "We'll all move away, or get different jobs, or whatever. And then Moh will have his family. But now it's like—his family may never come."

··

I WANTED TO GET A sense of the sentiment in Toledo that helped President Trump win in Ohio—the people who didn't want more Syrian refugees showing up in their town. So Matt and I visited some of the working-class dive bars near the Chrysler plant.

We had a harder time than I would have expected finding people who didn't want refugees in Toledo. Even the Trump voters we met didn't seem to mind. People told us things like, "My grandfather came here from Slovakia, and people didn't think he was white." It reminded me that communities with the most immigration often have the most positive views of immigrants.

When we did find people with different views, most didn't want to talk on tape. One woman muttered, "They've got their own country; they should stay there." Then I met a navy veteran named Jon Johnstone, who seemed to be a few beers in. He told me, "If you want to come here and turn the United States into Syria, I'm against that. You want to come here and speak English, you want to assimilate, you want to have a pizza, you want to have a beer, you want to eat a chicken wing, I'm all for it."

Matt and I decided that was the closest thing to an anti-refugee quote we were going to get on the record. So we sat at the other end of the bar to order a round of beers for ourselves at the end of a long day reporting. And then Johnstone stumbled back up to us and got in my face.

"Okay can I ask you a question?"

"Sure."

"You seem gay. Are you gay?"

"Yup."

"Well, they throw people like you off buildings. Why would you want them to come here?"

I stepped outside myself. I thought how strange it was that my pulse hadn't jumped. This wasn't a live interview on the radio. As much as part of me wanted to say, "You should see what they do to the gay *Jews*!," I didn't need a snappy reply. The guy seemed drunk and harmless. I muttered something like, "Well, I have a lot of gay Muslim friends from the Arab world. Shouldn't they have a safe place to go?" The woman he was with was already dragging him back to his chair.

He wasn't even being homophobic, exactly. In a twisted way, it looked like he was trying to find solidarity with me against what he perceived as our shared enemy. "America is a place that'll even tolerate people like you," he seemed to be implying. "Why would you want to jeopardize that?"

It reminded me of political stories I had reported from Scandinavia, where far-right anti-immigration parties had looped around to join forces with ultra-liberal politicians in an effort to defend traditionally permissive Scandinavian culture from Middle Eastern and North African refugees. In northern Europe, the political alliance of those strange bedfellows often meant that more moderate parties wound up in the minority.

I felt weirdly lucky to be able to sit at that Toledo bar and talk to people I would never otherwise meet. I was the one invading his bubble; he wasn't in mine. By the same time tomorrow, I would be back home in my familiar routine. Matt and I slowly finished our beers.

··

TWO MONTHS LATER, THE GUYS in Toledo texted me to say they had some good news. I called them up and everybody hopped on the line.

"Who wants to share the news?" I asked.

"Moh, say it. What'd you get?" Doug prompted.

"I have the green card!"

I could hear Mohammed's grin down the phone line.

He had been checking the mailbox every day for months, and when it finally arrived, the guys weren't sure at first what it was. Mohammed handed the piece of mail to Johnny. "And I started reading it. *You are now a resident of the United States* . . . and I was like, 'This is the green card! You've got a green card!'"

The roommates threw Mohammed a party with a green cake. Doug told him, "This is a great day for America, because we get to keep you."

But the story had another twist. When Mohammed told his family about the green card, they shouted and cried. His mom said, "Get on a plane! Come right now! Visit us!" Mohammed replied, "No, I can't."

He wanted to get on that plane to Jordan, more than anything. And legally, he could have left the country and come back in. But this was March 2017, at the height of the controversy over Trump's Muslim travel ban. Mohammed was afraid that without a US passport, if he visited his family in Jordan, he might not be allowed back into the US. Immigration policy under the Trump administration had become so chaotic and unpredictable, leaving the US was a risk he couldn't afford to take. So he told his family he would have to wait until he had American citizenship. That process would take another five years.

At least he was relieved that the green card meant he could stay in the US permanently. And he told me he wanted to thank everyone who helped him and made him feel welcome.

That month brought more good news. Two weeks after Mohammed's green card arrived in Toledo, I heard from Monzer in Dortmund. NPR's producer in Germany, Esme Nicholson, took the train three hours west from Berlin and showed up at Monzer's apartment building. It was surrounded by parks and trees, with birds singing. Esme rang the buzzer, and she heard children's voices. Monzer opened the door—a baby in his arms. His wife and daughters had arrived from Syria.

Lamar was four. Lojain was two. And the youngest, Lossin, was one. His wife, Walaa, had arrived with them two months earlier. Monzer laid out a banquet of Syrian food for Esme's visit. There was lamb, tabbouleh, and cakes.

"I was in a German course when I received the email from the German embassy in Turkey," Monzer said. "They told me, you can send your family to get a visa." He started jumping and shouting in the middle of class. His teacher asked, "What happened?" and Monzer yelled, "I just heard that my family will come!" The whole class applauded.

Walaa and the girls had their own challenges getting out of Syria. In November, a smuggler led the four of them across the border into Turkey by foot. They had to walk ten hours in frigid cold. Since Walaa was carrying the baby, the two other girls walked the whole way.

In the middle of January at 1 a.m., their plane from Turkey landed in Germany.

"I was waiting in the airport, looking at each person getting off the airplane. No, no, not my wife . . . not my family . . . then I saw my little girl carrying a big bag. She saw me, and I ran immediately to hug my daughters. I was crying with my daughters and my wife. Everyone in the airport was taking photos of us."

In the background, I heard his oldest daughter asking for more cake.

I reminded Monzer that the last time I talked to him, he was afraid he might never see his wife and children again.

"And now they're with me every day," he said.

"For five days after they come, I can't sleep. I wake up and look at my daughters sleeping beside me. I'm not dreaming? I ask myself. I'm not dreaming. I speak with my wife, and we're together again. We're not dreaming."

He put his wife, Walaa, on the phone. Over the years that I had followed Monzer's story, this was the first time I'd spoken to her.

"Welcome to Germany," I said.

She replied, "Thank you."

"This is a happy ending," Monzer laughed.

People all over the country had been accompanying us on this journey, listening to the stories in their cars and their kitchens. Each person followed Monzer's travels from their own specific place in the world, at the same time that millions of others did the same.

As this final chapter aired on the radio, listeners tweeted their congratulations to Monzer, Walaa, and their family. When I got home that evening I scrolled through the posts on social media and saw listeners describing crying into their soup or onto their toast, showing up at the dentist red-eyed or pulling over in rush hour traffic. They were people Monzer and I would likely never meet. I didn't know anything about them or who they were. But in that moment, I understood exactly how they felt.

11

THE WHOLE WORLD FALLS IN

Even at the age of ninety, Hector Black was handsome. He was sitting on his walker, which doubled as a chair, the sun just touching the treetops in late afternoon, while people adorned with body paint and glittering costumes danced around him with ribbons—multicolored streamers embracing a maypole.

I was camping on a mountain in the woods of Tennessee, celebrating May Day at a gathering of the radical faeries—a countercultural queer movement that started in the 1970s. My friend Mitchell Kulkin pulled me out of the crowd to introduce me to Hector, suspecting we might hit it off. Mitchell knows that I love a good story, and Hector was full of them.

Hector drew a bottle of clear liquid from the pocket of his overalls. (In the years I knew him, the overalls were his constant uniform.) "Would you like some blueberry brandy?" he said with a twinkle in his eye. "I distilled it from the blueberries on my farm." He told me he had learned the distilling techniques from friends in Germany. I don't usually drink beverages from strangers at faerie gatherings, since you never know exactly what might be in the potion. I politely declined, but I sat next to Hector and listened to him as he began to tell me about his life.

I've spoken about Hector publicly over the years, including on NPR. But people who heard those stories would never have known that we met at this bacchanalian celebration. The radical faeries like to keep a shroud of privacy around their doings. That's one of the things I appreciate about the movement: it nurtures people who shape American pop music, theater, literature, movies, and more. But the creative source, the geothermal vent that nourishes this hidden ecosystem, remains deliberately obscured. Out of respect for that practice, I've left some key details out of this account.

The faeries have their roots in a culture of nonconformity. When the gay rights movement was gaining steam after the Stonewall riots, mainstream LGBT activists urged respectability. Their message was "We're just like you, and so we deserve the same rights as you." But the activist Harry Hay had a different outlook. In the 1950s he had established one of the country's earliest gay rights groups, the Mattachine Society. He dismissed what he called "the middle-class mentality more concerned with respectability than self-respect." And in 1979, Hay wrote a manifesto laying out his vision for the radical faeries, calling on queers to "throw off the ugly green frogskin of hetero-imitation."

The faeries had no formal rulebook or membership process. There were elements of back-to-the-land, free love, paganism, and above all, the practice of radical acceptance. Intentional communities of faeries where people lived year-round sprang up around the country, and many of them hosted larger gatherings on special occasions. Many of the residents took on faerie names. As my friend Hush McDowell, who lived at one of the communes for years, told me, "We take ourselves very seriously, except when we decide not to. Then we take not taking ourselves very seriously very seriously."

When I started to get curious about the faeries in 2007, I called my friend Jeff Whitty, who wrote the book for the musical *Avenue Q.* Knowing that he had been going to gatherings for years, I asked him what to expect. "Sexy bearded queers in dresses, raising goats for food," he replied. I was intrigued, and so I went. My husband decided not to join me. Camping isn't really Mike's thing, and he thought it would be better for me to have this experience to myself.

I've always thought of myself as a defiant queer person who happens to live in a mainstream, homonormative way. To state the obvious, my life does not scream "radical." I married my college boyfriend; I've worked at the same company for more than twenty years; my gender expression these days is so unremarkably mainstream that I have actually been harassed on the street for wearing the khakis-and-button-down uniform of a DC conformist. I once asked a queer NPR colleague why he was so shocked to learn that I identify as a faerie. "Because I have seen you riding your bike in a suit, carrying more suits," he said. He wasn't exaggerating—he had passed me picking up dry cleaning on my way home from work.

Early in my adult life, new acquaintances would pretty consistently guess that I grew up in the Pacific Northwest. A few years after I moved to DC, they would more frequently guess that I was from someplace like Connecticut or New Jersey. That hurt. I recognize that in some ways I embody the "middle-class mentality" that Harry Hay spoke of so contemptuously. But the hemp-necklace-, polyester-thrift-store-shirt-, ear-cuff-, corduroy-knickers-wearing teenager that I was back in Portland still pulls many of the levers inside my brain. And so the people I met at my first faerie gathering . . . the cabaret singers, weed farmers, filmmakers, sex workers, poets, bartenders, ceramicists, and aerialists . . . they felt like my tribe. Their way of listening without judgment and approaching one another with openness and vulnerability reminded me that there is a different way of moving through the world, of telling stories, of relating to strangers.

At the first gathering I attended in 2008, one of my most memorable experiences took place in the sauna, after midnight. A friend and I had run in seeking shelter from a spring downpour, and the room was pitch-black, smelling of cedar and an essential oil that someone had dripped on the wood stove. No one could see one another. I couldn't even tell how many other people were sitting on those wooden benches around me. After some settling, we sat silently, breathing in the steam, the only sound the occasional hiss of water poured over hot rocks.

Suddenly a voice cut through the darkness.

"I'd kill for a burger," they said. (We had been subsisting on tempeh, brown rice, and other hippie food for days.)

There was a quiet chuckle, then a pause.

Another voice, taking the order. "How do you want it?"

"Medium rare. Ketchup, mustard, pickles. No onions."

Then, after a few moments, "Here's your burger."

"Thank you," said the first voice.

The moment was perfectly surreal. An imaginary, absurdist fast-food restaurant in a sauna. If, the next day, I had run into any of the people who shared that moment with me, I wouldn't have known it. I felt gratitude that the faeries' definition of radical acceptance extended wide enough to embrace someone like me, who didn't wear his radicalism on his sleeve.

The performer and playwright Taylor Mac (another faerie) once told me, "I think so much of our attention has been placed on trying to identify what is wrong. I want to create work that is about making the world that I want, as opposed to commenting on the world that is." That, to me, is the heart of the radical faerie project: dreaming the culture forward and creating the world as we want it to be, rather than investing our energy in critiquing the world as it is.

Year after year, I would come home from the gatherings and try to internalize a specific lesson as I returned to the straitlaced world of the Washington press corps. One year I would focus on pushing past my knee-jerk assumptions about people. Another year I'd try to remember to go slowly, or not to let technology hijack my attention. The insights I gained in the woods didn't always stick, but then I would go back again the next year and refresh my memory. After more than a decade of doing this annually, I have to give the faeries credit. They aren't only influencing pop music, theater, literature, and movies . . . they have also subtly shaped the way I move through the world. And of course, that includes the way I practice journalism.

There are radical faerie fingerprints on *All Things Considered* interviews that millions of people hear every day. In the last letter he sent me before his death, an elderly calligrapher named William Stewart, who knew Harry Hay well, told me he caught flashes in my stories of "the way queer folks can simultaneously be preposterous and profound, using previously unexplored trickster opportunities to nudge reality into new and illuminating forms. I hear you doing this on the air now and then," he said, "and I always think—Aha! There's a member of our tribe."

I never gave my bosses too many details. "Radical" isn't a welcome word in most newsrooms. The folks I reported to up the chain at NPR only knew that I went on a camping trip with friends each spring. In 2011, as a board member of the White House Correspondents' Association, I attended the White House Correspondents' Dinner. Nerd prom, as people in DC call it. I sat in my tuxedo at the head table with President Obama and First Lady Michelle Obama, pulling out my phone to sneak photos of George Clooney and Barbra Streisand mingling with the House Speaker and the secretary of state. The next morning, I flew to Tennessee, my luggage crammed with caftans and sequins. I smiled to myself at the yin-yang of the situation, appreciating how lucky I was to be able to walk between such different worlds and feel at home in both.

By the time Obama gave a speech at the White House that weekend announcing that special forces had killed Osama bin Laden, my phone was turned off and buried at the bottom of a suitcase in the corner of my tent. When I returned to Washington, I powered on my devices to find a deluge of missed calls, voice mails, emails, and text messages from my boss. She couldn't fathom how I, one of NPR's White House correspondents, had been unreachable for a week of such monumental news. "Where were you camping," she asked, "the caves of Tora Bora?" I told her it was a remote part of Tennessee. Very remote. Every spring after that, she referred to my week off the grid as my "Osama bin Laden camping trip."

Hector Black had no inkling that this world existed when he moved his family to rural Tennessee decades earlier. He was just trying to escape the temptation of Atlanta, trying to stay faithful to his wife after decades of secret affairs with men. He had fallen into a pattern: transgression, confession, repeat. When he started a little organic plant farm in a hidden holler, he thought he would be safe from the cruising glances of men in the city. He didn't realize that he had landed on the doorstep of a hidden faerie commune. He figured it out when he showed up to his first meeting of the local organic gardening group and recognized the admiring eyes of the men looking him up and down.

..

THE DAY OF OUR CELEBRATION around the maypole, other curious faeries gathered around to hear Hector's story. We escorted him to dinner, as befits a revered elder, and he slowly ate as he described his youth. Hector was born in 1925. Growing up, he had no words to describe his attractions. "I felt like nobody in the whole dang world was a weirdo like me," he laughed. He studied social anthropology at Harvard in the

1940s, where he had his first relationship with a man. "And I thought, *This is not me. This cannot be me.* And I was just horrified. And then, you know, after a few months, I started thinking about it. And then I realized that I'd wanted to experience this again." So they started a relationship.

Hector served in the army in World War II as a combat engineer but soon recognized that he couldn't kill another human being. He was interested in social justice, pacifism, and communal living. A doctor took pity on him and gave him a diagnosis of hammer toes so that he could get out of the service.

His interest in different ways of forming community carried him to a commune in Paraguay, where there was zero tolerance for homosexuality. So, like many gay men in the middle of the last century, Hector agreed to undergo treatment. "It was the treatment that people felt was the right treatment in those days," he said. "You take estrogen. And so I took that, until I started growing breasts."

He quit the estrogen, returned to the US, and thought he had left his attraction to men in the past. That's when he met Susie Maendel. "I felt that I was cured," he explained. "I don't think I'd have done it otherwise. It wouldn't have been right." They were married and had children.

In the 1960s, he believed that the civil rights movement was the most important thing happening in the world. So Hector moved his family to Vine City, a majority Black neighborhood in Atlanta where Martin Luther King Jr. lived. He discovered that his same-sex attractions helped him to understand what it meant to be different and to connect to fights against injustice. Although he could conceal his difference in a way that allowed him to pass, "I knew what it was like to be a despised minority," he said.

Hector helped organize rent strikes and other acts of civil disobedience. He was arrested, and Dr. King protested for his release. "One of the biggest honors of my life was to have him picket to free me from jail," Hector told a reporter from the Nashville public radio station WPLN.

Hector talked to many reporters over the course of his life. He told his story on *Radiolab*, *StoryCorps*, and *The Moth*. When I met Hector on that May Day among the radical faeries, I didn't yet know that he was much more than just an old gay farmer in Tennessee. He became best known for an act of forgiveness, one that is difficult to fathom.

..

IN ATLANTA, HECTOR'S FAMILY ADOPTED an eleven-year-old girl named Patricia. Her biological mother was alcoholic and would drink away the rent money. After Susie and Hector took her in, "She just blossomed," Hector told *Radiolab*.

She was interested in reading and sewing. She made her own clothes and sewed bridal gowns for extra money. After college, she started teaching kids to read and adopted children of her own. And then, in November 2000, Patricia was murdered.

She came home while a man named Ivan Simpson was burglarizing her house for drug money, high on crack. Ivan hid in a closet, hoping to escape. But Patricia opened the closet door. He tied her up. She told him that he needed to get help with his drug habit.

"Yeah, that's Trish, she had no compunction about telling people off," Hector remembered. "He asked her for sex, and she said, 'You'll have to kill me first.' And so he did."

When Hector learned what had happened, his lifelong commitment to nonviolence wavered. "I'll kill the bastard!" he yelled. "I'd never been in favor of the death penalty, but I wanted that man to hurt the way he had hurt her. I wanted him to hurt the way I was hurting."

For almost a year, Hector couldn't stop imagining the awful things he wanted to do to Ivan. "It was like he had control over me, pushing my face in the mud." And then Hector decided that this was a test of his principles, his beliefs. So he chose not to seek the death penalty.

At Ivan's sentencing, Hector stood up to read a statement. "I don't know if I've forgiven you, Ivan Simpson," he read off the page. "But I don't hate you. I hate with all my soul what you did to my daughter." And then Hector worked up the nerve to turn around and face Ivan, to say the last thing he'd written. "I wish for all of us who've been so wounded by this crime, I wish that we might find God's peace. And I wish that also for you, Ivan Simpson."

When Hector looked up from the page, tears were streaming down Ivan's cheeks. "That's the first time I looked into his eyes. And it was like a soul in hell."

Ivan was sentenced to life in prison without parole. That night in the hotel room, Hector couldn't sleep. "Because I really felt as though a tremendous weight had been lifted from me, and that I had forgiven him." So Hector picked up a pen and paper and started writing a letter.

> I forgive you for what you did to our beloved daughter. I don't know if this will be any comfort to you, but I wanted to tell you. We both have to live our lives with the pain of this deed always there. Patricia tried to make the world a better place. We should also try.

Weeks later, Hector received a reply from Ivan.

> I know God has forgiven me. You have forgiven me. But I can't forgive myself.

Hector wanted to understand what could make a person do something so cruel. So he wrote to Ivan again, asking for details about his life.

Again Ivan replied, describing his childhood being raised by an abusive mother with schizophrenia. When Ivan was eleven, she took him with his two siblings to a swimming pool and tried to kill all three of them. The two boys escaped, but Ivan watched his mother drown his little sister.

Ivan and Hector continued to exchange letters for years. More than a decade passed. Hector would send Ivan Christmas packages. "I'd say to myself, *You crazy old man, you're sending Christmas packages to the man who murdered your daughter. What the hell is wrong with you?*"

Hector would visit maximum security prisons around the country and speak to the inmates about restorative justice and forgiveness. At the local high school in rural Tennessee, next to the table where the military recruited students to enlist, he would sit at his own table and hand out flyers advocating for peace.

He began telling me these stories on May Day. Generations of flamboyantly adorned queers huddled around us, listening, with small hurricane lamps holding off the spreading darkness. Hours into his storytelling, I had decided I could trust Hector's blueberry brandy. It looked like water and tasted like summer, and I sipped it as he unfolded his life before us.

Gay people don't get a lot of opportunities to learn from the generations that preceded us. We aren't raised by queer parents and grandparents. We're more like foundlings, growing up foreigners, lucky if we find our way back to our people. In my life, the AIDS crisis wiped out almost the entire generation of men who would have been my gay mentors and guides. That's another reason I'm drawn to the radical faeries. The gatherings are places where I can learn from my elders, men like Hector.

And, Hector told me, the gatherings were valuable to him for the same reason. We were like his gay grandchildren, holding up and celebrating the generations above us who fought so that our lives could be easier.

··

THE SEPTEMBER AFTER THAT GATHERING, I went to visit Hector at his home in the Tennessee holler. It was the time of year when everything seems abundant, as though winter will never come. I made pesto from piles of his basil and braised fish in olive oil with sweet late summer cherry tomatoes. We dug up ginger from his garden and harvested fat black scuppernong grapes from the wooden trellis where they were climbing. I simmered down the fruit with the ginger and poured that syrup over ice with rum. As we sipped our drinks, he told me how he finally came out of the closet.

When Hector was seventy years old, one of his daughters came out to him and Susie. "We both loved her just as much as ever," he told me. "More, even, because I knew how much she had been through. How much she suffered because of who she was. And I just said, how can I love her and hate myself for what I am?"

He told Susie that he wasn't going to fight himself anymore. After forty years of marriage, he offered her a divorce. She declined his offer. But, Hector told me, "she set me free to find somebody. And she said she hoped she'd like him."

That was twenty years before I met Hector. Any time I think I'm too old to start something new in my life, I remember that he only began living as an out gay man at the age of seventy.

After our dinner, he sat down at the piano and played Schubert's impromptu number 3 in G flat major.

Susie had died just a few months before that September visit. The next morning we walked to her grave site, in a clearing under a canopy of trees, overlooking the creek that runs through their land. Their daughter Patricia was buried there too.

Hector told me that while he might have regretted some of the choices he had made, he didn't regret the life that he had lived. "I really think that suffering can be a way of understanding people," he said. "You know, Mother Teresa said, 'Lord, break my heart so completely that the whole world falls in.' I can't say that. But I really am grateful that my heart has been broken a good many times. Because it does help me to love."

In the final months of his life, Hector marched in Black Lives Matter protests in Tennessee. He died in 2020, at the age of ninety-five. He now lies buried next to Susie and Patricia, in that clearing by the creek. As one of his many friends around the world said, "He fought with love until his dying breath."

Hector had a lifelong passion for plants, and at the end of one of my visits to his home in Tennessee, he sent me on my way with a jar of calamondin jam that he had made from the fruits of his citrus tree. It was sweet and tart, the fluorescent orange color of the sun touching the treetops on that first day I met him by the maypole. I went back to Washington and bought a calamondin tree for myself, to remember him by.

12

ANSWERS VERSUS QUESTIONS

Hosting *All Things Considered* offers a gift that comes with a catch. The gift? I can ask almost any living author to tell me about their work. It's an English major's dream: a private book club where I get to talk with my favorite writers one-on-one (with, give or take, a few million eavesdroppers). Sometimes when I finish taping a book interview, I'll ask the author a question that I know won't make the final edited cut, just because I'm curious about the answer. I don't do that with lawmakers, who tend to hang up the phone as quickly as possible.

Early on in this job, I set a rule for myself that I would read a book cover-to-cover before interviewing the author. That isn't standard in my profession; many hosts skim a book or read a chunk. Sometimes they'll ask a producer or editor to do the reading and write a book report. But my philosophy is that if someone has spent a couple of years writing the thing, the least I can do is spend a couple of weeks reading it. It's a sign of respect. And that brings me to the catch.

Although I read more as a host of *All Things Considered* than I have at any other time in my life, if a friend recommends a title that came out last month, or last year, it will almost never make my list. My mother is a voracious reader, and she has learned that I won't take her recommendations—not because I think she has bad taste, but because every book she reads has already been published. *All Things Considered* is a news program. If a book is already out in the world, we've missed the moment. I sometimes hear an author interviewed by another NPR host and think, "I'd love to read that book. Too bad I never will." My stack of forthcoming titles that I must read for work is so tall, I don't even bother keeping a list of books I want to read for my own enjoyment. I know I'll likely never get to any of them.

And so, when I took four consecutive weeks off in the fall of 2020 to burn through the vacation time I had accumulated during the pandemic lockdown, I carefully contemplated the books that I would carry with me. I would be spending my hiatus at Salmon Creek Farm, a former commune that my friend Fritz Haeg has turned into an ever-evolving work of art in California's Mendocino County. And for the first time in many months, I would read for pleasure.

My plan was to burrow into one of the eight wooden cabins Fritz had restored and spend the month of September doing manual tasks that didn't demand much from the verbal part of my brain. I harvested apples, pickled zucchini, chopped firewood, and preserved chutney. The redwood duff on the forest floor dampened every sound, clearing space for the shush of the Pacific Ocean just over a mile away. And each day, I would sit in a nook with the words of Richard Powers, Robin Wall Kimmerer, and Colson Whitehead. I didn't take notes or jot questions in the back of the book; I just consumed what they had written. Powers described the slow, silent growth of redwoods as I leaned against the trunk of one and watched the canopy wave above my head. Kimmerer explained how our eyes have evolved to perceive colors in nature, and I foraged for ripe huckleberries among the brush. Whitehead carried me far from modern-day Northern California to the Deep South in the mid-nineteenth century.

..

I WAS PAINTING CHARTREUSE TRIM on the new Salmon Creek Farm greenhouse when the sky started to turn orange and hazy. Ash drifted onto the raspberries like snowflakes. California's wildfires weren't directly threatening us, but the air was toxic enough to send everyone to their cabins. As I sat looking out my window at the haze blotting out the sun, I remembered something the author N. K. Jemisin had told me in an interview a few years earlier, about apocalypse.

Jemisin was the first Black woman ever to win the Hugo Award for Best Novel, and then she became the only author ever to win that award three years in a row for her *Broken Earth* trilogy. The first book in the series begins with a mother losing her son. The setting is a post-apocalyptic fantasy world, where people with extraordinary powers are seen as a threat.

In our 2018 interview, I asked Jemisin why she wanted to begin her story with the end of the world. And she told me, "In a lot of cases, what's considered an apocalypse for some people is what other people have been living every day." Apocalypse was subjective, she explained. For her main character, "The world ended when this woman's son was killed," she said. "This is nothing new." She wanted to explore when we consider a cataclysm to have begun and ended.

That's why I recalled Jemisin as I looked out my cabin window at the smoke from the forest fires in the summer of 2020. My experience of climate change, the pandemic, and racial justice protests made me think of her gentle reminder that the shock and horror that felt novel to me were familiar to others.

I've met many people in my reporting who live in the maw of apocalypse. On the Indian island of Ghoramara, a man named Rubil Saha watched rising seas swallow his homeland. Every time the tides destroyed his house, he rebuilt farther inland. "This is my motherland, so I can't abandon it," he told me through tears. "And the pull of the motherland roots me here. I'm drowning."

In Zimbabwe, I met a woman named Florence Machinga who resolved to work as a poll monitor in national elections, even though her neighbors burned down her home and slaughtered her livestock after she supported the opposition in a previous campaign. "I will make sure there is peace during this election," she told me. "I am brave enough."

In Colombia, a Venezuelan woman named Reina Ballestero walked 350 miles from the border town of Cúcuta to the capital city of Bogotá. She told me she was going to earn money for her nephew suffering from leukemia back in Venezuela, where the economy had collapsed. "My feet are torn up, but I have to keep going," she said under a cold drizzle in the mountain town of Pamplona.

Jemisin gave me context to understand the experience of those people in a way that interviews with scientists, politicians, and business executives never did. And now that I have spent every workday for years speaking to leaders in all walks of life, I've reached a conclusion. The conversations that help me see the world most clearly are generally not with researchers, policymakers, or so-called experts. They aren't with the people journalists crassly call "newsmakers" at all. They're with artists—especially writers.

··

I HOPE IT GOES WITHOUT saying that I believe in the importance of news. Democracy depends on accurate and truthful stories. But in these times that can feel apocalyptic, as we seem to grow increasingly alienated from the world and from one another, I keep returning to the truths I find in fiction.

"That's the beauty of reading," the novelist Nathan Englander told me. "That's why it's subversive—because it crosses time and space and culture."

I was interviewing Englander about *Kaddish.com*, a novel that immerses readers in the intricacies of Orthodox Judaism. It isn't a flattering portrait of the religion; the characters often behave in ugly ways. Englander told me the point isn't flattery but empathy. "You want to make a genocide; we all know the ingredients, from the Holocaust to Rwanda. You start making people less than human. You compare them to animals, to cockroaches. It always starts the same," Englander said. "We dehumanize the other, and then we can kill them, you know? And to me, what literature does is—if you can enter into the world, if you can connect with a character, what else does that do but make connection?"

In this time of mutual mistrust and tribalism, we have few incentives to reach across divides. And then, we pick up a book and see the world through someone else's eyes. When I interviewed Salman Rushdie about his novel *The Golden House*, he put it this way: "One of the great beauties of the novel as a form is that it shows us that human nature is the great constant. Human nature is the same in all places, in all times, in all languages."

The Israeli author Etgar Keret told me he used to write lots of op-eds, but he doesn't any more. "The moment that you express an opinion about something in this world, then it becomes more and more tribal," he said. So these days, he writes fiction instead. In Keret's short story "The Birthday of a Failed Revolutionary," a rich and lonely man buys everyone's birthdays. Each morning, someone's mother calls and sings happy birthday to him. Which makes perfect sense, in a sort of dream logic. If you have more money than you can possibly spend and you're still unhappy, why wouldn't you buy up all the birthdays?

"I think that the moment that you write things that are more meta-phorical and not a statement about reality itself, people let some of their defenses down," Keret told me. "And maybe, if I'm lucky, then they get disoriented enough that they can rethink something." Not to mention, the reading experience is far more entertaining than a screed about income inequality.

In 2019, after I spent two weeks in Colombia reporting on the mass migration of Venezuelans fleeing their imploding country, I returned home to Washington and interviewed a Venezuelan journalist named Karina Sainz Borgo. She had just published her first novel, *It Would Be Night in Caracas*. The book reads like a nonfiction account of her country's collapse, with leaps in time from Venezuela's prosperous past to its violent present, but the scenes and characters come from the author's imagination. Since I had just returned from covering Venezuela's implosion as a journalist, I wanted to know why she chose to tell this story through fiction. "Journalism and nonfiction provide us answers," Sainz Borgo told me, "but I think fiction provides us questions."

..

MY REPORTING TRIP TO INDIA'S Ghoramara Island only happened because fiction provided me with questions. In 2004, long before I became a host of *All Things Considered*, I read a book for pleasure called *The Hungry Tide*, by Amitav Ghosh. The novel describes a real place on the border of India and Bangladesh, where borders blur as freshwater merges into salt. It is the world's largest mangrove forest—a patchwork of islands known as the Sundarbans.

Ghosh's vivid portrayal of this watery landscape burrowed into my psyche, only to reemerge more than a decade later. In 2016, I was planning a trip to India to report on climate change. My team had decided to start in New Delhi. We would investigate whether a developing country could provide more than a billion people with cars, refrigerators, and air conditioning in a sustainable way that didn't bust the world's carbon budget. I knew that beyond our reporting from the Indian capital, we also needed to show the present-day impact of climate change on the people experiencing it the most. With voices from *The Hungry Tide* still whispering in my ear, I decided to visit the Sundarbans.

I contacted Amitav Ghosh and told him about our plans. He told me that climate change had already transformed the place since he had written about it. "Years ago, when you went to the Sundarbans, the mud banks would turn red with crabs," he said. "That never happens anymore. You never see trees lighting up at night with fireflies." Mangrove islands are defined by change, but he told me this kind of change was different—noncyclical. Tides were taking away chunks of land that wouldn't return.

My team flew east from New Delhi to Kolkata and drove hours from the city to the water's edge. The experience felt adjacent to déjà vu, feeling my feet squelch into mud that I had read about in stories years ago. We launched our boat into the brown brackish water where three rivers converge, and as we motored past islands, an Irrawaddy dolphin popped out of the water beside us—a sign of good luck, according to local folklore. We reported stories about an ancient goddess named Bonbibi and man-eating Bengal tigers that were encroaching on humans as water swallowed the tigers' habitat.

After a few days, we reached Ghoramara. The island's shoreline looked like a block of cheese that had been nibbled by a giant mouse. The coast was gouged open, and palm trees leaned precariously out over the waves, their root balls partially exposed to the air. The island had been home to forty thousand people not long ago. By the time we arrived, just three thousand lived there. Ghoramara had lost half its land compared to fifty years ago.

A wizened man in his eighties named Debendra Tarek led me into his hut made of mud and straw. He took out a handful of rough brown rice. "This resists the saltwater," the village elder told me, a last-ditch effort to avoid this particular apocalypse by planting a new variety of rice. As I told Tarek's story on the radio, I hoped the narratives that I wove through my chosen medium of journalism might somehow lodge inside a person and subtly change their path in the same way Ghosh's *Hungry Tide* had changed mine.

A few years later, I interviewed Ghosh once again—this time about his novel *Gun Island*. It was a modern retelling of a Bengali myth, weaving in themes of climate change and migration. When I asked Ghosh what ancient stories could tell us about our present-day experience, he said, "I realized that what these old legends were about were exactly what we are living through today. Catastrophic floods, droughts, famines, storms." Today, he said, "when we have these catastrophes unfolding around us, we don't seem to be able to even imaginatively grapple with what's in front of us." Stories from thousands of years ago provide what our contemporary life cannot.

..

IF I EVER HAD ANY doubts about the power of literature to change the real world, a man named Behrouz Boochani wiped them away. In 2019, he won Australia's biggest literary prize for his book *No Friend but the Mountains*. Boochani didn't attend the awards ceremony, though. He is Kurdish, born in Iran, and he wrote the book while detained on Manus Island off the coast of Papua New Guinea.

In Iran, Boochani was an investigative journalist who was persecuted for his reporting and his support of Kurdish independence. He came to Australia by boat, seeking asylum. By the time he won Australia's Victoria Prize for literature, the Australian government had kept him imprisoned for six years on Manus Island. Manus was where Australia held asylum seekers indefinitely. Not where Australia held asylum seekers while processing their claims—there was no system process-ing the claims of the people there. Imagine the indefinite detention at Guantánamo Bay, but unlike the men at Guantánamo, the detainees on Manus were not even suspected of any wrongdoing.

Boochani wrote *No Friend but the Mountains* by text message. The book defies genre, incorporating aspects of memoir, mythology, history, and folklore. Boochani sent the texts to a professor at the University of Sydney named Omid Tofighian. Tofighian translated the book into English, which ultimately led to the book being published in Austra-lia. I was unable to reach Boochani because of his imprisonment, but I spoke to Tofighian after *No Friend but the Mountains* made inter-national news. "They could be released tomorrow," Tofighian told me. "They could never be released, and you wouldn't know. And I think that is part of the systematic torture that Behrouz really tries to convey."

Although Boochani couldn't attend the awards ceremony to deliver his acceptance speech in person, he recorded a video that was played at the event. "This proves that words still have the power to challenge inhumane systems and structures," he said. "I have always said that I believe in words and literature. I believe that literature has the potential to make change and challenge structures of power. Literature has the power to give us freedom."

Later that year, in a demonstration of the truth and power of his own words, Boochani was freed.

..

IN JUNE 2020, I WENT to Louisville, Kentucky, to spend time with the people who best knew Breonna Taylor, the young EMT who was shot and killed in her own apartment by police executing a no-knock search warrant. I wanted to tell the story of who Breonna Taylor was before she became a hashtag or a headline.

Taylor's best friends told me about how she could never stay awake during a movie; her aunts and uncle told me about her favorite card games, Skip-Bo and Phase 10. They talked about how surreal it was to hear people around the country chanting, "Say her name," about this woman whom they knew better than anyone.

That story aired, and then I returned to Washington, where I interviewed the author Alice Randall about her novel *Black Bottom Saints*. It tells the story of the Black people who created the "Caramel Camelot" of Detroit in the middle of the twentieth century, a shining city of Black art, activism, and industry. The book insists that Black joy is radical, that trauma can lead to transcendence, and that memory and stories are powerful tools of rebellion. Randall celebrates fifty-two secular saints of old Black Detroit, real people who orbited the city's Black Bottom neighborhood.

Randall and I didn't talk about Breonna Taylor by name. But I thought of her family and friends, men and women trying to marshal their energy and make sense of the senseless, as Randall said, "Dipping into art can be an act of self-care. It can be a cure. And if it's not a cure, it can be a relief that allows you to rest, to go back out to fight again." In that moment of national protest, when the gravitational pull of despair at times felt inescapable, Randall's fiction helped me see a different path. One in which tragedy, loss, and grief can metamorphose into something powerful and radiant.

At the last Tony Awards ceremony before the pandemic shut down Broadway, the night's big winner was *Hadestown*, a musical retelling of the myth of Orpheus and Eurydice. It's a familiar tale: Eurydice goes to the underworld, Orpheus follows to save her, and he sings a song so beautiful that it melts the heart of Hades. That part of the myth speaks to the power of art. And then comes the catch: they can leave, but Orpheus must walk first, with Eurydice following behind. If he reaches the surface without turning around, they're free. If he looks over his shoulder to make sure she's there, she'll be doomed to spend eternity in the underworld. Whether or not you remember your Greek mythology, you know how this tragedy ends.

In her speech accepting the Tony Award for best director, Rachel Chavkin said, "Power structures try to maintain control by making you feel like you're walking alone in the darkness. Even when your partner is right there at your back." We have all been on both sides of that walk out of hell. We know what it feels like to believe that we are solitary in the darkness. And we have also been the person at someone's back, reminding them that, in the words of Stephen Sondheim, "No one is alone." But as Salman Rushdie said in a speech months before an attacker brutally stabbed him, "We are not helpless. Even after Orpheus was torn to pieces, his severed head, floating down the river Hebrus, went on singing, reminding us that song is stronger than death."

Fiction serves as that reminder for me. Newsroom bosses sometimes treat author interviews as a treat, or a diversion—a break from the daily work of chronicling the world's politicians and corporations. But for me, those conversations are not a novelty. They help us find a path leading out of the darkness. Despite what power structures may want us to believe, writers help me see that we are all walking together in the same long journey toward the light. I don't have to glance over my shoulder to make sure it's true; I can just look down at the page.

13

YOU CAN'T SEE SCHVITZ ON THE RADIO

Here's something you wouldn't know if you've only heard me on the radio or read me on the page. When I get nervous, or anxious, or self-conscious—or pretty much any emotion in that universe of feelings—I sweat. And if you ask me to list my ten most embarrassing moments in life, most of them will involve my doing so too much, in the wrong place, at the wrong time.

I don't get dewy. I don't perspire. I'm not talking about "I could use a handkerchief." I'm talking about "I could use a towel. And a mop. And a change of clothes." The kind of sweating that makes people wonder if I'm unwell, or on drugs.

It starts slowly. I feel a tingling, blooming around my hairline. I know what's coming. And so the feedback loop begins. It's like showing fear to an aggressive animal. Panic only accelerates the inevitable.

Within moments, a steady drip is falling off the tip of my nose like a leaky faucet. My earlobes are melting icicles on a warm spring day. The moisture from my back soaks through my undershirt, my dress shirt, my suit jacket, and onto the back of the chair. It's not charming.

When I covered the US Department of Justice, I was invited to a background briefing with the new attorney general and a handful of reporters. I sat immediately to the left of Eric Holder at the long wooden table in the AG's office. I had bicycled to the DOJ on a hot, sunny day and didn't anticipate how warm the meeting room would be. My reporter's notebook still has the ink smudges from where my sweat dripped onto the pages. To Holder's credit, he pretended not to notice. But given that I was sitting just inches from him, my effusive performance was hard to miss.

After I graduated from the Justice beat to the White House beat, I was excited to get a question at my first White House news conference, sitting outside in the Rose Garden. I made it through the query all right. But as soon as the camera cut away from me, I lost my cool. The anchor Jake Tapper was sitting right behind me and watched me start spouting water like an open fire hydrant. When the press conference ended, he asked if I was okay. Jake has always been considerate like that.

I was invited to emcee a gala dinner in New Hampshire in 2013 for the launch of a new institute at the UNH Law School. There were senators and governors—John McCain among them. In an enormous conference room full of donors and civic leaders, I sat at the center of the long table on the dais, introducing one speaker after another, progressively becoming thoroughly drenched. When the sweating had started earlier that evening, I had used a tiny paper cocktail napkin to wipe my face. My ever-present stubble shredded it. So I was both sweaty and covered in white flecks of paper. Mercifully, the only press coverage of the event said simply that I "conducted the proceedings with great skill." Thank you, *NH Business Review*!

My waterworks do not respect national boundaries or religious affiliations. On a reporting trip to South Korea in 2015, I visited a Buddhist monastery outside Seoul where nuns had been preserving the ancient art of temple cuisine for centuries. I sat on the floor of the temple grounds, opposite a beaming woman with a shaved head. Sheathed in gray robes, she poured a pot of steaming hot tea into the delicate ceramic cup before me and gazed into my eyes. "You must become the protagonist of your own story," she told me. I was a protagonist—the swimming starlet Esther Williams in one of her MGM blockbusters from the 1950s like *Dangerous When Wet* or *Aqua Spectacle*.

Don't ask why I sweat so much. I don't know why. To keep me humble, maybe? Ultimately, the "why" is beside the point. It's not a morality tale or the lesson of a fable. It just is. I've learned to make the joke, "On the radio, no one can see you sweat!" It breaks the tension, unless the sweating just keeps going, which it does.

In the movie *Broadcast News*, there's a famous scene in which Aaron Altman, played by Albert Brooks, can't stop schvitzing. I recognize every gesture and detail. The finger swipe along the eyebrow. The damp ring where the collar meets the neck. The deep "inhale . . . exhale" as you try to visualize yourself making snow angels.

A guy in the control room says, "This is more than Nixon ever sweated." And in my finest moments I think, "This is more than Aaron Altman ever sweated." Altman concludes the broadcast, "At least twenty-two people dead," then the camera cuts away and he adds, "I wish I were one of them." I've never related to a movie scene more.

The members of Pink Martini have learned to ignore it. God bless the lead singer, China Forbes, who gamely dances onstage with me and gives me a dazzling smile even when I look like a drowned rat. In 2012, the band was invited to Paris for fashion week. It was the tenth anniversary of Alber Elbaz becoming creative director at Lanvin. We were to be the entertainment at the party for him after the fashion show.

Months beforehand, each member of the band was told to send in measurements for the custom outfits that Alber was planning to build for each of us. When we arrived in Paris, China Forbes was given a custom red gown. Each man received a bespoke red velvet jacket with a matching red velvet bow tie. The fabric was cozy as a fur coat.

While the models stalked the runway, we stood waiting on a circular stage under a towering chandelier, concealed by sumptuous ruby-red ruffled curtains. Tilda Swinton and Pharrell were in the audience as the fashion show unfolded and the temperature climbed.

The designer typically walks the runway last, but when the final model finished her runway walk, Alber was nowhere to be seen. Once she made her exit, the red curtains at the end of the venue parted to reveal us all in a tableau.

Alber stood at the center of our stage—his stage, really—lit by that cascading chandelier and twinkling strings of white lights above his head. Thomas began to play waltzing minor chords on the piano, and Alber sang "Que serà, serà."

The circular stage slowly rotated, turning us from the side of the venue where the fashion show had been to the cavernous space where everyone was streaming into the party. Gorgeous young men wearing velvet blazers in an array of jewel tones held trays of champagne glasses and delicate French macarons. Their foreheads were smooth and dry, while the twinkling lights sparkled off my dripping, shining face. I was a puddle before Thomas played the first note. But you'd better believe I still wear that red velvet Lanvin jacket today.

When I lived in London, my friend Ruthie Rogers invited me to an intimate dinner for eight at her Italian restaurant, the River Cafe. Two of the guests were members of U2, including the lead singer, Bono. Ruthie didn't know this, but as a teenager I was more than a U2 fan. I was a completist: I owned every album, some on both CD and cassette.

In my high school bedroom, I would sing harmonies to every track from *The Joshua Tree*. I fantasized about a day when the band would need an emergency backup singer, with no advance warning. I imagined myself running up to Bono, breathless. "No time to teach someone the parts? Well, I just so happen to have some harmonies for every song ready to go! I've got your back, Bono!"

My freshman year at Yale, I auditioned for my a cappella group with a U2 song: "Running to Stand Still"—from *The Joshua Tree* of course. I didn't see the band live in concert until I was an adult. And still, after all that time, I had never met Bono.

In 2016, Ruthie and the other guests knew none of this. The dinner was literally the stuff of my teenage fantasies. My heart was a fish flopping on a dock. And somehow, through most of the meal, I actually managed to hold it together. My internal switch stayed in the "off" position through the langoustines, the puntarelle salad, the saffron risotto, and the chocolate nemesis cake.

Bono masked his Irish accent to do uncanny impressions of Bill Clinton and Marco Rubio. He told stories from behind the scenes of his international antipoverty work. "So I said to Obama, *Why do you think you're above doing karaoke?* And he says, *Because I can actually sing.*"

Bono described trying to get a meeting with Xi Jinping to discuss poverty. He couldn't get through to the Chinese leader at first, "So Quincy Jones says, *China's First Lady is a singer, I'll give her a call.*" After Quincy's intervention, Bono got the meeting.

Near the end of the night, after plenty of wine had been poured and we'd moved on to grappa, US ambassador Matthew Barzun brought out a guitar that he'd stashed somewhere. He handed it to Bono, who plucked out the Beatles song "Norwegian Wood." Off the cuff, he improvised new lyrics, referencing everyone at the table and calling back to topics we had discussed that night. My teenage Portland soul left my body and ascended.

And then it plummeted back down to earth as I heard Matthew telling Bono that I sing with Pink Martini. Matthew insisted that I sing something for the table. My teenage Portland soul sank through my chair, into the floor, and down among the tubes of the London sewer system. "Do one of the Spanish love songs!" Matthew urged. It was the kind of thing that might feel totally natural in other circumstances—a woozy, late-night, post-dessert giddiness that segues into something like a sing-along. In normal times, this would be my favorite sort of transition, from a dinner party to music. But this wasn't normal. This was Bono.

What do you do when the US ambassador to the UK insists that you sing for your childhood idol? You open your mouth, and you sing.

Viniste a mí
Como poesía en la canción
Mostrándome
Un nuevo mundo de pasión . . .

And that's when the floodgates opened. By the time I finished the song, I was drenched and shaking. Bono gave me a bear hug. He didn't even wipe himself off afterward.

When I departed London after two years to move back to the US, Ruthie gave me a personalized River Cafe cookbook as a going-away present, containing some of her favorite recipes with handwritten notes. The back page has a photo of us, sitting around the table at that dinner. I am gleaming like a glazed ham.

When my friends Sam Kass and Alex Wagner were getting married, they asked me to officiate. Sam was close friends with the Obamas, going all the way back to their days in Chicago when Barack was a senator. Sam started as the family's personal chef and went on to lead Michelle's initiatives around healthy eating. I was honored when they asked if I would be part of the ceremony. They joked that it was because they needed someone who they knew wouldn't get nervous about having the Obama family in the audience. I knew it was also important to them that this day be about the two of them, not about the Obamas or anyone else. And certainly not about a sweaty officiant.

The ceremony was at Stone Barns in upstate New York, in late August. It was outdoors. The afternoon was humid. I was wearing a suit. You know where this is going. While the wedding party was gathering in the moments before the ceremony, I was running cold water over my wrists and holding ice against the nape of my neck—tricks that I had been told cool the body quickly, but that never seemed to do much for me. I was in the bathroom, holding cold damp paper towels under my armpits, as the bride and groom signed documents and took photos. Finally, I pulled myself together and dried myself off.

We walked outside to where the guests were seated in a circle, surrounding Sam and Alex. I looked into the eyes of the bride and groom, and then I looked just past them at the guests facing me. I locked eyes with Barack, Michelle, Sasha, Malia, and Michelle's mother, Marian Robinson. I felt that familiar tingling, blooming sensation at my hairline. And in my mind, I slapped myself in the face—hard. THIS IS NOT ABOUT YOU, I told my rebellious body. YOU ARE NOT ABOUT TO FUCKING RUIN THEIR WEDDING DAY RIGHT NOW.

Miraculously, I snapped out of it. I did not ruin their wedding day. At the reception, the president told me if I needed a change of pace from journalism, I could do this as a backup career. I wanted to write a thank-you note to my biochemistry.

I know that perspiration is not actually a medical hardship. There's even a pill I could take to stop the sweats, called a beta blocker. It suppresses the outward symptoms of nerves, without making you sleepy or hazy like a Valium. Classical musicians sometimes take the pill for auditions, to maintain steady hands and even breath. I've tried it. It works. But for reasons that I'll explain, I almost never take it (although I have occasionally second-guessed that decision).

All through my adult life, my friends and colleagues have mocked my seemingly effortless achievements. When they ask what I'm doing on my vacation and I say, "Touring with Pink Martini," they roll their eyes. "Of *course* you are." I know how I come across. My friend Jon Lovett once did an impression of me. In a flawless re-creation of my slightly lilty, swishy NPR voice, he said, "Oh, that chair? Funny story about that chair. Martha Stewart and I actually carved that chair together . . . out of a larger chair!" What makes my telling you this story even worse is that in the process, I'm name-dropping Jon, founder of Crooked Media and host of the podcasts *Pod Save America* and *Lovett or Leave It*.

I get it. I am aware of how blessed and lucky I am. I pulled a good card from the deck. I have a job I love, I'm happily married, and millions of people pay attention to what I have to say. I even sing with a band! But the cliché end of that sentence would be, "And I do it all without breaking a sweat." Well, that's where I refuse to fit expectations. I sweat like a goddamn snowman in heat.

That is one reason I've decided to embrace this biochemical tic and try to feel gratitude for it, even when it threatens to ruin the party. Sometimes, things that look like a breeze are actually terrifying. Things that seem effortless are exhausting. I push myself all the time to do things I might fail at and to stay present in moments where I feel like I don't belong. I have jumped and missed on so many occasions, humiliating myself in ways that have nothing to do with perspiration. But the sweat stains are my own evidence to myself that I kept going, even when it scared me into a *Waterworld*-ian panic.

I once sang a couple of songs in a ballet adaptation of *The Sun Also Rises*. For most of the show, when I wasn't onstage, I perched just behind the curtain at the edge of the Kennedy Center stage and watched the dancers float through the air. The moment they crossed the threshold into the wings where I stood out of the audience's view, they crumpled into gulping, sweating creatures who experienced gravity like ordinary humans, gasping for breath and wiping their faces with towels. Then they'd jeté out onto the stage again, transforming back into dandelion seeds drifting on the wind. That peek behind the scenes told me more about their experience as ballet dancers than anything I had ever witnessed from seats in the audience. I understand why they strive for the illusion of effortlessness, but I find it so much more interesting to know the truth about what goes into the grace and elegance that we see under the stage lights.

I love going for a run in the middle of summer in Washington, DC. When the temperature is in the nineties and humid, I start sweating the minute I leave the house. Miles later, I can wring out my tank top and create a small pond on the sidewalk. And it's okay. That is a place it's allowed.

Of course, if I have to meet anybody afterward, I'll need to explain myself. "Sorry I can't stop sweating. I went for a run several hours ago, and my body still hasn't figured out that it's over."

14

MUSICAL INTERLUDE 2:

CROWD SURFING WITH CIGARETTES

I first met Alan Cumming backstage at *Cabaret* in 2014, when he was taking a second Broadway turn at the role that won him a Tony in 1998 (which was itself a remount of a production he had done in London in 1993, which was a revival of the original 1966 production starring Joel Grey). The setting tells you something about me, and about Alan. He's been famous for longer than anyone I know personally. He can talk about the shift over time from autograph-seekers to selfie-seekers and why the latter are so much more annoying. He has an uncanny ability to look at someone walking up to him and guess what they recognize him from. The millennials clock him from movies like *Spy Kids* and *X2: X-Men United*. The boomers know him from TV shows like *The Good Wife* and *Instinct*. The gays, Broadway, of course. Which is why it makes sense that

I first crossed his path in a dressing room at Studio 54, the Broadway theater and former nightclub where he had just finished a Sunday matinee of the Kander and Ebb musical.

I was swinging through New York on a quick visit to the US before returning to the UK, where I was based at the time. I might not have gone out of my way to catch the revival of the revival, but one of my best friends from college, Ben Eakeley, was in the cast. Once the party at the Kit Kat Club ended and the blackout fell on (spoiler alert) Alan's Emcee in a concentration camp uniform, Ben brought me back to meet the stars. I didn't know whether Alan listened to NPR or had any idea who this friend of Ben's was. Years later, Alan told me that he recognized my voice as he heard me chatting with Ben on my way up the stairs to his dressing room. I joked it couldn't have hurt that I walked up those stairs repeating, "From NPR News, this is *All Things Considered*, I'm Ari Shapiro."

Alan welcomed Ben and me into "Club Cumming," his dressing-room-turned-bar (perpetually stocked thanks to a sponsorship by Campari America). Having seen him on-screen in roles that required American, English, and German accents, I found his natural Scottish lilt a bit of a surprise. He kindly said hello as he took off his makeup and apologized that he couldn't host me for a proper cocktail. Club Cumming was the scene of post-show carousing most nights, and years later the name would transfer to a brick-and-mortar bar in the East Village that hosts events from knitting to burlesque. But that Sunday, Alan was about to jet off to his birth country to spend his one free day a week campaigning for Scottish independence. As it happened, I would fly to Edinburgh the following morning to report on the referendum. We said a quick hello/goodbye as Alan rushed off to catch his plane. I didn't ask for a selfie, and he didn't offer. I assumed that might well be our first and last encounter. Five years later, we created our own cabaret-style show together.

..

IF YOU HAD KNOWN BEN and me in college, you might not have expected that years later I would be the one going to see him on a Broadway stage. At Yale I spent my free time doing plays and musicals with the thought that I might pursue acting, while Ben intended to be an architect. We joined the same a cappella group our freshman year. Between the finger snaps and doo-wahs before rooms full of wealthy elderly New Englanders, he and I became platonic partners in crime. When we graduated, Ben moved to New York and made the leap to performing full-time, while I made the equally surprising swerve to DC and journalism.

Reporting the news on the radio scratched more of my performance-related itches than I would have expected. I got to use my voice, tell a story, connect with an audience, and on the best days maybe even change someone's view of the world. The news was dynamic and fast-paced enough that I didn't miss being onstage. I definitely didn't miss auditions. I liked that my full-time job came with a 401(k) and health insurance, and that I didn't have to go back to square one after every closing night. Not to mention, as a reporter I got to write the script and choose the stories I would tell. I didn't have to settle for reading whatever a director handed to me.

When I started singing with Pink Martini several years into my journalism career, I remembered that a live audience does provide some qualities a radio broadcast lacks. There is a moment that everybody shares, together in one place. An experience that will never exist again in quite that way. Everybody breathes the same air molecules for a brief stretch of time. There's an audible reaction as you walk the high wire and nail the performance, or tumble off the tightrope and try to climb back on and salvage your dignity. I love how intimate and personal radio can be; those qualities appeal to my instinct to connect. But I also love how communal live performance is; that appeals to my instinct to form a collective.

After I had been touring with Pink Martini for a few years, friends started asking me whether I would ever create a solo show, a cabaret-style evening of stories and songs. (That's cabaret with a small "c," not to be confused with the Kander and Ebb *Cabaret*.) It seemed a logical enough next step. Pink Martini's singer Storm Large had done it. She wrote a book about her life called *Crazy Enough* and adapted that memoir into a one-woman stage show. Some of my favorite performers were cabaret artists—people like Joey Arias, Meow Meow, Rizo, Taylor Mac, and Justin Vivian Bond. I would go to Joe's Pub in New York and watch them bare their souls and/or their bosoms. Meow Meow would crowd-surf while holding two (fake, but real-looking) lit cigarettes and belting out a song about the apocalypse. As other members of the audience and I held her aloft and passed her over our heads to the waiting outstretched arms behind us, we felt a literal connection to her corporal form, to her straining muscles and heaving ribcage. No matter how much a radio story might move someone, the listener never winds up with the reporter's makeup smeared onto their shirt.

Justin Vivian Bond, who goes by Viv, once said they wanted to be an actor as a kid because as a trans person, "I grew up not wanting to be myself." After they grew up and explored the world, "I realized what I really wanted to be was myself." That desire to be authentically true to themselves onstage comes through in every one of Viv's performances. Watching their shows helped me understand the vulnerability and specificity inherent in cabaret as an art form.

A friend in London named Ben Walters wrote his PhD on cabaret and queer performance art. He told me that he thinks too many performers—Americans especially—confuse cabaret with musical revue. A musical revue, he said, is just a bunch of songs strung together with some anecdotes. But a cabaret needs to grow and change over the course of the evening. It needs to create a relationship with the audience and end in a different place from where it began. It needs to have a reason to exist—to be alive, and dangerous. Kind of like crowd surfing with cigarettes.

Ben Walters and I had that conversation a few days after a friend asked me to consider putting together a solo show of my own for a cabaret festival. I declined that invitation. I had no experience being vulnerable in quite that way. When I perform with Pink Martini, I don't sing about myself or tell stories from my life. And when I'm on the radio, if the stories I report and the interviews I conduct center on my vulnerability or pain, I'm doing it wrong. That's one of the fundamental tenets of my profession. *It's not about me.*

I was confident that I could string together a bunch of show tunes and American songbook standards for a musical revue. But nobody needed another gay man belting out Stephen Sondheim and Irving Berlin classics for an hour. Watching performers like Viv, I aspired to clear a higher bar. If I ever did a solo show, I wanted to tell a story that no one else could tell—one that was uniquely mine. And I wasn't sure what that story was.

··

THE SCOTTISH INDEPENDENCE VOTE FAILED, *Cabaret* ended its Broadway run, and Alan and I both moved on to other projects. A couple of years later, in 2016, I was living back in the US when I got a call asking if I would moderate a conversation with him in Washington, DC, about his new book, *You Gotta Get Bigger Dreams.* We cackled onstage together and swapped stories about some of the things we had in common: Scottish independence, gay marriage, and singing at the Hollywood Bowl. I think both of us were surprised by our rapport.

Around the same time, the artistic director of the Washington Ballet, Septime Webre, called me with an idea. He had previously invited me to sing a couple of Maurice Chevalier–style French songs in his ballet adaptation of Ernest Hemingway's *The Sun Also Rises*, in 2013. I crooned a Maurice Chevalier tongue twister called "Valentine," with French lyrics recounting the particular dimensions of the titular woman's body parts. The song was misogynistic and creepy, yet bouncy and alliterative. In other words, extremely French.

When Septime called me in 2016, his pitch had nothing to do with ballet. He was assembling a cabaret series for an old DC mansion in Georgetown that had been converted to an event space called Halcyon House. He planned to bring some of my favorite performers down from New York for the series. Having seen me with Pink Martini and in his own production, he offered to commission me to create a show for his inaugural season. If I agreed, he would find a musical director, pay for the band, and cover all the logistics. All I had to do was make the thing. Plus, he said, if I didn't want to fill a full hour, I could take the stage for just thirty minutes and he would find another performer to do a short set for the other half of the program.

I knew that the bar would never be lower than this, that I would never get an opportunity with so few hurdles to jump. If I couldn't say yes under these conditions—where someone else would handle the venue, the finances, and the musicians—I knew that I would never do it at all. So, having no idea what I was going to actually make, I said yes.

Deadlines can clarify the mind. I decided to take a different approach to some of the same stories I'd been telling all my life. I gave myself permission to center my own experience reporting on wars and revolutions. Taking a page from the Pink Martini playbook, I found tunes from Ukraine, Syria, and Iraq that were relevant to the events I had reported on. I learned lyrics in half a dozen languages, with a few English songs thrown into the mix to keep the party moving. I called the show *Homeward*, which came from the song I had chosen about Scottish independence.

It was uncomfortable. I wasn't sure the show held together or made sense. As I rehearsed the songs at home by my piano with my musical director Gabe Mangiante, I felt self-indulgent and sort of a traitor to journalism—like a vegetarian who sneaks off to scarf down a hamburger despite his professed belief in the sanctity of animal life. But I figured, what was the worst that could happen? We were scheduled to perform the show only once at Halcyon House. And I was curious, perhaps in a slightly masochistic way, to know how the burger tasted.

I took the stage with a five-piece band: piano, percussion, guitar, cello, and bass. Even in a suit and tie, I had never felt so exposed. My Jewish DNA has programmed me to expect the worst, so I was beyond relieved when the show went as well as I could have hoped. The venue was standing room only; people laughed at the double entendres in the Marlene Dietrich classic "The Boys in the Backroom," and they cried at the finale—a mashup of "Hard Rain" with "Here Comes the Sun."

The next week, feeling bold, I cold-called Joe's Pub in New York. I introduced myself, described what I had created for Halcyon House and explained how much of a dream it would be to bring *Homeward* to Joe's Pub. I asked if they would consider hosting me for an evening, and they said yes. We chose a Saturday night, scheduled an early and a late performance, and a couple of months later I sent the whole band from DC up to New York on the train.

After seeing so many people I admired perform at Joe's Pub over the years, it felt like a hallowed space. It's a cozy room connected to the Public Theater, with café tables and a bar. The sounds of clinking glasses and silverware are part of the ambiance for any performance. The lighting and sound technicians were so warm and encouraging, they made me feel like family. For years, I had been sitting in the dark at the edge of those footlights. Now, I was holding the microphone.

I stepped out onto the tightrope for the early show. And oh, did I tumble. I forgot my Arabic lyrics and ended that song prematurely, in the musical equivalent of a multicar pileup. I hadn't done any real advertising besides the occasional tweet and Instagram post, so the audience was more than half empty. In my panic, I overcompensated and pushed to create a connection that just wasn't there. A friend offered a review that I will never forget. "It was like listening to you shout the news."

I beat myself up, trying to fight the growing suspicion that I was just a pretentious dilettante and a poseur—an amateur who had convinced himself that he could play in the professional leagues. I couldn't allow that narrative to take hold in my brain. Because I still had to do the late show.

I tried to hit the reset button. To view the debacle as a badge of honor. *Every performer I admire has played to an empty house and fallen on their face*, I told myself. It's a rite of passage.

And then I got a text from Alan's husband, Grant Shaffer. They had seen my Instagram post and were coming to the late show. My heart sank. It's one thing to fail in front of a nearly empty house. It's another thing to fail in front of a brilliant artist whose work you've admired for years, who happens to be sitting in that nearly empty house.

The song that gave my show its name is one that nearly every Scottish person knows. "Flower of Scotland" was written in the 1960s by a group called the Corries. It tells the story of the Battle of Bannockburn five hundred years ago, when the vastly outnumbered Scottish army overpowered the English. It's an anthem for Scottish independence.

Getting ready for the late show, I figured I had nothing to lose. So I texted Alan to ask if he would be willing to come up and sing part of "Flower of Scotland." Alan, I now know, is the kind of person who says yes to things you might not expect. And he said yes to this.

In the middle of my second Joe's Pub performance, I invited him up onstage. The sparse audience hooted and cheered. He delivered a sweet, plaintive rendition of the song's first verse:

> *O flower of Scotland*
> *When will we see your like again?*
> *That fought and died for*
> *Your wee bit hill and glen*

And stood against him
Proud Edward's army
And sent him homeward tae think again.

It was our first time singing together. And I felt a connection. With Alan, and also with the people in the nearly empty house. Although I didn't know it at the time, a seed was planted that night.

..

THE SEED SPROUTED IN 2019. Alan came to Washington again, this time for an event at the Newseum that marked the fiftieth anniversary of the Stonewall riots. He invited me to join him in conversation onstage. And as we walked into the darkened wings at the end of the evening, he turned to me with a smile and said in his sweet Scottish accent, "You know, we always have such a good time doing these things. Why don't we make a show together?"

I stopped walking.

"Don't joke about that, Alan, because I will absolutely take you up on it."

He locked eyes with me.

"I don't joke about those sorts of things. Let's do it."

We went out drinking that night and brainstormed songs we could include in our show. The ideas became more outlandish with each successive cocktail. A gay bar called JR's was holding its regular Monday night show tunes singalong, so we popped in and belted along with the Broadway classics. When they played "Don't Cry for Me, Argentina," we stood on the indoor balcony and Alan extended his arms in the iconic gesture that Patti LuPone made famous. He took fistfuls of paper napkins and flung them fluttering down onto the crowd below, perhaps the only Scottish man ever to play Evita.

The next day, he sent me a classic "morning after" text. "I meant what I said. So when can you come up to New York and write this show with me?"

The entire thing came together in just two weekends. The first time we met to work on it, in June at his place in New York, we asked our followers on Instagram to suggest names for our creation. The suggestions included "Double Trouble," "The A Team," and way too many jokes that relied on Alan's last name. Somebody suggested *Och and Oy*, and that felt right. Scottish and Jewish. He'd be the *Och*, I'd be the *Oy*.

As we plotted out what we wanted *Och and Oy* to be, Alan and I found that we had more in common than just same-sex marriage and the Hollywood Bowl. We had both spent our lives pursuing the same values: empathy, connection, and listening. We had devoted our careers to telling stories in hopes of helping people better understand the world and one another. I told mine primarily through journalism, while he told his mainly onstage and on-screen. (Along the way, he'd dabbled in journalism and I'd dabbled in performance.) Different paths, similar destinations—we both woke up each day looking for ways to bridge divides.

We started to envision an evening that would combine the kind of cheeky, entertaining musical numbers you would expect from an Alan Cumming show with the thoughtful conversations you might find on public radio. For our opening song, we settled on a mashup of some old Broadway tunes about friendship and friendly competition—"Bosom Buddies," "You're the Top," and so on.

Alan knew an up-and-coming composer and pianist named Henry Koperski who had been doing some gigs at the brick-and-mortar Club Cumming. We commissioned him to figure out how the songs could fit together as a medley. We didn't tell him that this was also an audition to be our musical director, but Henry figured it out and passed with flying colors. We hired him as our accompanist and the third member of our troupe.

In July, Alan and Henry came to my place in Washington for our second workshop weekend. I had rewritten the lyrics to "You're the Top." The first verse was mine, sung to Alan:

You're the top, you are joie de vivre
You're the top, you're a Broadway diva.
You're a graceful swan, your name is on a bar.
You are wild and frisky, a Scottish whisky, a movie star!

Then he would sing the next verse to me:

You're the top, your career is glittered
You're the top, you're All Things Considered
An effete aesthete, a garden's bumper crop
But if baby I'm the bottom, you're the top!

That Sunday morning, Alan and I stood next to Henry at the piano and ran through the show for the first time before an audience of one: my husband. Mike scribbled his show notes for us on the back of a pizza box. I sent Alan and Henry back to New York that afternoon with corn on the cob and pesto pasta made with basil from my garden.

The next time Henry, Alan, and I saw one another was our opening night. We had decided to launch the show over Labor Day weekend in Provincetown, Massachusetts, where we knew we would find a friendly crowd to warm up with before launching into a national tour. Alan was filming a TV drama in Albuquerque called *Briarpatch*. After a long day in front of the camera he caught a midnight flight to New York, then on to Boston, and then a puddle jumper to Provincetown. He arrived at noon the day of our show, having traveled all night, and still, when the performance was over, stayed at our opening night party later than I did. *That* is how Alan rolls.

For those performances only, we introduced our show as "Alan

Cumming and Ari Shapiro: A Soft Opening." We kicked it off with jokes about how many people had enjoyed our soft openings over the years.

Friends asked if I was intimidated sharing the stage with someone as accomplished as Alan. But the truth was just the opposite. He was so talented and experienced, I knew that any time I jumped, he'd catch me. I knew that if our show was going off the rails, he'd steer it back on track. Performing with Alan is one of the least frightening, most fun experiences I've ever had onstage. And he made the vulnerability part easy. I didn't have to think about baring my soul to an audience of strangers; I could just sit onstage and confide in my friend.

We went back to our dressing room after our final bows opening night, and a parade of artists I admire came through to congratulate us. The director John Waters showed up; he told us this was his fifty-fifth summer in Provincetown and regaled us with stories of how wild it had been in the early days. Justin Vivian Bond arrived, applauding! They had seen our show and loved it. That affirmation from Viv meant more to me than any review. The owner of the venue brought us a bottle of champagne to celebrate.

..

SINCE THE SHOW SEEMED TO be a hit with the gays, we decided to book a performance the next month on Fire Island, the quintessential summer beach destination for queer New Yorkers. The producer for that production would be Daniel Nardicio, who has thrown a weekly underwear party on Fire Island for about twenty years. When I asked him how he balances his various projects, Daniel told me about a German expression that I have never been able to confirm with any actual German person: "You have one leg to stand on, and one leg to dance on."

I related to this idea: one thing pays the bills; another feeds your soul. Producing a show like *Och and Oy* was Daniel's leg to dance on. The underwear party was his leg to stand on. Not a bad gig when an underwear party is your standing leg.

On a Friday in late September, I went to Capitol Hill to interview House Speaker Nancy Pelosi for *All Things Considered*. The minute the radio show was off the air, I changed out of my power suit, made a beeline to the airport, and flew to Long Island, where I caught a car to the port and then a ferry to Fire Island. It was my first visit there, and the boat docked under a massive rainbow flag waving in the breeze. The air was still warm when I pulled in after midnight, and I found Alan and Daniel waiting for me with a gin and tonic.

Daniel put us up at his rustic multibedroom boardinghouse with adjoining barracks for the go-go dancers who came over from New York to work the underwear party. The place was called Big Dick's Halfway Inn. On Saturday morning, we all had coffee together—Alan, Henry, Daniel, the go-go boys, and I.

I had urged my parents to wait and see the show once we'd ironed out the kinks, but they insisted on coming to Fire Island (where they would encounter kinks of a different sort). These two straight Jews in their seventies spent the day strolling along the boardwalk among the twinks, bears, and muscle boys of Fire Island Pines (or "Fire Pines," as my mom kept mistakenly calling it). They popped into a swimsuit shop, where the man behind the counter offered to sell my dad a leopard print speedo. "Unless you've got a matching bikini for me, no sale," my mom said.

My parents were right to make the trip. Our Fire Island performance had a surprise special guest—one that I didn't know about when I tried to talk them out of coming. See, Daniel had produced Chita Rivera in her Carnegie Hall debut a few years earlier—another leg to dance on, I guess. Near the end of *Och and Oy*, Alan always told a story about this legendary trailblazing star of *West Side Story*, *Chicago*, and *Kiss of the Spider Woman*. Alan's anecdote about Chita segued into our finale,

"Nowadays," from *Chicago*. Daniel had the idea to invite Chita to join us onstage for that number. I enthusiastically endorsed his proposal.

Chita's presence on the island was not being advertised. But Fire Island Pines is a small enough place that word got around. Over dinner, someone approached her and gushed about her performance on the reboot of *One Day at a Time*. That was actually the work of Rita Moreno, not Chita Rivera. (I had shared the stage with Rita at a Pink Martini show in Oregon a few years earlier, and the same thing always happened to her.)

Saturday afternoon on Fire Island, a few hours before showtime, Alan and I stood with Chita (not Rita) in front of a mirrored wall, holding straight black canes. She taught us the choreography to "Nowadays" that Bob Fosse had taught her more than forty years earlier. Chita was smart, bawdy, funny, generous, and, at eighty-six, quicker than most thirty-year-olds I know. She and Alan gossiped about how Liza Minnelli was doing, and about Ryan Murphy's TV show *Fosse*, where an actress named Bianca Marroquín played a young Chita.

That night, the zany drag performer Dina Martina opened the show for us with an absurdist monologue about earthquake clowns. Chita sat in the wings, laughing so hard she had to wipe tears from her face. Ninety minutes later, as our sold-out show for a crowd of Fire Island queers (and my parents) came to a close, we segued into our final bit. It was a game of celebrity roulette, where I named a bunch of famous people and Alan dropped a funny story about each of them.

Liza Minnelli!
Ian McKellen!
Kristin Chenoweth!
And then . . . Chita Rivera.

"Oh, lovely Chita," Alan said. He spun a long tale about the legendary triple threat. And then he said, "But what I've really learned from working with titans of stage and screen like Chita and Liza is how to live life. Chita taught me that . . ."

At this point, Henry rolled a chord on the piano, and Alan started speak-singing:

> *It's good.*
> *Isn't it grand?*
> *Isn't it great?*
> *Isn't it swell?*
> *Isn't it fun?*
> *Isn't it? Nowadays.*

A pause. And then, a spotlight on the side of the stage. The woman herself appeared, in the flesh, looking every bit the superstar.

I've never experienced such a wave of sound and energy. A force field of joy washed over me. Everyone leaped to their feet, screaming. This was more than connection; it was combustion. In that moment I understood how the ancient Greeks would have felt if the goddess Athena had appeared before them. A lifetime of worship, culminating in a manifestation.

Chita laughed, bowed, blew kisses, and waited for the roar to diminish. It didn't. Finally, what felt like many minutes later, she picked up the song.

> *There's men everywhere [that line got a big laugh],*
> *Jazz everywhere,*
> *Booze everywhere,*
> *Life everywhere,*
> *Joy everywhere, nowadays.*

She slowly walked to center stage, as she has done thousands of times in her performing career. And then, the three of us joined in song together:

You can like the life you're living,
You can live the life you like.
You can even marry Harry,
But mess around with Ike . . .

After the show, Chita went back to the rental house where she was staying. The rest of us (minus my parents) went to Daniel's underwear party. The go-go dancers we had had breakfast with that morning greeted us like old friends. We checked our clothes at the door and mingled, as strangers who had been in the audience came up to congratulate us. Alan was in a jockstrap; I wore bright blue briefs.

When Alan went to the bar to buy us a round of drinks, his husband, Grant, pulled me aside. Grant is an illustrator with an understated, deadpan sense of humor. In a low whisper he said to me, "Have you ever had that dream? Y'know, the one where people keep coming up and telling you how much they liked your performance? And then you realize, you're only wearing your underwear?"

I laughed and pinched myself. But there was nothing to wake up from. Alan arrived with our cocktails, and we made our way, nearly naked, onto the dance floor. There was booze everywhere. Life everywhere. Joy everywhere.

15

YOU CAN'T KILL ME.

I'M AN IDEA. I'M TIMELESS.

Every year when Christmas rolls around, I hear Mariah Carey's "All I Want for Christmas Is You," and I think of the Pulse nightclub shooting in Orlando. This is, to put it mildly, an unpleasant juxtaposition. What happened at Pulse on that night in June 2016 is as far from the idea of Christmas as you can get.

When the massacre occurred, I volunteered to fly to Florida and cover it for NPR. Each time my producer, Jinae West, and I climbed into our rental car, she would plug in her phone and the car stereo would start to play the first song in her iTunes library, in alphabetical order. This meant that after every interview about trauma, loss, and death, we closed the car door, heaved a big sigh, turned the keys in the ignition, and heard that familiar *Ding ding ding ding*

*ding ding—I don't want a lot for Christmas, there is just one thing I
need* . . .

The previous day, on a warm Sunday morning, I had left my house
for a run through my neighborhood in Washington, DC. The first headlines about the shooting came through as I was hitting my stride. A
brief mention of an incident at a gay nightclub in Orlando. Half an hour
later, there were more details. Some reports were calling it the worst
mass shooting in modern American history. Panting and sweating, I
paused my run in the middle of a park and called my boss.

"Do you want me to fly to Florida?"

"We'll let you know."

By the time I'd gotten home and taken a shower, I was booked on the
next flight to Orlando.

It wasn't that I thought only I could cover this massacre. Any of my
colleagues could have done so. (And lots of others did. NPR sent a
whole team of journalists to Orlando that day.) As a journalist, I know
that there can be value to approaching a story as an outsider, to seeing
a situation with a fresh, clear perspective. That's where I sit for lots
of stories I tell. I'm used to being on the outside looking in. But lived
experience can be worth something too. And I brought a unique set of
experiences to this particular story.

I had been bar-hopping in Orlando more than a decade earlier. In
2004 and 2005, I spent almost a year in Florida filling in for a colleague who was away on a fellowship. I covered whatever news the state
offered up. That included the Bush-Kerry presidential race, a national
right-to-die debate involving the care of a woman named Terri Schiavo,
and four hurricanes that I can still name from memory: Charley, Fran-
ces, Ivan, Jeanne.

On a Monday night in Orlando in 2004, I had just finished filing
a story about bald eagles rebuilding their hurricane-shattered nests.
Very on-brand for public radio—plus, eagles make great sounds. I

decided I had earned a night out, and so I made my way to a nearly empty gay bar.

As I walked through the front entrance, I saw to my left a dark dance floor with platforms for go-go boys, and to my right a bright-white, futuristic-looking cocktail bar with a vibe more *2001: A Space Odyssey* than the moment we were living in. I turned right, grabbed a stool, and chatted with the bartenders. By the end of the night, I felt like I had made some new friends. Tuesday was their day off, so they invited me to go out with them the next night.

This is what gay bars have done for people across cities and generations. They're havens for strangers, places to make new friends, anchors of community, and oases of safety in a hostile world. Gay bars helped birth the fight for LGBT rights, and they provided meeting places for AIDS activists. They have been secular churches for people rejected by organized religion. And they've offered a cure for the loneliness and isolation that have characterized so much of gay life over the last century.

The bartenders were named Nathan Jokers and Bobby Mills. They picked me up at my hotel on Tuesday night and took me to dinner at the Hoop-Dee-Doo Musical Revue, an absurdly campy, country-and-western-themed Disney cabaret. Tuesday was also gay night at Mannequins Dance Palace, the club that was part of Disney's Pleasure Island complex. So that was our next stop, dancing late into the night with a gaggle of Disney queens. Ahem, "cast members."

I accidentally left behind a brown corduroy jacket that I loved. I flew home to Miami the next day, but Bobby and Nathan promised to retrieve it for me from Mannequins. It arrived in the mail a week later.

∙∙

WHEN I FLEW TO ORLANDO to cover the Pulse shooting in 2016, I didn't seriously consider reaching out to Nathan and Bobby. It had been twelve years since I'd last spoken to either of them. I didn't remember the name of the bar where they worked, and I assumed they'd long since moved on. Besides, it would have been a tacky moment to pop out of the woodwork.

I checked into my hotel and took my recording equipment to a gay venue called Parliament House, which had been a center of queer nightlife in Orlando for decades. The complex included a hotel, swimming pool, dance floor, and bar. Two police cars sat outside, and a sign read, "WE ARE PULSE—UNBREAKABLE." It had been less than twenty-four hours since the shooting.

I ran into two friends walking toward Parliament House—guys in their twenties named Arturo Ugalde and Edgar Gomez. "We spent most of the day terrified that everybody we loved had died," Arturo told me.

He shared a bit of wisdom that a drag queen whispered into his ear earlier in the night.

"She said happiness is the ultimate rebellion. And I think that the man who hurt so many of our friends last night, his goal was to make us too scared to leave our houses and to make us feel like we were alone and like our community didn't exist. And just by being here, we're proving that that's wrong."

For these two, a glimmer of light started to shine through the despair when they heard that the Parliament House drag show would go on at 10 p.m., as scheduled.

"And I will be in the front row tipping a drag queen far too much, with my best friend, having an amazing time because no one can tell me to do otherwise," Edgar said.

Inside the club, I saw every kind of LGBT person. Drag queens, big leather bears, butch lesbians, trans people, all ages and races. Some were drinking and dancing. Others were hugging each other, crying, or just talking in quiet corners.

I knew this bar. Literally—I had stopped by Parliament House for a drink on a trip to Orlando years before. But I also knew it in a broader sense. This was a place I recognized. A place where I could find my people.

A twenty-one-year-old named Julius Ortiz was wandering around with a friend. He had the shell-shocked look of someone who had just walked off a battlefield.

"Well, I haven't slept since last night because I was actually with my friend," he told me. "I was at Pulse."

After Julius left the club, he started getting text messages from friends who were still there, telling him someone was firing a gun inside. He stayed up all night trying to reach them. When day broke, he went to Orlando's LGBT+ center to volunteer. He left there and went to a bar, where he started to see victims' names on TV. One was a good friend, Luis Omar Ocasio-Capo. He went by Omar, and he was twenty years old.

When Julius's father kicked him out of the house for being gay, Omar let Julius stay with him.

Julius had a hard time telling me the story. I reflexively asked if he was okay, and then blurted out, "Of course you're not. How could you possibly be okay?" I asked Julius if he wanted me to stop recording. He said yes. So I put my microphone away. But he kept talking.

He pulled out his phone and showed me the text messages he had sent Omar all day. They grew increasingly frantic, with no reply, and stopped only when Julius learned his friend had been killed.

Omar was one of forty-nine people killed that night. More than fifty were injured.

At 10 p.m., as promised, Ms. Darcel Stevens took the stage at Parliament House. She wore a curve-hugging red dress and a blond bouffant wig. She lip-synced to a couple of songs while tears streamed down faces in the audience. She said some words in consolation, reminding everyone standing in that room of our collective strength and resilience.

..

JINAE ARRIVED ON THE FIRST flight the next morning (and the "All I Want for Christmas Is You" haunting began). During one of my earlier interviews, I had heard about a young man named Eddie Melzer. He left Pulse just before the shooting started and then volunteered as an interpreter, helping the FBI communicate with parents and family members who spoke only Spanish.

When Jinae and I met up with Eddie a few days later, he told me that some parents learned their child was dead in the same moment that they learned their child was gay. Some of the parents were in a daze; others screamed; some spoke gibberish without making sense.

"All I could think is, that could have been my dad," Eddie said. "And that was tearing me apart. I was so close. It could have been me."

He lost five friends that night. Another was injured. So I asked Eddie what he would say to his friend in the hospital when they were able to talk.

"I'll say, when are we going to go have martinis again?"

This took me by surprise. But Eddie shrugged.

"I'm just not going to subscribe to fear," he said. "You know, we're gay men. We live in a world where we get a lot of hate. And we're strong people, because we live in a world that wasn't made for us. And if tomorrow somebody took over this country and said, we're going to kill all the gays, I will be the first one in that square saying, shoot me—with my big flag all over the place—because I would rather die for what I stand for. You can't kill me. I'm an idea. I'm timeless."

On my last full day reporting in Orlando, I had an interview with the editor of the free gay weekly paper, *Watermark*. Billy Manes crackled with energy. Platinum blond hair shot off his head like an explosion in an old Road Runner cartoon, and he was wearing a favorite vintage leather jacket in bright lemon yellow.

Even in that moment of grief, Billy couldn't help but crack a joke about the fear he felt doing interviews. "It puts me in the spotlight. And then I'm like Whitney Houston in *The Bodyguard*, y'know?"

I always try to relax a guest with small talk before an interview, especially during a tragedy when people have recently experienced trauma. So I mentioned to Billy that I had been bar-hopping in Orlando more than a decade before, when I made friends with those two bartenders.

Billy asked for the name of the bar where they worked.

"Oh, I don't remember," I said. "I'm sure it closed years ago."

He prodded. "Well, what did it look like?"

I described the layout: dance floor to the left, cocktail lounge to the right.

"That was Pulse," he said.

Of course it was. I don't know why it hadn't occurred to me earlier. Maybe I didn't want to put myself at the center of the narrative. Maybe I didn't want to imagine myself on that dance floor. I started to wonder about Nathan and Bobby—where they had landed, what had happened to them.

I looked up Nathan in my phone. And there was his number, along with an email address that ended in *@pulseorlando.com*. A little more searching told me that he was now living in Chicago, working in advertising. And two days later, when I was back in Washington, I decided to call him.

To my shock, he still remembered that night in 2004.

"We saw you there by yourself, and we wanted to make sure you were part of the group," he said. "We didn't want you to feel alone."

Nathan told me that the other bartender, Bobby, still worked at Pulse. He wasn't there the night of the shooting. Any pretense of journalistic distance popped like a soap bubble. I sighed to Nathan, "A gay bar is so much more than just a place to get a drink."

"Right. It's a home. It's a family. It really is a place for us to connect and feel safe," he said. "I couldn't tell you how many stories I've seen of people who have walked through the doors as their first gay bar they've ever been to, and really felt welcomed."

The gay rights pioneer Harry Hay used to talk about "Subject-Subject relationships." He argued that society raises straight people to think about relationships as Subject-Object. The pursuer and the pursued; the conqueror and the conquest.

Journalism often feels that way. I arrive in a community and gather up stories from people who live there. Their voices become ingredients in a recipe that I mix, bake, and serve to an audience of strangers. Then I drift off like some Mary Poppins who hasn't actually improved anybody's life before floating away on her parasol.

Hay believed that one reason gay people exist is to demonstrate a different way of relating to one another. Not in service of a selfish goal, but in mutuality and recognition of one another as more than a means to an end. Not Subject-Object, but Subject-Subject.

..

ONE YEAR LATER, JINAE AND I returned to Orlando for the anniversary of the shooting. Back at Parliament House, we sat backstage with Ms. Darcel Stevens, interviewing her as she dabbed on makeup for her midnight drag show.

"You know how Stonewall got started?" she asked, sponging foundation onto her cheeks and chin. "It was the drag queens who had just had enough of it, wasn't going to be bullied any more, wasn't going to be arrested, y'know? So whenever there's a social movement within our community, it's usually the queens who go to the front."

For the previous year, I had wondered what it had taken for her to walk onstage that night in 2016. "I could profoundly say in that moment, I had no idea what I was going to say," she told me. "I had prayed to my maker and asked him to give me words of encouragement."

She told me she didn't want to know what she had said that night. Someone had sent her a recording of it, and she hadn't listened. But even all these years later, I still think of those words often. "You are brave, and you are stronger than you think. We are going to get through it."

16

PLAYING FAVORITES

I never know what to tell people when they ask what my favorite interview has been. And they ask me all the time.

First of all, I refuse to rank my conversation with Bette Midler above or below my interview with Patti LuPone. That is a Sophie's Choice if I've ever seen one, and I'm not going anywhere near it.

And second of all, the premise of the question always seems like a setup for failure. If I spend my career thinking wistfully back on the one great interview that I did way back when, something in the system has broken down. I should be excited about an interview I did last week, and one that I'm doing next week. Hosting a daily news program is like sprinting on a treadmill at the gym. If you pause to gaze at the hot guy walking by, you'll fall on the floor.

My point is, when you try to Consider All Things, picking your favorite thing to consider kinda misses the spirit of the project. I'm not here to compare apples and oranges; I'm here to make a delicious fruit salad. So when I get asked about my favorites, here's what I do. I smile, say "great question," and pivot. "Let me tell you about an interview I did just last week that I loved."

Pro tip: if someone asks you a question you don't feel like answering, whether at a dinner party or in an NPR interview, begin by thanking them for the excellent question. Then pretend they asked something else and confidently answer the imagined one without missing a beat. Do it with enough conviction, and nobody will care.

I don't play favorites because even now, having filled this book with memories of people who poured their stories into my microphone, with dozens of favorites embedded in these chapters, there are still more that I can't leave behind. I've crammed these hundreds of pages with humans (and one kitten) I will never forget. My suitcase is stuffed to bursting, I can barely zip it closed, it's time to leave. And yet—as I sit on the floor contemplating the straining seams of my baggage, I just have to squeeze in a few more before I go.

Fine. I'll shove them in and hope the zipper doesn't break. I'll pay the overweight fee and tip the taxi driver extra for waiting.

These are three people, on three continents. They've never met one another, but if they did, I would want to be at that dinner party. Their lives and their stories appear to have little in common, but their shared thread is what has kept them in my mind for years, even as I've forgotten thousands of other people I've interviewed. Each of them brings a sense of defiant joy to their shared project of reshaping a world that might just as soon have left them on the sidelines.

··

THE FIRST IS A YOUNG man I met when I was covering the White House during the Obama administration. I was working in NPR's little basement cubbyhole under the briefing room. NPR's White House team shared the space with some mice, the occasional cockroach, and correspondents for other news outlets. We squeezed into "radio row," a hallway full of identical tiny rooms with soundproof doors, one short flight of stairs below where the White House press secretaries held their daily briefings. The TV folks had larger rooms on the ground floor, which tells you something about the press corps hierarchy.

(On the other side of the wall, behind the briefing podium where the press secretary would spar with reporters, you could squeeze down into the drained swimming pool where all the wiring and electronics ran for the TV cameras. White House correspondents signed their names on the swimming pool walls over the years. I've been accused of taking up too much wall space with my signature, but I swear my autograph really isn't all that big.)

One afternoon just after Thanksgiving in 2011, an announcement went out to the White House press corps that the preview of that year's Christmas decorations would be starting shortly. Holiday decor is a visual story, not great for radio. But it was a slow news day, so I decided to go. If nothing else, it would be an opportunity to get out of the basement a bit, wander through the White House, and see the famous gingerbread replica of the mansion that was an annual part of the Christmas display. Maybe I would even spot the Obamas's dog, Bo.

I didn't yet understand that being a White House holiday decorator is an *experience*. The volunteers who do it may apply for years, from all over the country, hoping to be selected. They write letters explaining why the White House should choose them. More than one hundred decorators ultimately show up and get assigned to teams in various parts of the building. It's like summer camp for the HGTV set, in November, at the most famous address in America.

As I walked through the Red Room, the East Room, and the State

Dining Room, the volunteers told me the stories of how they had ended up there. A man named José, from Rhode Island, came with his ninety-one-year-old dad, Pedro. José told me that his father had always dreamed of visiting the White House. José kept his application a secret, surprising Pedro with the news at the last minute.

Maybe this was a story after all, I thought, even if I didn't have images to go with it. I kept recording as a woman in the next room named Denise, from North Carolina, told me that she never got to spend the holidays with her son, who was in the military. The previous year, her husband had died. So her best friend decided that decorating the White House together would be a way for them to bring back some holiday cheer, and she sent in their application. They, too, were invited to Washington together.

And then I met David Bondarchuck, a rosy-cheeked, exuberant young man from Colorado. He wore a sweater vest, the cuffs of his shirt rolled up just so. "Tell me how you ended up here, decorating the White House for the holidays," I prompted him. He answered with the focus and poise of a student who had been preparing for a speech and debate tournament.

"Well, fifteen years ago I was homeless. And I saw Martha Stewart with then-First Lady Hillary Clinton in a White House special," he told me. "And I decided—that's something I'd love to do! So I stayed in school, and I watched Martha Stewart every single day, and started sending pictures of my events and my tablescapes to the White House, and this last August I got an acceptance letter!"

I was so glad I had gotten out of the White House basement to meet him. I later learned that he had experienced homelessness as a teenager, after his abusive father was arrested. He watched Martha Stewart at the youth shelter where he lived for six months. "How did you feel when you heard that you'd been accepted as a volunteer White House decorator?" I asked him.

"There was some screaming," David said. He blushed and giggled. "There was some crying. And I ultimately have attained my goal!" So I had to know—now that this dream had come true, what was his next goal?

David looked me straight in the eye, leaned into the microphone, and replied as though he had been rehearsing the answer for days. "Martha Stewart in New York: If you're listening, here I come!" In someone else's voice, this might have sounded stalker-ish. Coming from David, it was more "aspirational Disney protagonist."

Those snippets from José, Denise, David, and more went into a short audio postcard that aired on Saturday morning, with holiday piano music playing underneath their voices. A few days later, the phone in my basement cubbyhole at the White House rang. The woman on the other end introduced herself as a producer for *Martha Stewart*. She had heard my story and wanted to know how she could reach David Bondarchuck. I let out a gay gasp, took a moment to regain my composure, and then gave them the number for the East Wing, where the First Lady's staff handled the holiday volunteers. I hung up and held my breath.

On December 22, David joined Martha on set to make holiday decorations. They assembled a winter wonderland, making miniature trees out of sisal rope and wire. David, in a hot pink shirt, kept up with Martha like a pro. "Yours is even better than mine!" she said. And then, the queen of home crafts revealed another surprise. She asked David to look at a TV screen, and a video message began to play. It was Michelle Obama.

"You are proof that if we keep our dreams in our sights, if we work hard enough, if we weather the bumps that are sure to come along the way, then we can achieve anything we set our minds to," the First Lady said. "And that is a beautiful gift for all of us this holiday season."

David declared it "officially the best Christmas ever!" Even as a Jew who doesn't celebrate the holiday, I had to agree.

Today, David has his own food and events company in Denver called Scratch Catering Services. He has been on the Food Network and written a cookbook. And look—I've done stories that have led to federal policy changes. I do interviews every week with people whom the world deems *Important*. My little audio postcard about White House holiday decorators was not going to change the world. But I will always squeal a little bit when I think about David going on *Martha Stewart* and getting a personalized message from the First Lady, thanks to a story that I hadn't even planned on doing in the first place.

My friend Sam Sanders, who created the podcasts *It's Been a Minute* and *Into It*, has a philosophy about the artificial divide between "hard news" and "soft news." He says it's structurally oppressive—a way of diminishing marginalized groups.

"All the stuff that the old school voice-of-God journalists want to call the 'soft' stuff, that they don't care about, always happens to be stuff about women, and Black and Brown folks, and gay people," Sam says. His podcasts are a testament to the idea that you can't understand so-called hard stories about "just facts" until you understand the cultural significance and emotional stuff that's in the softer stories. There is a place for reporting on policies around homelessness, incarceration, or LGBT youth. And there is an equally important place for hearing David Bondarchuck describe how he came to be a volunteer White House decorator. I prefer not to elevate either one above the other.

After I heard Sam articulate that perspective, the distance that I had observed between some of my bosses' values and mine started to make more sense. Of course my career is a testament to the fact that I do care about politics, war, and business. I'm happy to interview a senator or a cabinet secretary about the political controversy du jour, and I understand why that is an important part of the mix of stories that we tell. But I think news organizations often make a mistake by valorizing those bone-dry interviews over flesh-and-blood stories of culture, emotion, and personal experience.

And so, in deference to Sam and his philosophical approach to hard versus soft news, I am not going to rank my interview with a volunteer White House decorator above or below the day I spent with Savanna Madamombe, a freedom fighter I met in Harare, Zimbabwe. Everyone calls her Sava, and I will shove Sava's story into this overcrowded suitcase right next to David Bondarchuk's. If I have to sit on my luggage to force it closed, so be it.

··

WHEN I DESCRIBE SAVA AS a freedom fighter, I use the word *fighter* loosely. On the day I met her, her weapon of choice was flowers.

Sava was born in Harare. But she moved to New York in 2000, got a green card, and spent most of her thirties and forties working in American hotels and restaurants. From across an ocean, she watched her country crumble under the oppressive dictatorship of Robert Mugabe. She felt helpless, like she didn't even recognize her Zimbabwe any more.

So she got on Facebook and started speaking out, talking to other members of the Zimbabwean diaspora. She organized protests when Mugabe visited the United Nations. Hundreds of people showed up. And she streamed it all on social media.

In videos on her page, you see her black halo of curls and her mischievous smile as she exhorts the crowd outside the UN building in New York. "Get up! Speak!" she shouts, "before they knock on your door! Before it's your brother!"

Her videos had tens of thousands of views, and the success of her activism meant she couldn't return home. Mugabe's security forces crushed any dissent, and public protest was forbidden. Activists in Zimbabwe were beaten, arrested, and mysteriously disappeared. Going home to Harare could have been a death sentence for Sava. She hadn't seen her family for almost twenty years.

She kept her activism limited to the US, where she would lead the crowd in call-and-response chants through the streets of New York.

"Mugabe must do what?"

Go!

"Mugabe must do what?"

Go!!!

And then, in late 2017, he finally did. After almost forty years in power, the military ousted him. The interim leader, Emmerson Mnangagwa, had his own record of human rights abuses. But after Mugabe left, Mnangagwa started talking about a new era of openness and free expression. And so one month after Mugabe was forced out, Savanna Madamombe did something she thought she might never be able to do. She returned to Harare.

That's where I met her. My team flew to Zimbabwe in that window of openness, to see what it looked like when a country experienced something like freedom for the first time in decades. We arrived in June 2018, when the low angular sunlight of the Southern Hemisphere's winter cast long shadows. Towering poinciana trees flaunted their scarlet foliage. Sava sat on a couch in the sunshine by a window in her sister's house. She had come home and brought her activism with her. "If it was still Robert Mugabe, I would never dare to do it," she told me.

Week after week, Sava walked through the center of Harare, livestreaming on social media, pointing out piles of trash and crumbling buildings. She had been doing it for six months by the time I arrived, calling out city councillors by name, tagging them in her posts. In all that time, she hadn't been arrested or even questioned by police. And the other thing that seemed so incredible to me was that her activism had a real impact. Elected officials could have brushed her off or ignored her, dismissing her work as the entitled complaints of someone who had spent too long in the United States. But that's not what happened.

In one video, she pointed out a fountain overflowing with garbage in the middle of downtown Harare. When she went back days later, it had been cleaned out. Rusty Markham, a councilman, told me that her video was the reason for the clean-up. "It's activism in its truest form," Rusty said. "Put it this way: in 2008, I don't think she could have done what she's done."

You could have said the same of my reporting trip. Colleagues who covered Zimbabwe under Mugabe told me stories about sneaking into the country under false pretenses, then being trailed by police or questioned by security forces. Meanwhile, my team and I were walking around freely, speaking with people in public, our microphones fully visible.

On the day we met up with Sava, her plan was to flower-bomb First Street. That plaza was once the grand promenade of central Harare, what Piccadilly Square is to London or Times Square to New York. As a teenager in the 1980s, it was where Sava would go to meet boys. By the time I met her more than thirty years later, decades of poverty and neglect had left the area run-down. Concrete planters were full of weeds and trash. Sava's plan was to clean them up and fill them with flowering plants, demonstrating for the people of Harare what activism and free speech could look like, while beautifying her city at the same time.

We piled into the back of her brother's pickup truck and rumbled down potholed streets under the dappled shade of jacaranda trees. With every bump, I clung more tightly to the edge of the truck bed. Sava, meanwhile, started livestreaming, holding her phone at arm's length. "Hi, guys, I know I haven't done a live video in a bit," she shouted over the engine noise, greeting her followers as they tuned in. "Good morning, Mark! Hi, Jacob. Hi, Sam! Do me a favor, guys—share the video!"

The truck pulled over at a roadside nursery, and Sava hopped out.

Narrating for her followers the whole time, she told the staff to pile the truck bed full of flowers. She had been collecting donations online for this project. Sava counted out a mix of US dollars and Zimbabwean bond notes, thanking her social media followers for their support. More than 450 pansies, snapdragons, petunias, violets, and marigolds were carefully lined up, ready for the journey downtown.

We got to First Street around lunchtime. People crowded the sidewalks, leaning on the giant planters, eating food from street vendors. A man sitting on the curb sold used shoes lined up on a blanket.

Sava and her friends got to work, jumping on top of the planters, picking out empty liquor bottles and used napkins, attacking the dry clumps of dirt with hoes, rakes, and shovels. The crew wore matching T-shirts that said *Fix Zimbabwe or Die Trying* on the front, and *We the People* on the back.

As Sava and her friends hacked away at the soil, bystanders stopped to ask what was going on. They offered suggestions or encouragement. Sava handed them T-shirts and garden tools and told them to join in. The project gained momentum as more pairs of hands started nestling plants into the soil. What had been brown and gray became orange, pink, yellow, and green.

Sava gave her phone number to the new volunteers to keep in touch, then she popped into each of the storefronts along the block and asked the shop owners to help water the plants after the guerrilla gardeners left. I felt like I was watching a society transform in real time.

By midafternoon, the concrete cubes had metamorphosed into a rainbow quilt of new life. The trash was gone, and a crowd of people who had begun the day as strangers were congratulating one another on their role in making it happen. The scene was beautiful. But as a journalist, I wasn't quite ready to get swept away in the moment.

"How much can it really accomplish?" I asked Sava.

"Forget the flowers," she told me. "It's a symbol. I'm hoping that this will start a conversation"—among citizens, and also between citizens and their government.

I was both hopeful and dubious. I decided that I couldn't broadcast the story until I knew whether the transformation would hold. So a few days later, my producers and I returned to First Street, bracing for the worst. I knew that whatever we found would be the last scene of our piece.

As we turned the corner, bright colors caught our eye. The flowers were still flourishing. The man selling used shoes on the sidewalk told me he had been looking after them—watering the plants, removing trash. He didn't want the street to go back to the way it was.

So many people I met in Zimbabwe expressed hope for the future of their country. Eventually, I couldn't help but share their optimism. But life is more sprawling than journalism. Beyond the confines of a news report, no story ever truly ends. And the peace in Zimbabwe didn't last.

A month after my team visited the country, Zimbabweans went to the polls to vote. Mnangagwa declared victory. And when the opposition party claimed election fraud, Mnangagwa cracked down on peaceful street protesters with the same kind of violence that had become routine under Mugabe.

From Washington, we called Sava in Harare.

"I feel like something has just been stolen from me," she said. The water tanks that the military had used to blast peaceful protesters had also sprayed the planters at First Street, ruining the flowers. "But the flowers are the least of my worries," Sava said. "People died today."

The period from Mugabe's exit to Mnangagwa's election was a small window of light, shining on people who were ready to bloom. When I think back on my time with Sava, I remember how colorful, beautiful, and self-sustaining a community can be—if political leaders give citizens space to create the world that they envision.

..

BUT SOMETIMES, EVEN IF POLITICAL leaders neglect a community, people find ways to take root in the cracks and grow. Which brings me to the third person in this trio of favorites-that-I-refuse-to-call-my-favorites. She is someone who built a community and a family in the face of a society that would just as soon have shut her out. The phrase *chosen family* may be overused, but Vinolia Wakijo helped me understand what it can mean.

I met "Mami Vin," as everyone calls her, in the Indonesian city of Yogyakarta. She was in her sixties, wearing a hijab, cherry-red lipstick, and a modest brown dress patterned with dogwood flowers. She is the matriarch of a family of transgender women known as warias.

Like the hijra of India, warias exist on the fringes of Indonesian society, all across the wildly diverse archipelago of islands. You find them in the strict Muslim Aceh province in the west, where people live under shariah law. And warias are in the majority Hindu island of Bali, more than two thousand miles to the east, where international tourists frolic on beaches. Warias typically do sex work, or they sing for tips on the street. Both of those practices are technically illegal, but tolerated, and warias have been part of Indonesian culture for as long as anyone can remember.

I went to Indonesia in 2017, wanting to learn more about what held together a sprawling diverse democracy that was also the largest Muslim country in the world. I thought maybe I could find some lessons that would help me understand the strains tearing at America's societal fabric.

A young doctor named Sandeep Nanwani introduced me to Mami Vin. He told me one of the reasons he loves the warias is their insistence on responding to suffering with laughter. "If they get caught by the police and there's a lot of media, they will literally go to the cameras and strut their stuff. They're shameless," he said. "And I just love that."

I thought of the queers and drag queens outside New York's Stonewall bar in the 1969 riots that launched America's gay rights movement.

In the face of arrests and beatings, they famously formed a Rockettes-style kickline in front of police and chanted, *We are the village girls, we wear our hair in curls. We wear our dungarees above our nellie knees.* Even on the other side of the world, in another language and another decade, high camp could bring down authority structures like a high tide on a sandcastle.

Mami Vin grew up in Yogyakarta and dreamed of becoming a teacher. As a waria, that path wasn't open to her. She dropped out of school and started doing sex work, which seemed like the only option. As time passed, she became an organizer and an advocate for other women like her. And so it was with tremendous pride that nearly forty years after she ended her formal schooling, she showed me a wall full of certificates and awards from universities and medical schools that have recognized her work as a leader in the community. These days, the waria who could not pursue a career as a teacher is an honored guest lecturer all over the world.

Mami Vin clung to me and insisted on taking photos with the American who had come to interview her about her work. Given how hard she had fought for everything in her life, she wasn't about to feign humility. We were standing in the front room of a group house that Mami Vin established for people with HIV. The place is called Kebaya—a mashup of the phrase *Keluarga Besar Waria Yogyakarta*, or "Yogyakarta Transgender Family."

That word, *family*, is literal here. In Indonesia, people carry a card listing their biological relatives. It's like a social security card that also ties everyone to a community. That card gives Indonesians access to health care and other benefits. So when warias come out as transgender, if their families cut them off (as they often do), the warias are effectively excluded from society—with no way of getting health care or other benefits.

Mami Vin helped the warias organize. And eventually, the government granted their chosen families legal recognition. In a society that wanted to shut out Mami Vin and everyone like her, this matriarch found a way to punch a hole in the wall and bring her entire community through the opening along with her. That became especially necessary when Indonesia's HIV epidemic started to ravage the waria community in the early 2000s, some twenty years after the disease first swept through the US.

At Kebaya, Mami Vin pulled out her family card to show me. It was a full-size sheet of paper, listing the street kids who were now legally considered a part of her family. Without her, those young people wouldn't have had access to medicines that prevent or treat HIV. As the leader of Yogyakarta's waria community, she helped make sure that no one fell through the cracks.

It wouldn't quite be right to say that Mami Vin won a battle against society. She told me that in the decade that she had been running the group home, forty-six residents had died of AIDS-related complications. Her entire generation of warias was nearly wiped out. There is no number of honorary degrees or policy changes that could make those losses disappear. Kebaya is full of photographs of people who did not survive to see the age that Mami Vin has reached. But the home that she built had a future. And her chosen family was growing.

Mami Vin introduced me to an eleven-month-old baby with big brown eyes named Nira. After Nira's mother died of complications from AIDS, the warias took the baby in. A member of the community named Ma Ona was in the process of officially adopting her. The Kebaya residents gathered around as Nira cooed, fussed over by the protective mothers who surrounded her.

..

AS I REPORT THE NEWS every day, I keep returning to these memories of people who not only refuse to break but actually somehow bend the universe to their will. I sniff around for stories that illuminate the shift that occurs when people move from trauma to transcendence.

A young Samoan climate activist named Brianna Fruean articulated this instinct in a way that I will always remember. (Shh, maybe nobody will notice if I squeeze in one more favorite.) I met her at the 2021 UN Climate Change Conference in Scotland known as COP26. I noted that in a sea of black and navy suits, she was dressed in pink and lavender with a flower in her hair. Brianna told me she didn't want images of despair and devastation to be the only thing that moved people to action.

"I think images of beauty, of hope, of culture, should be what also push us into action because that's what's at stake," the twenty-three-year-old told me. "For me as a Pacific Islander, a lot of people think my role here at COP is to come and cry, like I owe them my trauma, when I don't owe you my trauma," she said. "I want to come here in bright pink and neon colors and be like, I'm a very happy person. And this is the happiness I'm trying to save."

I don't believe that suffering is inherently noble or that misery is a prerequisite for greatness. But I look at David, formerly homeless, going toe-to-toe with Martha Stewart. I see Sava wielding flowers as a weapon against oppression and a tool to inspire. I remember the warias protecting one another as they sang sweet songs for tips in a night market. And I feel lucky to carry them with me, as examples of how to confront life's ugliness with beauty, how to meet horror with humor, and how to smile in the face of whatever might come next.

ACKNOWLEDGMENTS

As someone who prefers to engage in forms of expression with a brief shelf life (radio, cooking, live music), I always believed that I would never write a book, right up until the moment I discovered that I had started writing this one. That realization took place at Fritz Haeg's Salmon Creek Farm. Thank you, Fritz, for creating a space where I could slow down and open up to new possibilities.

Others who believed in me as an author before I saw myself as one included my perceptive and patient agent Mollie Glick, who spent hours talking with me about the shape and focus of this book before it existed, then played yente with Rakesh Satyal, my insightful and encouraging editor at HarperCollins. Speaking of yentes, I'm grateful to the entire team of agents at CAA for bringing me into the fold—most especially Josh Lindgren, who connected me with Mollie in the first place.

My early manuscript readers, Jolie Myers and Sandy Rowe, struck just the right balance of positive reinforcement and tough love. Other friends provided thoughtful feedback on early drafts of specific chapters: Ahmed Badr, Alan Cumming, Monika Evstatieva, Barrie Hardymon, Thomas Lauderdale, Rich Preston, and Fatma Tanis. Thanks to Kat Lonsdorf for snapping the photo that became the basis for the book cover and to Cassidy DuHon for creating the work of art that provided me with a title.

A version of the essay about Pulse nightclub first appeared in the *Atlantic*, and I am grateful to the team there for showing me that it's okay for a journalist to get personal sometimes. Kim Hastreiter first published a version of the chapter about fiction in her pandemic publication, *The New Now*. Thank you, Kim, for your friendship and for allowing this DC interloper into your New York broadsheet. I am grateful to Rosemary Hill for allowing me to quote her late husband Christopher Logue's poem "Come to the Edge." And of course, I first introduced listeners to many of the people in these pages with the guidance and collaboration of NPR producers, editors, audio engineers, local fixers, and other colleagues. To everyone at NPR, including my many mentors and co-workers whose names do not appear in these pages, thank you for teaching me how to tell a story. I am especially indebted to my *All Things Considered* cohosts, past and present, for always having my back.

Thanks to my parents and my brothers for a childhood that taught me to be curious about the world. And I would never have reached this point without the love and support of Mike: two islands in a sea of— well, he knows.

Above all, I am grateful to the thousands of people who have entrusted me with telling their experiences, on the air and on the page, over my years in journalism. This book is a testament to them, and I hope that I have done their stories justice.

ABOUT THE AUTHOR

Ari Shapiro is the award-winning host of NPR's flagship daily news program, *All Things Considered*. He makes frequent appearances as a singer—with the "little orchestra" Pink Martini, as a solo cabaret performer, and alongside stage and screen star Alan Cumming. Shapiro lives with his husband in Washington, DC.